Out in the Blue

Letters from Arabia – 1937 to 1940

A Young American Geologist Explores
the Deserts of Early Saudi Arabia

Thomas C. Barger

Selwa Press

Selwa Press
1101 Portola Street
Vista, California 92084 U.S.A.
www.outintheblue.com

Printed in the United States of America

Publisher's Cataloging-in-Publication
(Provided by Quality Books, Inc.)

Barger, Thomas C.
    Out in the blue : letters from Arabia, 1937 to 1940 :
a young American geologist explores the deserts of early
Saudi Arabia / Thomas C. Barger. – 1st ed.
    p. cm
    Includes bibliographical references and index.
    LCCN: 00-90642
    ISBN: 0-9701157-3-3

    1. Barger, Thomas C. 2. Geologist–Biography.
3. Deserts–Saudi Arabia–Biography. 4. Petroleum industry
and trade–Saudi Arabia–History. 5. Geology–Saudi
Arabia–Biography 6. Saudi Arabia–Social life and
customs–History. I. Title

QE22.B37A25 2000   551.092
                              QB100-500025

2 3 4 5 6 7 8 9 10

To the two women named Kathleen,
from a man twice blessed

Contents

Maps

Notes

The photographs published in this work are from the Thomas C. Barger collection, unless otherwise noted. Photographs within the collection attributable to a specific photographer other than Tom are credited accordingly.

Transliteration of Arabic words into English can be a difficult task. As some Arabic letters have no equivalent in English, several systems of transliteration have been developed. *Out in the Blue* uses a transliteration system loosely based on contemporary American journalism of the 1930s. In this system, the name of the King, for instance, is written Abdul Aziz, rather than 'Abd al-'Aziz, which is the currently accepted spelling. The definite article "the," *al*, is used in small case with a hypen before common nouns and place names, as in al-Hasa. The similar Al, which means "house (or family) of," as in Al Saud, uses a capital A without a hyphen. Arabic words and phrases are italicized; proper names of people and places are not.

Tom wrote scores of letters both to Kathleen and to his parents. The latter provided Wallace Stegner with valuable primary material used in writing his book, *Arabian Discovery*, later released as *Discovery!* Every letter that appears is written to Kathleen, but details from Tom's letters to his parents have been used liberally to add, clarify or amplify a subject.

The passages printed in italics represent direct extracts from either Tom's writings or from transcribed interviews conducted by me as well as others. My editing of the interviews as well as the letters has been chiefly a task of selection. Once selected, a letter or passage has been modified only for clarity.

The beauty of reading a letter comes from the fact that it is preserved in time. Tom arrived in Saudi Arabia knowing nothing about the country, though he was eager to learn. It is a joy to watch this learning grow into knowledge throughout the course of these letters.

Acknowledgments

In 1983, I agreed to help my father, Tom Barger, write his memoirs, portions of which he had started to write in the late 1970's. Unfortunately, soon into the project I realized that he no longer had the stamina for a book of the scope that he intended to write. Instead, I suggested that I transcribe and edit the voluminous and complete sets of letters that he wrote to my mother, Kathleen, and to his parents during his first three years in Saudi Arabia.

With the able assistance of Margaret Maher, Tom's former executive secretary, who was also retired, I worked with my father to edit the letters into a collection called *Out in the Blue*. Tom's short-term acumen remained as strong as ever throughout the editing process, and he was delighted when we finished in the spring of 1984.

Although I still needed to add a narrative commentary and select the appropriate photographs, I sought to find an interested publisher. My earliest attempt began with a submission to a leading New York literary agent. He replied that he had enjoyed the letters immensely, but there wasn't a commercial market for this story. Meanwhile Tom's health began to decline, and over time the urgency to publish *Out in the Blue* diminished.

My father passed away in 1986. Over the years, people occasionally requested copies of the letters or wrote to let me know that there were readers interested in this story. One retired Aramco employee, Howard Norton of Austin, Texas, was especially persistent, and I would like to thank him, as well as his wife, Mary Norton, for being instrumental in my final decision to finish this book.

Whatever success I may have achieved is in no small part due to the assistance of many people from Aramco and Saudi Aramco who share a common interest and affection for the Saudis and their country. For their intial comments and suggestions, I would like to thank Charles Homewood, one of the early Casoc pioneers; Ismail I. Nawwab, the author and Islamic scholar; Robert Norberg, former editor of *The Link,* a periodical published by the Americans for Middle East Understanding; and Paul Nance, founder of the Nance Museum, the largest and most diverse collection of Saudi art and artifacts on continuous display in the United States.

F. S. Vidal, a leading authority on Arabian society from antiquity to the present, provided many important suggestions as well as a priceless insight into the work as a whole. Regarding oil wells and production, Donald R. Fate, formerly a Senior Vice President of Aramco, provided me with facts as well as an education. John R. Jones, a veteran of Aramco's Government Relations Department, and his wife Lola, were personal friends of my parents throughout those many years in Dhahran. Their contributions were fundamental to the final form of this book.

Three men have been been especially invaluable and they have each in turn taught me to aspire to their higher standards. Peter C. Speers, editor of the *Aramco Handbook* and later, *Saudi Aramco and Its World;* has given me only solid information and sagacious advice from the beginning. His dedication to discipline in both fact and expression has made this a much better work.

James P. Mandaville, retired after many years spent in Aramco's Arabian Affairs department, patiently responded to scores of inquiries. His extensive personal knowledge of Saudi Arabia and its people is unequalled, and he shared this wisdom with articulate grace.

Finally, William Tracy, a long-time writer and current editor of *Al-Ayyam Al-Jamilah,* the magazine for Aramco's annuitants, elevated this entire project to a higher level when he meticulously critiqued an early manuscript. He is an editor's editor and I will always be grateful for his enthusiasm as well as his skill.

The copy editor, Lynn Barry, proofed the final manuscript and her many suggestions strengthened the text throughout. For background material about North Dakota and details about my mother's family, I am indebted to three women from Dickinson, North Dakota: my mother's sister, Virginia A. Hewson; her daughter, Kathleen; and one of my parents's closest friends, Virginia Reichert.

I owe much to my entire family. To my parents, I hope that this work does them credit. To my second mother, Kathleen V. Barger, I am obliged for the constancy of her support. Our three children, Khamisah, Luke and Sam, each have contributed in their own way, but it is my wife, Sydney, who made it possible for me to complete this book. She did more than her share of the tedious production work involved in this project, but more importantly, she gave me advice, perspective, and loving encouragement that never faltered.

Timothy J. Barger,
Editor, *Out in the Blue*

Preface

When I agreed to work in Saudi Arabia, I didn't even know where it was; now, after 32 years there, I know only too well. By publishing selected parts of the letters I wrote to my wife, Kathleen, during the time I first encountered Saudi Arabia, its people and its embryonic oil company, I hope to preserve a bit of the wonder I felt then and to present to the reader a glimpse at the way of life in Arabia before there was oil.

Tom Barger
La Jolla, California – March 1984

Prologue

It was September of 1937. After working for six years as a gold miner, a mining engineer in the Arctic Circle and a metallurgy professor at the University of North Dakota, I traveled to Butte, Montana, to take an engineering position at Anaconda Copper. Unfortunately, between the time of the offer and the time I arrived in Butte, the price of copper had dropped with the country's fortunes in the eighth year of the Depression. The man who had originally offered me the job explained that he couldn't hire me as a research engineer, but if I could mine, he could find me work. Something was better than nothing, so I joined the Mine, Mill and Smelter Workers Union, Local #1, and, before long, I was working far below the surface in Anaconda's East Colusa Mine.

During my tenure at the university, I was involved with various efforts to find oil in the state. In the course of these duties, I met a crew from the Standard Oil Company of California and had the occasion to write Dr. J.O. Nomland, Assistant Chief Geologist at Socal and a graduate of the University of North Dakota.

Though I was getting nowhere in the mines, there was something more pressing. I was madly in love with Kathleen Ray, a young woman from Medora, North Dakota, and until I could earn a living wage, I couldn't ask her to marry me. After a few more weeks in the mines, I was desperate, so I wrote Dr. Nomland to see if Standard Oil had any openings. This letter changed my life.

The Helena *at Pump Station H-4 on the Kirkuk-Haifa pipeline*

Chapter One
"Job, Marriage and Departure"

October 28, 1937
Butte, Montana

Dear Mom and Dad,

I have in hand a telegram that reads as follows: "Can you arrange to come to San Francisco for interview regarding employment? We pay transportation expenses but no salary for the trip." Signed "J.O. Nomland, Assistant Chief Geologist, Standard Oil Company of California." I had applied about six weeks ago; the word "salary" was underlined, which made me laugh.

The telegram came yesterday. Today I saw my shift boss about getting off for the interview. He is all in favor of anything to get a man out of "these damn mines." Tomorrow I leave for San Francisco. If all goes well, I will change from a miner into a geologist.

Tonight I'm working the graveyard shift on a timber repair job in a main haulage drift. It's a pipe. We go down in the mine about 11:00 and sit and look at our work until 2:00, as we can't start until the night shift leaves and the motors stop pulling trains through the drift. Then we have lunch at 3:00, rest until 4:00, and get out to the station by 6:30, so as not to miss the cage up.

Pray that I have luck in San Francisco. I must start scrubbing my hands and fingernails so I will look civilized by Monday.

November 2, 1937
San Francisco

Dear Folks,

Yesterday I interviewed with Dr. Nomland and today I have decided to go to Saudi Arabia as a geologist for Casoc, the California Arabian Standard Oil Company. It is a three-year contract at 300 dollars per month and expenses, with a three-month paid vacation every two years.

It was a most peculiar interview. I went into his office at 10 o'clock. We sat and talked for an hour and a half about everything except me, my experience and the prospective job. Finally, he asked me about these things and how much salary I would expect. I told him it depended on what I was to do, but I couldn't work for less than 200 dollars a month. He said they needed a man in Arabia to do surveying and to work with the geologists. Our preceding social conversation was simply to find out something about me irrespective of my resume. He stressed that I am to study my geology to fill in some of the gaps in my education.

The concession, on the northeast coast of Arabia, is about the size of California. On the island of Bahrain in the Persian Gulf, Casoc has several producing wells and is drilling more. I will be working on the mainland, opposite the island, at a place called Jabal Dhahran. *Jabal* is the Arabic word for a hill or high place.

Dr. Nomland is a big, genial fellow and, I suspect, the man responsible for obtaining the Arabian concession. He says that he was the fourth American to cross Arabia and the first not to write a book about it. He gave me a good many pointers on what to do and not to do. According to him, the success of a geological field team depends on 10 percent geology, 40 percent surviving your environment and 50 percent getting along with your partner. He also said that it is better to work for an oil company than for a mining company. When a mine closes, you have to start all over again, but when an oil field closes, you are simply transferred with no loss of seniority.

Tomorrow I will go to Butte, pack everything, come home, tie up the loose ends and send Dr. Nomland a wire that I'm ready to go on the payroll.

November 11, 1937
Butte, Montana

Dear Mom and Dad,

Kay called tonight from Grand Forks and told me that her folks have consented to our getting married. You see, when I told her about going to Arabia, she talked with Father Mac again, and he strongly advised that we be married before I go. Kay called her folks, but they were opposed to the idea. She talked to Father Mac again, and his opinion remained the same, so she called me in San Francisco to tell me. I wanted her to marry me before I left more than anything else in the world, but I couldn't have suggested it myself. Now her folks have not only consented but approve. I am to meet her in Dickinson Saturday night. It looks as if I'm going to be so late leaving here, I can scarcely hope to make it to Bismarck on Saturday night. I will be in Sunday to see you and possibly bring Kay along.

When I arrived at my parent's home in Linton, North Dakota, I was totally surprised by their vehement opposition to my marriage plans. My mother was in the hospital with cancer, so there was a stormy session between my father and me. Not wanting to upset my mother, and possibly aggravate her condition, I dropped the subject of my marriage and returned to Kathleen in Medora. *

* Italicized text represents narrative from Tom's papers and transcribed interviews. Italicized text within parentheses is editorial.

(Tom had been engaged to a young woman from a respectable family in Devil's Lake, North Dakota. Tom's mother, Mayte, liked her and approved of their marriage. She was shocked when Tom broke off this engagement in order to marry a rancher's daughter, especially as ranchers were considered, in her opinion, to be less than respectable.)

November 18th Kathleen and I were secretly married at her parents' home. We honeymooned on our way to New York City. The first of December, 1937, I boarded the *S.S. Manhattan*, waved goodbye to my wife one last time and sailed off to Arabia.

My journey to Arabia was faster than that of any of my predecessors in the California Arabian Standard Oil Company. Arriving in London the evening of the seventh, the next day was spent mostly trying to find a book on Arabic a bit less formidable than Wright's two-volume Arabic Grammar. *The morning of the ninth I boarded a train to Southampton. As I entered the dining car, an American voice guided me to breakfast with Mike Bush and his British companion, Slim Waters. Both were returning to Bahrain for a second hitch. I couldn't have fallen into better hands. Mike had been in the first drilling crew, and his lovely wife, Alice, had been the first American woman to join her husband.*

At Southampton we boarded the recently inaugurated Imperial Airways flying boat service to the Middle East. The routine for our flight with its nine passengers was to take off as soon after sunrise as possible so as to have as much daylight to reach the next overnight stop. Night landing facilities did not exist. Our first leg to Marseilles took eight and a half hours, refueling at St. Nazaire; nine hours to Athens, refueling at Lake Bracciano and Brindisi; and four hours on the third day to Alexandria, arriving early enough for sightseeing.

At Alexandria, we transferred to the Helena, *a wonderful Handley-Page four-motor biplane with a top speed of under 100 miles per hour. Our passenger list reduced to five, we took off before dawn and reached Baghdad some 14 hours later after refueling at Port Said, breakfast at Gaza, refueling at Pump Station H-4 on the Kirkuk-Haifa pipeline and lunch at Rutbah Wells. Another nine hours of flying, including a refueling stop at Kuwait, brought us to Bahrain, five days and some 45 hours of flying time out of London.*

Al -Khobar – December 1937

Chapter Two
"Arrival in Dhahran"

December 15, 1937
Casoc, Jabal Dhahran

Dearest Kathleen, *

Finally in Arabia. I'm quite comfortable here in my air-conditioned room. My roommate is a petroleum engineer from California, John Domercque. Incidentally, everyone in the camp is American; no British are allowed on the mainland. We landed at Bahrain Island day before yesterday and spent the night at Bapco, the headquarters of the Bahrain Petroleum Company. The island is about 20 miles from Saudi Arabia. Yesterday, I came over in a native boat with a crew of four and a wonderfully patched gas engine assisted by a sail.

* *The subsequent letters are to Kathleen with the exception of her letters to Tom, which are datelined North Dakota. Her letters are placed in context rather than chronologically to compensate for the delay in mailing time.*

The launch deposited me on the half-finished pier of al-Khobar, a small fishing village, where we were met by a clerk from the company. He drove us six miles inland over an oiled road to the company town at Dhahran. Remember how I thought I'd forget or lose track of the way cars looked? No chance. The Shaikh of Bahrain just got a new Studebaker, and the company has a fleet of cars, all Fords.

We arrived in camp at 3:30, just in time to return to al-Khobar and await the arrival of Crown Prince Saud, the eldest son of King Abdul Aziz Ibn Saud. He didn't whistle in with his new Chrysler Imperial until after sundown, so we didn't get pictures of his arrival from Riyadh, the capital city of Saudi Arabia, a three-day journey to the west of here. The reception was quite an occasion, with bunting out, flags flying and everyone dressed in his Sunday best.

The Shaikh of Bahrain had sailed over to meet Saud. The Shaikh's men had to repitch the Shaikh's tent because it was too close to the Prince's and they wouldn't be able to "visit" one another properly. Prince Saud drove up, was greeted by the local dignitaries, and escorted to his tent. After a bit of time, the Shaikh started to move out from his tent; the Prince and his retinue came forth and they met about halfway and kissed each other . All this was done in silence; they save the gab for the sitting and feasting that follows.

The next morning I was introduced to my boss, Max Steineke, Casoc's chief geologist. A big, burly man, he greeted me heartily, " I am certainly glad to meet you. I'm awfully glad to have you here with us; I don't know what I am going to do with you, but I am certainly glad to have you on board."

He continued that I should particularly read the reports that had been prepared by the geologists in the last four years and generally find out what was going on before I became immersed in work. As there was no mention made of my surveying for a seismograph crew, the ostensible job that I was hired to do, I never asked about the haste with which I was sent out from San Francisco. I made no further inquiries into the matter, as I was very pleased to be regarded as a geologist rather than a surveyor.

This morning, at Max's suggestion, I went back to al-Khobar to see the celebration. Every Arab was armed with either a sword or a rifle or both. The collection of rifles was the most varied I have ever seen. There were all makes and calibers, from the latest bolt action to ancient muzzle-loaders, such as you see in the movies.

Then the Arabs started dancing. Drums furnished the only music to which they sang out a sort of chant. Assembled in two lines, the dancers brandished their rifles and shuffled their feet back and forth like American Indian dancers. After a while the Prince and the Shaikh came out and sat in a sort of pavilion tent. Four of us were ducking about through the crowd and around the soldiers, trying to take pictures, when the captain of the guard invited us to come into the tent and take all the pictures we wanted. Charlie Herring, a young engineer, nearly sat in the Crown Prince's lap taking close-up shots of His Highness.

Afterwards, we mingled with the dancers, taking more pictures. Someone shot off a muzzle-loader into the ground beside Herring, and he really jumped. Everyone thought this was really funny, which provoked even more firing of weapons. They were only shooting percussion caps, but they made a fine noise.

After these festivities, the Shaikh and the Crown Prince embarked for Bahrain where the Shaikh is to present Saud with the fabled Studebaker. We were invited to come aboard and take pictures before the fleet set sail. There were many incongruities: Arab robe and headdress over a business suit and shoes, soldiers dressed in Boy Scout shorts and Arab head scarves armed with modern Mausers, but they wore elaborately carved swords and inlaid daggers in their belts.

Floyd Ohliger is superintendent of the Arabian operations; Harry Rector is his assistant, and Max Steineke is my immediate boss; they are all good eggs. The camp itself is fine. There are about 60 men here: drillers, geologists, mechanics, engineers, a lot of Indian clerks and a young army of Arabs. The food is fine; there are plenty of fresh vegetables, ice, and distilled drinking water. As a geologist, I will spend most of my time out in the blue.

Tomorrow, I am going with Max to locate some points by astronomical observations. We plan to return a couple of days before Christmas.

Christmas Eve, 1937
Jabal Dhahran

Yesterday we arrived back from the field just in time to attend a formal dinner for the Crown Prince upon his return from Bahrain. You should have seen some of the retinue wrestling with knife and fork and especially the surprised look on one Bedouin's face when the ice cream he put in his coffee disappeared entirely. Walt Hoag remarked that they did much better than he did at his first Arabian banquet of sheep and rice.

We spent all of today computing the star observations we made in the field. Tonight there was a Christmas party hosted by the five

Shaikh Hamad bin Isa Al Khalifa of Bahrain in the white robe and, to the right, Crown Prince Saud aboard the Shaikh's Dhow

wives in camp. It was a fine party, but it hardly seemed like Christmas without snow and familiar faces.

Max Steineke and I left last Friday morning in a Ford sedan, followed by an Arab named Ahmed in a pickup truck. The company has nothing but Fords, and I have gained a great deal of respect for them in the last week. Down the coast to a place called Oqair, we passed a few dunes that I thought were especially treacherous. Fortunately I didn't say anything as, it turns out we were on the main highway south. At Oqair we were to pick up two soldiers and give the Emir, the chief man, a letter.

We arrived and Max gave the Emir the letter. He was really the assistant Emir, and he had to call for a scribe to read the letter. It was from the government representative, and this fellow didn't like taking orders from anyone other than his direct superior, Saud bin Jiluwi, the Emir of al-Hasa, which comprises our concession and has its capitol at Hofuf. Oqair is the seaport for Hofuf and consists of a mud-walled fort and an open warehouse alongside the wharf.

Saud bin Jiluwi's father, Abdullah, a close cousin to King Abdul Aziz, participated in the capture of the Masmak fort in Riyadh in 1902. Abdullah threw a spear at Ajlan, the Al Rashid Emir of Riyadh, but it missed him and stuck in the door to the fort. Before Ajlan could close the door, Abdul Aziz grabbed him. He kicked the king in the groin and fled. Abdullah chased Ajlan down and killed him.

Abdullah was the King's right-hand man. They were companions in arms throughout the three decades of campaigns that ensued as Abdul Aziz built his kingdom.

In 1913 the King's Wahhabi army captured Hofuf, the capital of al-Hasa. At that time the oasis of al-Hasa covered an area of about 30,000 acres with about 60 villages, of which Hofuf itself was by far the most important. With a population of 200,000 people, al-Hasa was the biggest true or interior oasis in the world. The Ruzaiz date was the mainstay of the economy and the kingdom's biggest export; however it was the premium date of Hofuf, the Khulas, that was universally regarded as the finest date in the Gulf.

Al-Hasa, a name which the Turks also used to denote the entire area now called the Eastern Province province, was also home to the great pearling ports of Qatif, Jubail and Tarut Island. Hundreds of pearling ships generated the kingdom's second-biggest export, but the industry was waning when I arrived as the Depression had diminished the market for jewels of all kinds, and Mikimoto's cultured pearls were beginning to erode the market for natural pearls.

The Eastern Province was a vital commercial area that required someone absolutely loyal to the king but someone who could govern, so the King made Abdullah bin Jiluwi the Emir of al-Hasa.

Like most of these Arab men brought up to govern, Abdullah was a tough governor, but fair and just in most people's eyes. One story was that when Abdullah first took over the governorship, a man came to his majlis *and said that there was a sack of rice on the way to Oqair. Abdullah asked him how he knew that it was a sack of rice. The man replied that he had kicked it with his toe. Abdullah then ordered his men to take this man outside and cut off his toe as a lesson about meddling with other people's property.*

Under Turkish rule, raiding and pillaging wayfarers had been a fact of life, but now raiding was over for good. Shaikh Abdullah Al Mubarak, the judge in the Eastern Province at my time, remembered that when the fighting was going on in the Hofuf citadel, where the Turks had retreated; Abdul Aziz was already passing judgment on those Bedu, who had started looting even before the fighting was over.

Abdullah died in 1936, and his son, Saud, carried on as Emir in the same spirit as his father. The wrath of Saud bin Jiluwi was feared far and wide, from the border of Oman in the south to the Kuwait Neutral Zone in the north.

We all sat on a sort of low wall around a porch in front of the entrance to the fort. The Assistant Emir was at one end with the chief of the soldiers on his right; Max and I were on his left. Max and the Emir got into quite a heated discussion. I felt terribly awkward in my *ghutra*, a kind of head-scarf, and *agaal*, a couple of turns of rope used on the head to keep the *ghutra* in place.

The customs house at Oqair, the Emir's fort is to the far left

First, we were served cardamom-flavored black coffee poured into small cups from a brass coffee pot. It is good manners to drink two cups and even better manners to drink three. Max and the Emir continued to argue. Max was annoyed because the two soldiers were ready to go and the Emir was just stalling. Then they served us sweetened tea, but insulted us.

The Emir's cup had been filled first, forgivable but showing no deference to his guests, and then the insult. The chief soldier's cup was filled next. We finished our tea and left with the two soldiers. Dhahran to Oqair is about 80 miles; Oqair to Selwa is about the same distance and twice as far in time. Max wanted me to get the practice, so I drove most of the way and got stuck in the sand four times. We arrived about sundown to be greeted by two bearded geologists, Walt Hoag and Jerry Harriss.

In retrospect, it seems to me that Max had known perfectly well what he was going to do with me as soon as he found out something about me. This trip, which was for a job of relatively short duration, would give him a chance to do so without committing himself to future assignments. At dinner that evening in the dining tent, we sat at two card tables shoved together. Jerry told several "shaggy dog" stories, a genre in which the punch line is pointless. Max and I laughed a bit at the proper moment, but Walt kept right on eating. Weeks later I learned that Jerry and Walt had stopped speaking to one another long before the

1936-37 field season. Once one of them going to work in the morning passed the other, whose car had broken down. The passer, who had the lunch, continued on his way, went about his business and picked up his partner on his way back to camp in the evening. If I got the barest of passing grades, I would be substituted for one or the other.

In the evening we practiced taking star shots before going to visit the soldiers, of whom there were 10, not counting the cook and the camp boy. These soldiers are armed Bedouin sent by Emir bin Jiluwi to escort our field parties in the desert. They make sure that everyone knows that we are here at the invitation of King Abdul Aziz ibn Saud and are not to be disturbed. They live in a large white canvas tent supported by two tent poles, American 2 by 4's, which the Arabs say are much better than the traditional poles. There is a door in the middle of one side and a sort of bolster on the opposite side covered with rugs, as is most of the floor. The soldiers' rifles and cartridge belts hang from the tent poles and give the place a martial flavor.

Emir Saud bin Jiluwi, Governor of the Eastern Province

These soldiers were generally Bedouin who were impressed by the government into service, given a rifle if they didn't have one of their own, rations and a monthly salary. As I wrote, their role was to make sure everyone knew we were working on the King's business and were under his protection. Since we always had more soldiers than we needed, we speculated that the government assigned us these men as a way to keep their services without having to pay them, as they were on Casoc's payroll.

We arranged ourselves along the bolsters. Walt and I are much too tall to sit with crossed legs in the approved fashion, but the main thing is not to insult anyone by pointing the sole of your foot at him. In the center of the tent, the coals of the incense urn glowed while a hunting hawk sat on its perch near the entrance. The place was lit by two kerosene lanterns and the campfire, which burned just outside of the door. We had coffee and then tea. Max, Jerry, and Walt talked with the soldiers, particularly Hussein, the Emir of the soldiers. Though it seems every third person around here is an emir, the word means the leader or headman of any specific group of men.

December 31, 1937
Bay of Selwa

Here we are back in Selwa to do the star work I wrote about. Jerry has established a cache half a day from here, which we can use as a base on our way to a place called Sufuk Wells. Before bed, we went over for coffee with the soldiers only to discover that Hussein, Emir of the soldiers, had orders for us to go to these wells by a different route. His route was much longer and unknown both to us and to the guides. We could have gone that way, but we never would have finished our work in the time allotted us. Jerry left at midnight, drove nine hours to Dhahran and explained the situation to Max. For the last two days, Walt and I have been in camp listening to the radio every hour for further orders. Tonight Jerry returned to tell us to start work on some closer boundary points while the manager at Dhahran awaits word from the King regarding a deadline extension on this survey.

Medora, North Dakota – December 23, 1937

My Darling,

Believe it or not Bing Crosby is singing "Adeste Fidelis" on the radio; it really isn't bad either, though I'd say he is definitely not the type.

It gets harder and harder to write you; I date a letter and think four Thursdays ago, and five Thursdays ago. I can't forget those few short days and nights together. Now Bing is singing, "She's Tall, She's Lou." Incidentally I like dancing with you more than anyone in the world, that covers a lot of territory but then you are really extraordinary and I mean really.

A definition of hope: "Hope is like a fish leaping out of the water. A certain longing drives every man to it, but he's better off below." But I still hope that this is the last Christmas we must have to be so far apart.

Good night, my dearest. Merry, Merry Christmas and a very good year for my best husband.

All my love for you,
Kath

January 1, 1938
Selwa

A Happy New Year to you. I dreamed of you all day. Perhaps, Kath, it will be happier than we think. Yesterday, Well No. Seven blew in with a roar. No. Two, the second well drilled at Dhahran, came in with much gas and some oil at about the same geological depth as the producers on Bahrain. The company prepared itself to produce oil and drilled more wells. Unfortunately, none of them produced satisfactory amounts of oil. Now this No. Seven was drilled much deeper than the other wells, almost as a last desperate chance. They have had a devil of a time drilling it. Though it is too early to know much, everyone is optimistic. The more oil we find, the more people will come and the sooner I'll have you here with me.

Walt is just now breaking open a can of prune juice for me to celebrate the New Year. He and Jerry are whooping it up with warm apricot juice. Salih bin Mijhud, the cook, just came in to help Jerry make out the food order for the next four months. About all I can understand is the numbers.

The other day we met an old camel herder at a well. He asked Walt if it had rained in the north. Walt said, "Yes, and perhaps it will rain here."

"Yes," replied the old man, "*Allah kareem*," God is generous. Later, the old man brought us a big aluminum bowl of camel's milk. It tasted good. The Bedu can live on the salty water of this well because they let the camels drink it and they drink the camel's milk. It is not unusual for a man to go for months without drinking water at all.

Today Walt and I went eighty miles south to Mishash al-Iziba, where we have our gasoline cached for the Sufuk Wells trip. A *mishash* is a shallow well with drinkable water. We took down two soldiers as watchmen to replace the two already there. They had been there for three days – this was the fourth – and the first people they had seen were a couple of Bedu who came in with a herd of camels just before we arrived.

To get back to the coffee ceremony, when we approach the tent, we all say, "*Salaam aleikum,*" Peace be with you, and the soldiers all reply, "*Wa aleikum es salaam,*" And to you peace.

Then everyone says to everyone else, "*Mesak Allah bil khair,*" Good evening, but more literally "the peace of God be with your evening." All the time, everyone is shaking hands all around while continuing with "How are you?" to which you reply, "Good," to which the host says, "*Al Hamdulillah,*" Praise God. Then you say "How are you?" He says "Good," and you say "Praise God." It is considered good form to repeat this several times. It is as if you are so delighted that your friend is in good health, you want to hear it over and over again.

After we are seated and the Emir has inquired after our health some more, he signals the server to bring in the tea. It is served from a brass pot into glass cups about the size of a demitasse. The server fills the cup to the brim and offers it to you. The first round you wave away to the host, the Emir, who declines and waves it back to you. The tea is without milk, but very sweet; the sweeter it is, the more you are being honored. One night we were treated to tea with camel milk.

You should drink at least two cups, but three cups is best. At first I sipped mine quietly, but I have since learned that noise is a mark of appreciation and I can now slurp with the best. Likewise, belching is in high approval and fills the heart of the host with joy, as it is proof that everyone has had plenty of food.

After the tea comes the coffee. The coffee beans are roasted in a shallow pan at the campfire, ground with a mortar and pestle and made into coffee immediately. It is served in little cups, smaller than the teacups, which are half filled with the black unsweetened brew. Sometimes it is flavored with cardamom seed, sometimes with cloves. To get a full cup of coffee is a sign of high disfavor, the implication being that you should drink up and be gone, the sooner you leave the better.

All this time there is much talk and joking. This business about Arabs not laughing is baloney. The Emir Hussein's hawk sits on his perch by the door and blinks like an owl unless he has his hunting hood on; then he just sits. After the coffee, the talk turns to business, if there is any, but only after the coffee. Finally the server brings in the incense urn with fresh coals in it. The Emir unlocks a chest, takes out some incense and places it on the coals. The server then takes the urn to each in turn. While he holds it under your nose, you make a sort of tent around it with your *ghutra* and take a couple of whiffs. The Arabs say incense is good for the nose. The urn comes around four or five times and then you are free to go home. Everyone shakes hands all around again and says, "*Fi aman Allah,*" in the care of God.

In the morning we drove to the well at Selwa, about four miles from our base, shot the sun and shot the stars that evening. Max returned to Dhahran while Jerry, Walt and I set out to determine the latitude and longitude of a place called Ain al-Nakhla. *Ain* means well and *nakhla* means palm tree; in this case the well is two five-foot deep holes in the sand and the *nakhla* comes from a lone palm tree about a kilometer away.

Ain Selwa, notice the gurbas in the bed of the pickup truck

Jerry and I drove in the sedan with our two guides, Khamis bin Rimthan and Salih bin Qamra, and a soldier named Hamud. Khamis is from the Ajman, a big tribe in the north, and is said to be the best guide in eastern Arabia. Salih is a Murra tribesman. This is his home territory, but he hasn't been in this country since he was a boy, so he's not much help. Salih says that he is 58 years old, but few desert Arabs know their exact age. Hamud is descended from Africans sold into slavery and is reputed to be the best shot of our 10 soldiers.

Walt drove a pickup followed by our mechanic, Shauby, who drove another pickup with a soldier named Saud. Shauby comes from the Hejaz, the western province of Arabia, and is quite a character. He is the only one of our crew who has been abroad; he worked on the coaling gang of a British steam ship for a year or two. He has a wife in Mecca, but, being diplomatic, he took another wife from the town of Jubail on this coast, so he's one of the hometown guys now.

Because his first wife is coming from Mecca to find out what it's all about, Shauby told Walt that he's glad to be out here in the desert. Of course, any man is entitled to four wives, but sometimes the old ones don't approve of the new one.

Khamis bin Rimthan during the 1935 field season as photographed by the geologist, J. W. "Soak" Hoover

We shot the stars at Ain al-Nakhla and left the next morning to a place called Rimth, where we camped and took more starshots. The exact time is critically important in determining longitude, so we check our chronometer every night against the radio time signals from England and France.

The next morning we set out for a well called Ain al-Khufus. Salih bin Qamra was supposed to know where it was. Eventually, we found a well with a Bedu woman and child standing beside it. Salih hopped out of the car and said to them, "This is Khufus, isn't it?", which made Jerry furious.

Jerry saw a Bedu man approaching and rushed over to interview the fellow before Salih could prejudice him, too. It was not Khufus. Undaunted, Salih took us to a second well that was not Khufus, but turned out to be another well we were looking for. We finally found Khufus with the help of a Bedu we met. We persuaded him to get in the car and direct us there. The poor fellow got in the back and tried to cross his feet and sit up on the seat, but there was no room after Salih got in. When we started driving, he hung on for dear life. Salih nearly died laughing, though it's not so long since he was in the same boat. After reaching the well, our new-found guide disappeared; we later saw him walking back alone.

After Khufus, we continued our survey to the shores of "the new lake" Bertram Thomas claimed to have found in his book *Arabia Felix*. We think it is an arm of the sea. By the way, don't take Thomas too seriously. He says he couldn't go to Selwa and Iskuk because of the possibility of attack by fanatical Ikhwan, a dangerous religious sect. I asked Walt about these dangerous zealots, and it seems some of our soldiers were Ikhwan!

Selwa, located a few miles away from our tin shed, consisted of a tiny grove of bedraggled palm trees, several shallow wells and an abandoned mud fort. The fort had been built some years ago only to be abandoned shortly after its completion. Like Iskuk, it had been an Ikhwan settlement.

The King had founded the Ikhwan as a religious group of brothers who foreswore their tribal allegiance in favor of absolute loyalty to the King. They were encouraged to settle on the land and become agriculturists. In the early flush of enthusiasm, Ikhwan colonies sprang up all over the kingdom. Most of them were eventually abandoned, but a few grew into sizeable and prosperous towns of great importance because they were a reservoir of military manpower that not only could be called upon to defend the Kingdom, but could also be used against internal rebels. Having foresworn their tribal allegiances, they were ready to fight anyone, anywhere, as part of their duty to the King.

More in another installment. Tomorrow we go out to map Sabkha al-Amarah and shoot the position of Ain al-Amrah. Thomas says his guide took him to the Sabkha, and lo, it was a lake. Passing the lake going north, he then beheld "a great salt plain here called Amrah." A *sabkha* is a great salt plain and has nothing to do with lakes.

The work is good, darling, and I like the desert, but sometimes I am so lonesome for you that three years grow into three centuries. Before we arrived here I hadn't a letter from you for three weeks. The night before we left Selwa I dreamed of you the whole night, both waking and sleeping in fits and starts.

It is better, though, to have memories of those few days and nights together than should I have come here with only yearning in my heart. I love you so; may you never regret marrying me. For you, in the midst of people, it must be far more lonely than it is for me. Love me always; perhaps someday I can repay you.

Happy New Year to you. We'll be here for a period of two or three weeks locating points, so don't be anxious if you don't hear from me.

More than 40 years later, I am still amazed that in a month's time I met and became good friends with perhaps the two most remarkable men I was ever to encounter in my life. Max Steineke and Khamis bin Rimthan, though born on the opposite ends of the earth and as physically different as they could be – the one, big and boisterous; the other, a rangy and slightly self-effacing man of medium height – were essentially cut from the same cloth. Energetic, intelligent men, when subjected to physical hardships, stinging winds, poor food and worse water, they never mentioned it unless it was an occasion for a good joke.

On the desert, Khamis was never lost. For in addition to his sixth sense, a sort of infallible, built-in compass, he had an extraordinary memory that could recall a bush that he had passed as a young man or the directions to a well that someone had told him about 10 years before.

Under the desert, among the strata of rocks and sediment that are the geologist's domain, Max was much the same as Khamis, able to relate an outcropping he might find on the coast to a paragraph in a thick geological report he had read years earlier. Figuratively as well as literally, they both seemed always to know where they were and where they were going next.

Khamis bin Rimthan and Max Steineke – 1936
Picture by J. W. "Soak" Hoover

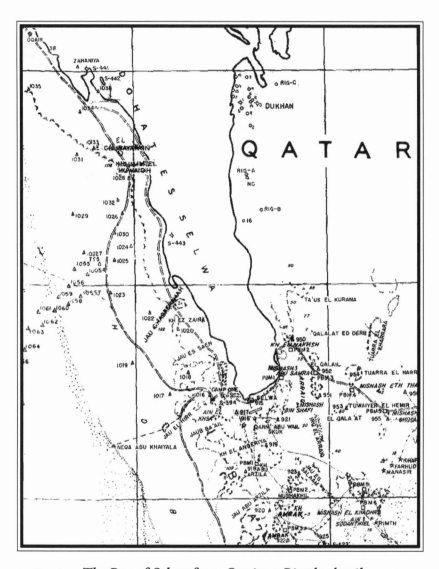

The Bay of Selwa from Oqair to Rimth, detail
of a field map drawn by T.C. Barger - July 1938

Unloading the supply dhow on the beach at Selwa

Chapter Three
"The House at Selwa"

January 7, 1938
Al-Qasr, Selwa

A *qasr* is a house, a fort, a building or a pile of rocks, as far as I can find out. It sounds like "gusser," but better men than I spell it "*qasr*." As ours is the only house for miles and miles, the Arabs call it *al-Qasr al-Selwa*, the house at Selwa. Walt and Jerry have been gone for two days shooting stars at a couple of wells and are due back this afternoon. The supply boat from Khobar is also due, but I'd rather see Walt and Jerry. The radio transmitter quit on me last night, and it looks too complicated for a novice like me to tinker with.

There is a strong south wind today with dust everywhere. Normally the wind is from the north-northwest; all the dunes are formed and the drifts of sand are laid down so exactly in this north to south axis that you can never lose your direction. However, when a south wind arises, it sort of catches the sand by surprise and whirls it about in great style.

Most of the morning I sat upon a hill watching the bay for the supply boat. The wind came up gradually off to the south and formed dust clouds that looked like prairie fires or like the clouds blowing off the sandy country south of Linton. Gradually the far off *jabals* disappeared and even Qarn Abu Wail, a whopping big one only 10 miles away, became a gray shadow. A *jabal* is a hill or sometimes a range of hills, but a *qarn* is a hill only, a butte or peak isolated from any nearby hills or ranges.

There is someone coming across the *sabkha* now, but I can't make out whether it is a car or a camel. A *sabkha* is a perfectly flat salt plain, usually encrusted with a sort of salty mud cake, which is good for driving on in dry weather. There is one north of Dhahran on which you can drive at 60 miles an hour for hours. However, the earth is always damp a foot or so beneath the *sabkha*. When it rains, the surface becomes a combination of quicksand and wet gumbo that no car can traverse. In driving over bad *sabkha,* the rule is to stick to old tracks or a camel trail (with one wheel). In dunes and *dikakah,* knee-high drifts of sand behind bushes, it is better to break a new trail rather than drive in sand that is already churned up. Those are camels coming across the *sabkha.*

We are still making astronomical observations at various points that are likely to figure in the forthcoming boundary dispute between Ibn Saud and Petroleum Concessions Limited, the British oil company in Qatar. The government thinks that it is more secretive for us to travel in one car; consequently, our limit is about a three-day trip before we must return for more gas. They are very conservative here. Actually, we could stay out for five days, but the safety margin is maintained for unforeseen problems.

Besides being allowed only one car, we are also supposed to take four soldiers. We have an enclosed Ford station wagon with four-wheel drive that is made especially for this job. It is almost impossible to stick in the sand and can do sixty miles an hour on the *sabkha*s. The first day we loaded on all the equipment and put our cook and mechanic in the back; two of us got into the front and drove over to pick up our soldiers. There was only room for three, so the Emir rose to the occasion and told us we would only need to take three soldiers.

The purpose of our exploration was not simply to map the area, though that was of prime importance, but also, given the disappointment in the drilling to date as well as four and a half years of geological work, to determine if there were any more geological structures likely to contain oil. This meant primarily looking for hills that would expose the rocks they were composed of, or less likely, finding surface outcrops of some of the rocks older than those of the relatively recent date that blanketed most of eastern Arabia. All of the oilfields then known in the Middle East were associated with either oil and gas seeps at the surface or with structures that were prominent topographic features. We didn't have the time to attempt a minute geological investigation of such a vast area, so we narrowed down the search by quizzing our guides about the terrain around us.

l-r. Tom, Walt Hoag, Max Steineke and Jerry Harriss

Walt and I were out three days and two nights. The first night we camped at Ain al-Amrah, on the Qatar peninsula. It is a well that consists of some shallow holes amongst dunes, which are completely innocent of any vegetation whatsoever. It's the most barren place I've ever seen. That night it rained really hard so there was no star shooting.

The sprinkling began about eight o'clock. The soldiers were huddled in blankets around the coals of their campfire. Walt told them that if it continued to rain, they could sleep in the station wagon when we finished our radio work. Old Salih, the Murra guide, replied, "*Allah kareem*," God is generous, and the rest chorused, "*Allah kareem*." Nothing to be done about the rain. However, when it really began to pour, they all found cover, two in a corner of our tent, two in the station wagon and one under it.

The second night we had perfect weather and then back to camp the next day. The following morning Walt and Jerry left for Khafus, Farhud, and Manasir, leaving me here. These three points are close together, only about 40 miles from here, and the only ones of the lot that I know how to find. If they aren't back tonight, I will go out with a couple of trucks, gasoline and spare parts and find them. In case you should get some books on Arabia with maps in them, Walt and I were at Ain al-Amrah, the second and third Europeans ever to visit.

All these places we are locating are wells. Many of the names are applied to nearby *jabals* or *sabkhas*, but the really important place to a Bedouin is the well itself. Thus there are Ain al-Manasir, Sabkha Manasir and Aglaat Manasir. *Aglaat* comes from *agaal,* which is a camel hobble, as well as the rope which holds the *ghutra* on one's head; it designates a shallow well, three to four feet to the water, which is roughly the length of an *agaal*.

After leaving my perch on the hill this morning, I went over to pay my respects to the Emir. While the cook made the tea and coffee, we talked, but neither of us understood much. My Arabic consists of about four verbs, of which I know one or two forms in the present tense, and a handful of mispronounced nouns.

The Emir caught a new hawk four days ago. He named him Dahad and has begun training him. The old hawk, Fellah, has caught 113 *hubarrah*, a game bird something like a sage hen and about the size of a young turkey. The training begins by tying the hawk on a small round perch, feeding him and getting him to allow himself to be petted. Dahad, being a bright bird, allowed himself to be petted the second day. Next, he is taught to sit on a gauntlet worn on the left hand. Each time he is fed, his name is barked at him continually at a pitch audible for a few hundred yards. Later he is fed by making him sit on the gauntlet while the master pushes a piece of meat out through the end. I'm told that the bird soon learns to distinguish between the meat and the master's fingers.

From time to time, a leather hood is placed over his head and the drawstring lightly tightened. The new hawk promptly claws or shakes it off, but in time he becomes used to it. The hawk is allowed to get very hungry before he is fed. When he finally sees the meat, he hops off his perch and onto the gauntlet without any coaxing.

Still later, they'll take Dahad out and train him to light on a couple of flapping *hubarrah* wings. Besides stocking these wings, the well-equipped hawk hunter also carries a dove with him. The hawk rides along, perched on the gauntlet with his hood over his eyes and an empty stomach. When the hunter raises a *hubarrah*, he takes the hawk's hood off and unleashes him. The hawk gets the *hubarrah* and the hunter gets both. Sometimes the hawk refuses to return, and the dove is used for bait. Last year, Jerry bought a hawk for eight dollars. The soldiers carefully trained him, and on the first hunt the bird flew away, never to be seen again.

I was going to tell you more about this one-car foolishness. Most of these places we visit have only been seen by one or two Europeans, if any. As we have the only cars in this part of Arabia, it's hard to see how one car is more secretive than half a dozen. Anyone really interested could sit on Khashem al-Naksh in Qatar, less than 20 miles away, and watch us through a good telescope.

Had I been a little more experienced, I would have realized that the Bedu telegraph was an even better reason why this secretiveness was pretty foolish. In this sparsely populated desert with very small groups of people spending weeks at a time alone, whenever they met someone else, they would spend hours going over every little bit of news. Americans driving around in a car would definitely be big news that would quickly spread across the whole desert.

The more points we located and mapped relative to these border discussions, the more it dawned on us that with the exception of the King himself, no one on either side, British or Saudi, knew the slightest thing about the geography of this area. We often were requested to locate non-existent landmarks. One place, which the British negotiators claimed as an immutable landmark, we found to be some thirty-five miles further north, which is favorable to Saudi Arabia, than shown on the maps used by the English. They promptly lost interest in that site.

I have spent the last two days computing the data we took at Ain al-Amrah. Last night I got the coded message about the departure of the supply boat, then the transmitter quit working just as I finished signaling Jerry and Walt. We don't talk, but have some special signals we use. It is another aspect of the secrecy game; Casoc sends us coded messages pretending they are for another camp 100 miles north of Dhahran.

Muhammad bin Dhabit, secretary of the soldiers by virtue of being the only one able to read and write, came in for a visit and stayed for two hours of much hand motioning and broken Arabic. I have a book with English words in the center column, Arabic equivalents on the left and Arabic pronunciation in English characters on the right. Muhammad reads the Arabic when he can't understand my murdering of his native tongue. "*Wagid kelam fi Arabi,*" many words in Arabic, is right.

The Islamic conquest impressed the language on an enormous variety of people; thus a book on Egyptian Arabic may not be much good for a beginner in Mesopotamia. Even among the various tribes of Bedouin there are wide differences. The word Bedouin, meaning desert Arab, sounds more like "Bedu" or "Badu." Walt says it is spelled Bedouin because it was first transliterated by a Frenchman.

I hear the Emir out banging away with his muzzle-loading shotgun. He is probably hunting rabbits and field mice for Dahad's lunch.

The boat arrived about four and Walt and Jerry a half-hour later. We're unloading the boat by moonlight. No airmail this trip.

January 12, 1938
Selwa

Walt Hoag and I are going out tomorrow to a place called al-Akerish, another place that no European has ever seen before. After Akerish we will have only Sufuk Wells left to survey, though we still don't have permission to visit them. We've had some sandstorms, but there's no dirt to blow, only sand. They are not as dirty as dust storms in North Dakota, and the visibility is much better. It is marvelous how Khamis knows where he is all the time. Riding in the back of the station wagon, he knows his whereabouts better than we do with all of our maps and instruments. The current sandstorm has been blowing for the last three days. The thermometer doesn't go any lower at night, but the wind whistling through our tin-roofed warehouse sounds like a blizzard and makes it feel colder.

The supply boat brought us six ducks, but we haven't yet decided whether to eat them or their eggs. Muhammad, the houseboy, built separate quarters for the ducks, as the rooster wouldn't let them in with his hens. Salih serves us bacon, eggs and hotcakes for breakfast. The mystery is how he packs the eggs so they don't break after jolting overland all day.

Speaking of jolting, my respect for the Ford car increases. This Ford station wagon is fitted with a Marmon Harrington four-wheel drive that will do 60 miles an hour on the *sabkha*s and two miles an hour in the dunes. It is the perfect car for this job, as the big six-wheel trucks are too slow and no other car could carry two geologists, a cook, a mechanic and three soldiers, as well as a radio, the chronometer, a transit with tripod, four goatskins of water, spare springs and parts, a drum of gasoline and another of distilled water, food, bedrolls and tents for seven men.

Raghwan was quite a well compared to most of the ones we've visited. Situated in the cup of a dune, it is surrounded with bushes and plants, and the soldiers say its water is fresh "like rain water."

We spent the entire day on computations, as our observations are piling up faster than we can do the calculations. We are allowed only 21 days for this job. We have 10 days left to get to Sufuk Wells and make our last observation. In between, I am trying to study Arabic and read Doughty's *Travels in Arabia Deserta*, the best of all the Arabian books. Although it was written in 1875, I'm told it has never been equalled as a description of Arabia, the Arabs and the land in the north and western regions. Walt Hoag has read it twice, and says that I won't really appreciate it until I have been here a year and get to know the Arabs better.

Walt was working on the radio the other day and heard one of our engineers in Jubail calling Casoc to find out what day it was.

January 16, 1938
Selwa

So you may be pregnant? Much as I would love and be very proud of Ann or Michael, I hope she or he doesn't come just yet, but rather later when we are together. Then I can stand forth and say, "this is my wife" to one and all without hurting those who are dear to me.

(Next day) I've been thinking of Ann or Michael all day. If she or he comes, I shall have to write my folks and tell them; it will hurt them very much, and I have prayed that somehow they may come to know and love you in the meantime.

If you should cable me, word it so that the message can be passed over the radio without everyone knowing about our private business.

January 19, 1938
Jabal Dhahran

The soldiers are curious about everything. When Walt told them about winter in America, they couldn't understand why anyone would live in a country piled with ice and snow half of the year. Often when he tells them something particularly astounding, especially if it is man-made, one of them, usually old Salih, will say, *"Allah Akbar,"* God is the greatest. The others follow suit and say, *"Allah Akbar,"* presumably to show that after all it doesn't amount to much.

Thus far I like the desert fine. This is the best season of the year, and this winter is said to be much milder than usual. There is usually some wind, mostly just sort of a breeze. Sandstorms are not the common occurrence that I had supposed. Though there are lots of flies, they just walk on you without biting, unlike the blackflies and mosquitoes at home.

We had an interesting trip up here. At the stop for lunch, Muhammad, the houseboy, became violently ill with a pain in his stomach. I think he was car sick from riding in the station wagon. It is a rough ride, especially for someone not used to cars. Jerry theorized that it was caused by eating tainted shrimp. We made the poor guy drink a quart of hot water and put his fingers down his throat.

Meanwhile, the soldiers had brewed their coffee and had an iron in the fire. They announced that if we failed to cure him, they would try burning the soles of his feet with the hot iron. Muhammad made a quick recovery. I don't know what theory lies behind the iron; I suppose the burn hurts so much you forget about the original ailment. These poor people have no doctors and only the simplest and crudest of remedies. Despite their *"Enshallah,"* if God wills, they are desperately eager to be doctored. A geologist out here has to be an amateur physician.

We treat the simple ailments, but many are beyond our diagnosis, let alone treatment, so we give them something that won't hurt them and say, *"Enshallah,* you will be better tomorrow." Pills have to be doled out in single doses, as the Bedu are confirmed in the belief that if one is good, six would be better. Perhaps you could find me some books on amateur doctoring. All the first-aid manuals I've read say, "Make the patient comfortable and call a doctor."

In camp our soldiers pray five times a day. When we are traveling, they pray only three times a day. Most of them have no watches, so they tell time by the sun. They smooth a flat place in the sand, place the little finger on the ground, and, with the hand spread as much as possible and the thumb straight up, mark the point at the end of the thumb's shadow. If the distance from the little finger to the mark of the thumb's shadow is two hand spans, it is time to pray.

This place is worse than Great Bear Lake for money. No one ever has more than a few rupees. Everything you want, you charge to your account. If the customs people charge you duty, you sign a slip. When I went to Bahrain, Jim Garry introduced me in the stores as a geologist from Arabia and I could have anything in the place. A fellow could buy $500 worth of movie equipment without making any deposit or signing a check. It simply comes out of your pay. The company looks after everything; you don't even buy stamps. Just drop the envelope in the box with your name on the return address, and it is deducted from your account. If you overrun your field allotment, it comes out of your home pay.

Back in the field next week, we shall probably not return to Dhahran for two or three months and possibly not until the middle of May. First we are going to the Jabrin oasis, 250 miles southwest of Selwa; it has been visited by only two Europeans previously, Major Cheesman in 1924 and the explorer H. St. John Philby in 1931. Once a large settlement with large date palm gardens, the gardens have been abandoned and the population dispersed because of a fever, presumably malaria. There were groves of palms and ruined buildings and forts when Philby visited.

After Jabrin, we are going to explore to the southeast behind the Trucial Coast of Oman. The boundary is still in dispute, but we know the territory that is undoubtedly part of Saudi Arabia. It corresponds roughly to the sandy desert part of the Rub' al-Khali.

This is one of the largest unexplored tracts of land in the world outside of the Polar Regions. It is to the east of Bertram Thomas's route and never has been entered from the coast on the north and east.

Formerly on such trips they hauled gasoline by camels to an outlying base. We are going to try using a six-wheel-drive truck with big soft tires to haul two weeks' supplies from Selwa to a base camp and have the truck return to Selwa for a second load if needed.

Abu Sita, **the father of six,** *our desert-worthy truck*

Before this time, when the field parties were supplied by camel, it required as many as 25 camels to carry the gasoline, diesel oil, electric generator and all the other paraphernalia of a camp. After everything was unloaded, the camels would be set free to forage, and the geologists, in their red Fords with low-pressure tires, would survey the surrounding area, map it and then locate the site of the next base camp. Khamis and a couple of the soldiers would go out to find the camels. Since it might take a few days, if not a week, to find all the camels, it was not uncommon to spend two weeks just to move the base camp. Though we made fun of our "desert-worthy" truck, we always knew where it was.

Grand Forks, North Dakota - December 28, 1937
(At this time Kathleen is working as a caseworker for the County
  Welfare Board)

Write me very soon. I'm going to the doctor next week, though
I'm almost certain of the verdict. However I'm going to try to work
until March.

I love you so much, so much. You know that if I ever write
"off" letters, don't blame me too much. Tom, in case it is true we are
going to have Michael, will you write your folks? I suppose the
marriage will have to be announced; we'd can't have Michael think
he was illegitimate or something. Maybe you'd rather have me tell
them. Please answer me right away. Air Mail!

January 19,1938
Jabal Dhahran

Your letter of December 28 just arrived. So you think we will
have Michael or Ann? I do not know exactly how we should break
the news to my parents. I suppose that it would be best if first I
broke the news of our marriage before telling them about the baby.

It isn't a question of their dictating how I live my life, but
simply that they have been most kind and loving to me these many
years. I would be much happier if they would only accept you in
their hearts.

So it will be as I suggested long ago; Michael will want to know,
"Who is that funny-looking man coming down the gangplank?" Or
maybe it will be Ann. In either case, I am sure such parents could not
fail to have a most charming baby.

Grand Forks – January 3, 1938

Tom, I feel so wretched; I could have an out-and-out good
weep session. There isn't going to be any Michael, and now it will be
so long; honestly I had my heart set on having him. But maybe it's

much better this way; in fact, I know it is. Darling, I must be with you soon, my "soons" being measured in months. I never realized before how much having a baby really means to me.

Crazy question – I've been dying to know if it is cold there. I've been freezing so much myself I guess I can't think of anything else. Grandpa says that he read that it has snowed there; is that so?

Sometimes it's very lonely, but always I know that you love me and then my temporary unhappiness vanishes. I do miss Michael so, in spite of the fact that I prayed he wouldn't come. I always said, "Thy will, not mine, Oh Lord, be done" and hoped He'd want me to have him.

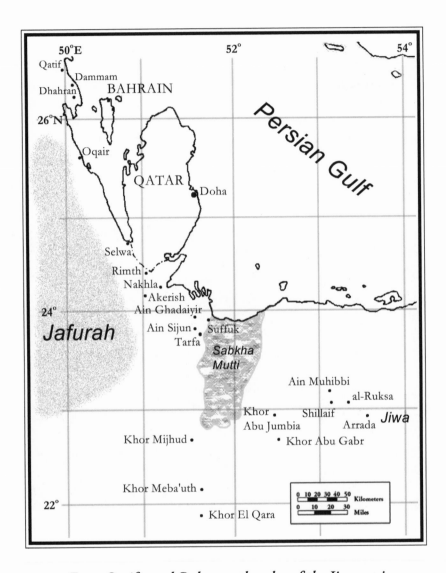

From Qatif to al-Ruksa on the edge of the Jiwa oasis

Leaving Casoc in January 1938
l-r. Jerry Harriss; Shauby and Ibrahim, drivers; Muhd. bin Abdul Latif, houseboy;
Salih, cook; Saud, Khamis bin Rimthan and Muhd. bin Sulman, soldiers; and Tom.
Note the warm clothing.

Chapter 4
"Jiwa"

January 25, 1938
Jabal Dhahran

Your letter announcing the non-arrival of Michael or Ann came this afternoon. I am not really glad, Kath, more sort of relieved. I was getting so swelled up at the thought of becoming a father that I wasn't worrying much about telling my folks.

Now I can write some letters to various people. I've sort of been holding off to find out whether we would have to announce our wedding to preserve your honor.

(Later) The wind whistles through the screen, Kass; most lonesome is the sound, and when it is snowing and cold, think of me in no blizzard, but I still shiver in the raw north wind of the Rub' al-Khali, wriggling into a set of damp clothes in a Bedu tent.

Sometimes when I am most lonely for you, I try to argue to myself that I really don't miss you so much because we were together for such a short time, but it's no use. It is as you said once, time has nothing to do with love. Perhaps it does make it stronger; if so, from a start like this, ours should develop into a right lusty sort of affection.

Grand Forks – February 14, 1938

You poor darling, how Michael must have worried you. By now however, you no doubt have been assured that he isn't coming. 'Twas with greatest irony I received your letter this morning when I was so sick with cramps I couldn't even read it. I was forced to stay home all day, as I had a fever.

Visited my folks and returned on the train that gets into Medora at 2:15 a.m. I got a berth and went to bed, waking up from time to time with an aching desire to be in your arms again. I wish you could have seen the hills in the moonlight. It was so bright and clear. There has been more snow than we've had in years. It was very lonely, and somewhere I knew you were trudging along in the sand or probably just having lunch.

January 31, 1938
Selwa

Yesterday we had the Emir and Khamis in for a conference. Jerry told them that from now on our orders were that we were to go where we pleased, as we pleased – no more of this one-car traveling. Thank goodness. We now know more about the official boundaries between Saudi Arabia and the Trucial Coast Shaikhdoms, so it will be our responsibility to stay on the Saudi side.

Before coming here, we asked the government representative to obtain for us a guide from the Manasir or Awamir tribes into whose territory we are entering. However, Emir bin Jiluwi already has sent us a new guide, Abdul Hadi bin Jithina, a Murra who is supposed to know the country to the east very well. His brother was the guide for Bertram Thomas. We had him over and tried him out. A toothless, sharp-eyed Bedu, he answered all of our questions without hesitation and a minimum of "*Yimkens,*" maybe, and "*Enshallahs.*" Either he knew all of the places we named or he didn't; this is most desirable in a guide. He knew the correct directions between places that we knew to be accurately placed on the map. In some cases he was at variance with the map, but the map is based on hearsay.

For instance, he knew Dhafra and a place shown on the map as "Liwa," which he said was east of Dhafra. The map shows it south of Dhafra. We asked him for the names of some of the wells in Liwa, and he named a dozen that were shown on the map. At first he spoke of a place called "Jiwa," which we couldn't find. After some palaver, with Khamis questioning Abdul Hadi because Jerry and Abdul Hadi don't yet understand one another very well, Khamis explained that the Murra call the district "Jiwa," but the Manasir and the Awamir call it "Liwa." It is hard for us to read the names off the map and pronounce them so the Arabs will understand. If Arabic is written in English, there is no way of knowing where the accent goes or how the letters are sounded. It is much better to get the guides to name the places and see if we can locate them on the map.

Abdul Hadi said that in Jiwa there is an oasis as big as Hofuf, which surprised us. The town of Hofuf has a population of about 30,000. Unlike many Bedu, Abdul Hadi has been to Hofuf and knows how large it is in fact. None of the explorers mention a town of such size in that part of Arabia behind the Trucial Coast, but then no mapmakers have ever been there. Much of the coast is only charted as a dotted line. The British, who speak in the name of the Sultan of Abu Dhabi at the boundary conferences, claim some sort of dominion over this coast. The best basis for their claim is that they eliminated piracy along the coast 50 years ago.

Tomorrow we go into the desert again, but not to Jabrin; instead we will strike off to the southeast into virgin territory. The maps are vague, though it really isn't unknown country because the Bedu inhabitants know every bit of it. No Europeans have ever been there, so instead of being third or fourth at a place, we'll be first. From a geological standpoint it should be quite interesting, as the country is so remote we have no idea of what we might find. The map shows mountains on the coast of Oman, but no geologist has ever investigated them or seen what exists on the Saudi side.

The senior geologist and my partner is a guy named Jerry Harriss. He's 35 years old and a graduate of Pomona College in Los Angeles. He worked for an oil company in California, taught at Pomona and spent three years in Hawaii working in marine geology. He was married for seven or eight years but divorced his wife just before coming here in 1936.

Max says Jerry is the best geologist in Casoc, though he is somewhat impractical with machinery. As Walt Hoag says, "Anything that runs is a mystery to Jerry." He is always ready to stop and explain geological details to me. Though his contract is up in October he may stay over for another year. If so, he and I will do some detailed geological work up north, which will be invaluable to my education as a geologist.

Each afternoon we have coffee with the soldiers. They invariably come with the invitation at the most inopportune moment, but I enjoy the sessions and am beginning to understand some of the conversations. Abdul Hadi provides much of the diversion. He is the only one of the soldiers who smokes, "drinks tobacco" as they put it, and being the newest, he would get a lot of ribbing anyway. After smoking his pipe, which is made of a piece of bone and an empty cartridge held together with a piece of black tape, he refills it, and sitting cross-legged on the floor, holds it between his big and second toes while he drinks his coffee.

The Bedu have a good sense of humor, but I'm not always sure what will strike them as funny. The Emir told Abdul Hadi that he smoked too much and that it made him weak and short of wind. Abdul Hadi, who is even now a tough old bird, admitted that before he began to smoke, he was tough as an elephant. Then, without thinking, I said, "Now you are like a *jerboa*," a small desert mouse, but he wasn't offended as the soldiers roared with laughter. The Emir said, "No, I think he is more like a *damusa*," a little sand lizard. Everyone laughed again, even Abdul Hadi, who hid his mouth with his *ghutra* as he laughed

The other night Abdul Hadi gave a simplified version of a raid he went on as a young man into the country of the Sa'ar, between the Rub' al-Khali and the Hadhramaut, far to the south. They got 22 camels, 26 sheep and one Sa'ar, who counted discretion the better part of valor.

The strategy of desert raiding was based on getting in, getting your loot and getting out as fast as possible. The tactics employed depended on whether you were after sheep or camels. Sheep were more difficult because you couldn't move them as quickly.

The ideal raid was to go in on horseback with your cow camels left behind. Dash in, get your victim's sheep or camels and make a quick retreat before he can respond in force. Meet up with your camels and head home. Of course, women and children were never to be harmed in these raids, and there was a tradition that you never took the victim's entire herd. If he had 10 camels, a raider would take nine of them, being sure to leave at least one cow camel so the victim wouldn't die of thirst.

In general there was very little killing. However if there were a blood feud involved, it might be different. The primary objective was plunder; the secondary goal was for the excitement and the sport of the raid itself. These two factors were always tempered by the realization that every raider could just as easily be the victim the next time.

The raids of the Ikhwan were an entirely different matter. The age-old codes and traditions of desert raiding were completely violated. Infant boys would be taken from their mothers and both of them put to the sword. Destruction of the infidels – in this case, anyone not an Ikhwan was more important than plunder. The soldiers never talked about these raids because they were deeply ashamed of what had been done.

In the early 1930s, the Ikhwan rebelled against the King and were soundly defeated. It was strange how quickly the fervor of the Ikhwan disappea.ed, so that when we arrived less than five years later, there was no trace of the zealous enthusiasm that had made the Ikwhan the most feared warriors of the peninsula. By this time the King had almost totally suppressed all raiding. On one occasion, Abdul Hadi bin Jithina pointed out a place and said, "Over there is where we caught a certain notorious raider."

Abdul Hadi and the posse had spent two and a half months inexorably chasing this gang of raiders, and when they caught them, they executed them on the spot, as the King had already passed sentence on them.

There is a certain mystique about the Bedouin way of life, but it was a hard life lived by tough men who were prepared to be absolutely ruthless if they felt threatened. They had to be this way to live in such an unforgiving environment.

A great deal of the firearms came legally or illegally from British India. The Snyder, the Polish Mauser and the rolling-block Martini were common arms. I was always amazed at the shooting that our soldiers demonstrated. I was a pretty good shot myself, but I had fired literally thousands of shells to learn. These men could never afford to learn this way, yet they were excellent marksmen. I don't know how they learned.

l-r. The soldiers: Hamud, Khamis and Salih bin Qumra; Tom, Shauby and Salih in front of the lone palm tree at Ain al-Nakhla

The Base Camp at Tarfa

Chapter 5
"Camp Tarfa"

February 4, 1938
Camp Tarfa

Here we are at Camp Tarfa, so named because it is in Batin al-Tarfa, a whopping big valley about a mile east of Ain Tarfa, a very bitter well. The camels will drink from it, but the water is so bitter that only a desperate Bedouin will drink it. Our position is latitude 23° 49' north, longitude 51° 40' east; that is also the best way of describing this place.

All in all, the trip was good. Before we left Selwa, we went into the desert on a half-mile chase after the saluki, who objected to riding on top of the lorry. Old Salih, the guide, caught him by walking out with the hawk on his wrist, as if he were going hunting. Quite a menagerie: the saluki, 11 chickens, four ducks, the hawk and a pigeon. The latter is used in lieu of a dove to retrieve the hawk should he refuse to return after catching a rabbit or *hubarrah*.

Most of the day we ambled along flat, gravel-covered plains. Even the lorry and its three-and-a-half tons cruised at 20 miles an hour. It was a fine day, calm and cool. We ate lunch at a lone dune in the middle of these plains. The soldiers called it "Crazy Dune" because the wind striking it from all sides has given it an unusual form and slopes. That night we camped in a bit of a hollow where the soldiers had plenty of firewood.

Awake long before sunrise, we started about sun-up and reached the dunes about nine in the morning. Khamis did right well; he picked out corridors on the plains between dunes that looked like solid sand from a distance. Most of the afternoon we drove through the dune belt, and the truck didn't get stuck at all. The saluki provided more diversion at lunch by running away again. The soldiers were aghast at my suggestion that we go on and leave him to follow the truck for a few miles. They said he could track a camel, a man or a gazelle, but never a lorry. Very fast, these dogs – the only breed not considered unclean by Moslems. I saw our saluki chasing a rabbit yesterday. He just about caught him, but the rabbit made his burrow.

Yesterday we moved the truck a few miles and left it while Jerry, the three guides and I went looking for wells and possible campsites. One well, Ain Sijun, was bitter. Just to see what the Arabs consider bitter, salty, and sweet, we take samples, bring them home, boil them and taste them. Ain Ghadaiyir was sweet. Our camp is about 12 miles south of it, quite a haul for water for the soldiers and servants.

In general, the water in the Eastern Province would be considered unfit for drinking according to the American sanitary codes which considered 500 parts per million of salt as the absolute maximum that should be found in drinking water. In Arabia, water with 1,000 parts per million was regarded as practically rain water. We commonly drank water with as much as 3,000 parts per million; at one well, we saw some small Bedouin boys drinking water that was later analyzed at 10,000 parts per million. Seawater is slightly more than 30,000 parts per million, so these young men were drinking water that was a third as salty as seawater. When confronted with a well too bitter to drink, the Bedu let the camels drink it and then they drank camel's milk. Among its many attributes, the camel also acted as a walking still.

We were driving along at 30 miles an hour, looking for Ain Ghadaiyir, when Abdul Hadi set up an awful fuss, yelling for us to stop, which was the only part I could understand, but Jerry didn't stop. Abdul Hadi wanted to get out and pick up a broken cigarette Jerry had just thrown away! He'll break Jerry of smoking. With us less than a week out, he's already bumming smokes like a diplomat. "I have lots of matches, but my tobacco is nearly all gone" is one of his better opening lines.

By the time we returned from scouting the country, it was too late to move camp, so we spent the night in a little hollow up on the plains. Just as the sun was setting, the north wind came up and blew lots of sand about just when we were struggling to put up the radio aerials.

Today we picked out the actual campsite, moved, and had the tents up by noon: our English army tent, the cook tent, the servants' tent, and two tents for the soldiers. We visited Ain Tarfa, six feet of water in a hole 13 feet deep and three feet in diameter. The top half is lined with gypsum slabs, and the rest has been dug through soft sandstone. Khamis said that the well is very old, maybe older than Salih. Salih bin Qumra laughed, hiding his mouth behind his hand, which seems to be a Murra custom. At first, I thought he and Abdul Hadi simply were hiding their missing teeth, but four Murra at the well today did the same thing, even though their teeth were perfectly good.

The wells must be fairly old, as there are two or three dead ones close by and the camel dung has built up a bit of a mound around them. When you consider that such wells may not be visited more than two or three times a month, it takes a long time for any sort of a noticeable mound to accumulate.

Each day just before lunch, we put on our shorts and play football with Shauby, who is becoming a pretty good passer. Thus we add

insult to injury; besides bringing chickens and ducks into the Rub'
al-Khali, we play football in shorts in about the same region where
Bertram Thomas was "marching furtively."

Tonight we ate some baby camel meat, part of some that was
given to the Emir today. It was the hump, which is supposed to be
the choicest bit. It tasted much like beef.

The radio worked fine; after our regular program with Casoc,
we talked with Bill Aldwell at Jiddah, clear across the peninsula. He
is the regular Dhahran operator, who is over there installing a new
station for the company.

*Abu Nasir, Khamis, Tom and Muhammad bin Dhabit on
an unusually thick-crusted sabkha near Camp Tarfa*

Our medicine is doing well. The night before we left Selwa,
Muhammad bin Dhabit came in with a nauseated stomach. We were
sure he would be all right by morning, but to maintain our reputation,
Jerry mixed up some soda and water; I put in a few drops of vinegar,
and the potion fizzed most impressively. The next morning he was
fine. Jerry has now begun to treat the old Bedu who gave our Emir
the baby camel. He has worms, and the book recommends that the
patient should not eat, but might drink water for 24 hours before
taking the medicine. Jerry had to compromise on the gentleman

drinking a little camel milk because the water around here is undrinkable. Tomorrow he returns, and the Emir, who has a watch, will give him the pills at the proper intervals.

One of our drivers is taking the lorry back to Selwa tomorrow for another load of gasoline. We expect a car to come down from Casoc with supplies, so we may get some letters out. Perhaps there'll not be another opportunity for two to four weeks.

February 18, 1938
Camp Tarfa

We plan to swing south, behind the Trucial Coast, and go as far east as longitude 55. Then, if time permits, we shall go further south into the Empty Quarter. In some of the books I wrote to you about, you will notice arguments about the name. Philby says that the Bedu use the name Rub' al-Khali; Thomas and Cheesman claim that it is not used by those Bedu who live in northern Arabia. Thus far, I am inclined to agree with Thomas and Cheesman, as our Murra and Awamir guides do not use the term; they refer to the district south of us as "the South" or "the Sands," *al-Ramlaat*. The Bedu here do use Rub' al-Khali, or something close to it, in referring to directions such as NE, NW, SE, and SW. Any direction between the four cardinal points may be Rub' al-Khali, the Empty Quarter.

Only a few of the Arabs with us speak English. Our cook, Salih bin Mijhud, has been with the geologists for three years, so he understands and speaks a few words. Though he doesn't speak much English, Khamis acts as a go-between for us and the rest of the crew. He knows approximately how much Arabic we can understand, so he rephrases their words for our consumption. Used to our accent and mutilation of the language, he polishes up our Arabic and passes it on for us.

I understand a bit of the language in the line of business and can make myself understood by much talking around the bush with my limited vocabulary. They have several letters of the alphabet that are difficult to pronounce, but the prize is "ain," usually defined in

English-Arabic books as "a sort of click in the throat." I can't produce it and can hardly detect it when it is spoken.

We are just back from having coffee with the soldiers. Salih bin Qumra, the guide who is going back to Hofuf tomorrow, recited a poem about 58 Murra engaging in battle with 154 robbers at a well southwest of here. Salih and his fellow tribesmen vanquished the robbers and got many rifles and camels. Khamis told us the story. The poem had a long rhyme in each line, and each line ended with the same syllable. I wanted Jerry to ask him who the robbers were, but it's likely that the robbers were from another tribe represented in our "army," so Salih was naming no names.

Abu Nasir recited a poem; Khamis told a "small story," and Salim, the new Awamir guide, recited a romantic poem about five Awamir who were held for ransom in the north and obtained their freedom by singing a song. I can understand very little of the stories and none of the poetry.

The Emir showed us how the saluki will shake hands when you say "*Salaam Alaikum*" to it. He says the saluki can catch two or three rabbits a day, but after that he is exhausted. By this time the incense was being passed, so we arose and departed.

Note what you say about Thomas's *The Arabs*. I am not familiar with it; however, he wrote one, *Alarms and Excursions in Arabia*, about the coast of Oman. Thomas is apparently a good linguist, but he has no aversion to dressing up the subject for the sake of excitement. Doughty's *Travels in Arabia Deserta*, although written about northern Arabia, will give a more accurate idea of Bedouin life and customs than any other six books. The biggest change in Arabia in centuries has been Ibn Saud. We have half a dozen tribes represented in our soldiers. Khamis is an Ajman; Abdul Hadi, a Murra. Fifty five years ago their two tribes fought a big battle at a well south of Selwa. Now these two crack jokes with one another. Abdul Hadi's home pastures are around Shanna in the southern part of the Rub' al-Khali, yet he's just come from the Iraq border.

Now I'm also an anesthetist. One of our drivers had such a fine toothache that he couldn't sleep for several days, so the other night I administered ethyl chloride and he "slept half the night, praise God."

February 5, our truck driver went back to Selwa with the big six-wheeler, *Abu Sita,* "father of six," for another load of gasoline. We stayed close to camp in order to save enough gasoline to go to Selwa, should the lorry not return. Our time was spent doing calculations based on our astronomical observations. Every afternoon we had coffee with the soldiers

After five days of fine weather, the lorry did not return, and we set out to look for it. A strong south wind blew the sand like drifting snow as we traveled west over 30 miles of dunes. The wind was so hot that it made our engines boil when we reached the *dibdibah,* gravel plains, and drove north to Selwa. We arrived at four o'clock to find the lorry in front of the storehouse with a broken steering gear. There was an hour of quiet, and then just after sundown the north wind, the *shamaal,* came whooping down, and the temperature dropped. The wind whistled through our corrugated tin storehouse, gradually increasing in fury. About midnight I began to wonder whether we might lose the building. The next day we waited all day for the cars from Casoc with spare parts. No paper or envelopes to write a letter and no books to read except the radio manual. Cold and sand and wind, our cook and our kerosene stove at Camp Tarfa, we made a banquet out of cold canned food.

In addition to getting the lorry, we got the Awamir guide that we had requested, Salim Abu Ar-Ru'us. With his white beard, he looks for all the world like one of the Three Wise Men. He had come to Selwa once from Hofuf, but arrived the day after we left. He then returned to Hofuf and was promptly sent back with orders to find us. He arrived at Selwa the same day our lorry returned so he awaited us. His home country is south of here, just where we are going.

The next day we returned to Camp Tarfa. It was like coming home. Though the *shamaal* roared all day and the motors heated as badly as they had on the trip up to Selwa, we were going south this time and were happy to see our warm tent, wash our faces and sit down to Salih's dinner with Muhammad Abdul Latif hovering about.

*Salim Abu Ar-Ru'us
brandishing his* jumbia

February 19, 1938
Camp Tarfa

I don't have much news on the chances of getting you here, as it all depends on oil wells in Arabia. They don't talk about the progress of wells over the radio. In our last letter from Max, he wrote that Well No.7 is cleared and drilling has resumed, so pray for its success.

The three guides, Khamis, Abdul Hadi and Salim, and the scribe, Muhammad bin Dhabit, have just left. We ask the guides for the names of various places; Muhammad writes them down in Arabic, from which we try to make English equivalents. Then we try to find the meaning of the names, which is quite a trick at times, but our two new guides have caught on quickly and now give us meanings before we ask for them.

For instance, Sabkha Mutti. At first we thought *Mutti* meant "donkey" because Walt found an Iraqi word of that meaning in the dictionary. The guides disagreed and said it was the father of all *sabkha*s. Finally, Khamis explained that it meant stretchy, like rubber, because this *sabkha* went farther than you thought it did. Sure enough, we found *mutti* in the dictionary under stretchy, and what a good name it is. We have mapped this *sabkha* for more than 50 miles south, and it still extends beyond the last dune we charted. In some places, where there are no dunes or sand hills, the flat, featureless surface stretches away to the horizon in all directions, devoid of vegetation or life of any kind.

The method of mapping was simply measuring distance with the car's odometer. With our surveying equipment, we would lay out a track two or three kilometers in length and then drive the car back and forth carefully over this track with our tires at a pre-determined pressure and heated up so that we could apply a correction factor to our speedometer. We quickly became expert at estimating whether the terrain we were driving over was slower or faster than the smooth ground on which we had calibrated the odometer.

We drove from point to point, and each point was called a station, a word that the soldiers rapidly picked up and understood. After we had gone 50 or 60 miles, we would stop and take time out for a star shot to give us longitude and latitude. Weeks later, I would lay out the longitudes and latitudes, refer to my notebook, and stretch or shrink the rest of the data to fit the longitude and latitude points. It was not very accurate, but it was perfectly good for our purposes.

Some of the other names we found out today were, "Well of the Doe Rabbit," "Sweetwater Well of the Mirage," "Dune of the Ravens," and the "Unknown Well." Salim and Abdul Hadi did most of the talking, as this is their region, while Khamis sat paging through a *Saturday Evening Post*. In great puzzlement he held up the page to show me a picture of the AC Sparkplug winged horse in a bathtub. When I told him it was a horse, he beamed, "Another kind?"

One bit of good news, Salim says "Jiwa" or "Liwa" is three days by *thelul*, fast camel, south of the coast so it may be within our boundary line.

The only good thing about our trip to Selwa was a dinner with the soldiers on the way up. It was Eid Mubarak, a big Muslim festival, so Jerry bought a sheep for the men: four had come with us, three with the lorry, our two drivers and two more drivers and a mechanic down from Casoc in the afternoon. We were invited to the feast, so after we read our letters and finished our radio work, we went over.

The soldiers had built a wall of brush about three feet high on the north, east and west sides, with the west wall about twice as long as the others. They stretched a canvas over this structure and banked the north wall with sand. This arrangement allowed them to do the cooking in front of the lean-to with the west wall for protection. Inside they built a smaller fire for coffee. Light was courtesy of a single kerosene lantern.

Two blankets were spread for us facing the smaller fire, and between us was a two-foot-high bolster on which to settle back stylishly on one elbow. We had tea, then coffee, and then the piece de resistance – sheep and rice. There were three huge aluminum platters, each with four inches of fried rice under a heap of sheep in the center. Four or five men knelt around each platter, and with the right hand only, gathered up rice, squeezed it to the size of a golf ball and popped it into their mouths like they were shooting marbles. As a mark of courtesy, everyone about our platter yanked off choice bits of meat and piled them in front of us.

The rice was a bit greasy, but the sheep was delicious except for a little sand. I don't think that I spilled any more rice than the rest, though my eating technique definitely lacked snap. Afterwards we washed our hands and settled down to talk and drink coffee. After an hour, Jerry and I left so the fellows could have another go at the food.

The other morning we went out for a short trip, and I shot two *kirwan* with Jerry's shotgun. When the soldiers picked up the birds, one of them had a broken wing so they brought it back alive for the hawk, Fellah, to practice. They placed the *kirwan* 100 yards away and then released Fellah, who sailed off two feet from the ground and hit the poor *kirwan* like an express train. Philby calls the *kirwan* a stone curlew. It is a little larger than a teal and has long legs and a long body. Roasted *kirwan* is delicious.

Since arriving here we have spent every day mapping the great Sabkha Mutti. Much of it has dunes or loose sand, or worse, a light coating of sand drifted into ripples six to 12 inches high. Since the prevailing wind is from the north, the rows run east and west. Driving over them in the north-south direction produces the finest jarring of the gizzard I have ever experienced. In some places the *sabkha* is smooth as a dance floor. Yesterday on our way home we covered 50 miles in less than an hour.

Khamis gave us another good demonstration of his sense of direction. To make our maps, we take a bearing and measure the distance by the car's odometer, but in this smooth place there was nothing visible on which to sight the compass. Jerry told Khamis to take the pickup truck straight south for two kilometers and stop. We could then sight on it, get our bearing and follow him in the sedan. We did this several times and covered about eight miles before we saw some sand dunes that we could use as a horizon point. When I plotted the eight-mile route Khamis had laid out for us, it deviated less than 20 yards from a true north-south line.

Last night we were late coming back and cut across three or four miles of gravel plains distinguished only by a few clumps of low bushes here and there. We wanted to find a place on our old road that we had marked by driving the car around in a small circle. Khamis directed from the back seat, "a little to the right," "left a little," until we drove right over the circle.

Salim Abu Ar-Ru'us came over to our tent for treatment the second day in camp. First he had a sore back, so we gave him some analgesic balm. Then he said he couldn't hear out of one ear. Jerry asked him if he could hear out of the other ear. When he said that he could, Jerry said, "Praise be to God, you can hear with one ear at least." Salim agreed.

Finally, Salim suffered from constipation. This common problem with desert Arabs is probably a result of not enough roughage in their diet. We gave him the standard remedy, a compound cathartic pill.

The next day he reported that nothing had happened, so we gave him another cathartic pill and a tablespoon of castor oil. The following day still nothing had happened. I found an empty tomato can, filled it with mineral oil and castor oil and told him to drink it. He refused. He wasn't being stubborn; he just couldn't stand the smell of the castor oil and couldn't keep the vile stuff down. I couldn't blame him, so I rummaged through our larder and found an orange. I squeezed some of the juice in the medicine and said, "Now, Salim, if you drink this, you may have the can," – he was still at the stage where an empty tin can was treasured – "and you can also have the orange." So he summoned his courage and drank this terrible brew, started on the orange and went away reasonably happy.

The next morning he told us that everything was wonderful; his "stomach had walked," as they say in Arabic. He said to Jerry, "I used to be perfectly happy if I had a good meal, a woman and a smooth piece of sand, but now I must also have an orange to be truly satisfied."

February 20, 1938
Camp Tarfa

Tonight rabbit for dinner. The soldiers used Jerry's shotgun to shoot five of them while we were out hammering at rocks. Khamis can spot a motionless rabbit half hidden in a bush that duplicates its coloring perfectly. Often times I can't see the rabbit even when he points it out, and I don't believe that the other Arabs always can, either.

The other night, when we were drinking coffee with the soldiers, Abdul Hadi lamented that he had been sent to us directly without the chance to visit his wife and son. Later Muhammad bin Dhabit came over for some medicine, and in the course of the conversation told us that Abdul Hadi had planned on buying a new wife in Hofuf. I suggested that it was just as well, as now he could save up more money. "No," said Muhammad, "it is not like America, you do not need much money for a dowry, just a camel, about $100 and a new bed, but the bed is negotiable."

March 1, 1938
Near Camp Tarfa

Broken down cars are giving me many chances to send letters to you. Yesterday we left camp in three cars on a four day-trip. An hour later the station wagon was stuck in soft sand with a broken transmission. Shauby and I took it apart, greased it and put it back in. Now it works, but makes a sound like a coffee grinder churning a handful of nails. Shauby is tearing it apart again to see what new parts we will need to order.

Last week we set out for al-Jiwa. We went about 60 miles east, through country we had already mapped, and then, staying two to three miles south of the boundary line, we traversed 20 miles of new country. Dunes everywhere. We had been spoiled by dashing around the flat surface of Sabkha Mutti at 50 miles an hour. Now we are thankful for patches of *dikakah*, rolling sand with knee-high bushes behind which the sand drifts into long lumps. It's rough driving, but at least the sand is firm. We camped in a sheltered hollow, and Shauby changed a spring in the sedan that had been broken for some time, but now was starting to fall out.

The next day we continued east towards Jiwa, keeping as far north as possible in the hopes that we could find the gravel plains that were supposed to lie to the north. If they are there, we didn't find them. By zigzagging through strips of *dikakah,* we managed to cover 17 miles in a day of driving. Hemmed in by dunes on all sides, we walked ahead of the cars looking for firm sand, but did not always find it. We got stuck, pushed out the cars and got stuck again. I took off my shoes because the sand felt so good between my toes, which are now blistered.

We have lengths of rubber belting that are 12 inches wide and cut to fit exactly between the front and rear wheels of a car. We lay the belts in front of the stuck car and between its wheels so that when we push the car, the wheels have something firm to run on and maybe the car can get up enough momentum to reach solid sand. Nine times out of ten, this doesn't happen on the first try. So the belts have to be dug out and carried forward as we push the car along four or five feet at each attempt. Shauby says the song of the Rub' Al Khali is, "*Shiyl al bultz, wa hatt al bultz; shiyl al bultz, wa hatt al bultz*," that is, "Remove the belts, and put the belts down; remove the belts, and put the belts down."

The four-wheel drive Marmon Harrington station wagon in a scene that sometimes would be repeated dozens of times in a day

Sometimes we can use one car to pull out another. The four-wheel drive Marmon Harrington is useful for this, if there is a place ahead of the stuck car where the sand is firm and slopes downhill enough to keep the Marmon Harrington from getting stuck, too. It doesn't get stuck as often as the other cars, but when it does, it is a great chore to get it out.

The pulling procedure requires practice and finesse. We use as long a rope as is practical. The trick is to start the pulling car slowly, then, just as the rope becomes taut, the drivers of both cars apply full power in low gear. If the timing is not right, either the pulling or the pulled car will bog down, often in a worse situation than when the operation started.

Jerry and I spent the night swapping stories with the soldiers around the campfire. Jerry told about Daniel Boone throwing tobacco in the eyes of his Indian captors and swinging over a river gorge on a vine to make his escape. I stumbled through Custer's Last Stand. The Indians are called "the American Bedu" and the soldiers, "the Army of the Government." Khamis and the rest are used to my terminology and especially love the Indian names such as Crazy Horse, Red Cloud and Rain in the Face.

Abdul Hadi hadn't heard of the Indians before and was fascinated with them. He wanted to know where they lived and finally ventured his opinion that they must be related to the tribes in Iraq. Salim Abu Ar-Ru'us doesn't take much interest in our stories because he can't understand our Arabic, so he sits crooning softly to himself. This can be disconcerting to the storyteller, but is apparently good Arabian etiquette.

After I related how the Indians cut out Custer's heart and ate it to make them brave, Khamis said the Bedu did a similar thing with a wolf's eye; they carry it with them when they don't want to be seen at night. Then he wanted to know how the war ended. I told him that the Indians surrendered and that their land, designated by a big circle in the sand, was taken from them, leaving a small circle. Khamis nodded and said the same thing had happened in Arabia. It was a personal remembrance for him because his tribe, the Ajman, had revolted against the King some 10 years earlier and was soundly defeated in battle. Many of them fled to Iraq; much of their land was given to other tribes, and they were forbidden to live in their largest city, Sarrar, which now has tumbled into ruins.

The following morning Salim took us to Khor al-Ghubar al-Dhaw, Salt Water Well of the Hidden Fire. A *khor* is a well with water that is only potable for camels. It was filled with sand. Shauby dug out the nearest shaft by going down with an aluminum pan and scooping sand into a five-gallon gasoline can, which the soldiers pulled up with a rope. There was much fun tapping Shauby lightly on the head each time the empty can was lowered to him.

Abdul Hadi bin Jithina poses with shovel in hand at
Khor al-Ghubar al-Dhaw, the Khor of the Hidden Fire

Abdul Hadi led them in Murra chants as they pulled the bucket out of the 15-foot shaft sunk into the soft sandstone. I think he is not long away from the tribal raiding parties of old. He is the only one of our soldiers who always has his rifle with him, and there are no clay plugs in its muzzle or enough cloth for an overcoat wrapped around its breech. He stripped to the waist to help with the well, but carefully buckled his bandoleer back on before going to work.

The night that I told the story of Custer's Last Stand, Abdul Hadi quietly took his rifle and slipped out of the tent. One by one the other soldiers followed him into the night. Abdul Hadi had heard something, and they stayed on alert until morning. This was the only time this happened to me, but this area, despite the peace of Ibn Saud, was vulnerable to incursions of raiding parties from outside of the Kingdom; a fact of which a veteran raider like Abdul Hadi was well aware. I never wrote home about this because I didn't want Kathleen or my folks to worry.

Just before sundown, we climbed a sand ridge beyond a belt of dunes to see *dikakah* stretching westward as far as the horizon, a most welcome sight as we won't have to struggle homeward as much as we did getting here.

That night we sat around the campfire again and listened to the soldiers. Abdul Hadi leans towards poems and songs rather than stories. Salim Abu Ar-Ru'us is a born actor. Though we can understand little or nothing of his Awamir dialect, his facial and vocal expressions are a show in themselves. I love to hear these men recite poetry. The lines all have the same rhyme, and the listeners repeat the last two or three syllables at the end of each line.

Tonight Muhammad bin Murdhi told a story about Abu Zaid, hero of Arabia and a man of many fabulous deeds. Usually Muhammad is a quiet, almost bashful, fellow. He was once a shaikh of some importance, but somehow lost his position and is now an ordinary soldier. When he tells a story, his eyes shine; he waves his hands, and his speech is quite deliberate with a different voice for each character.

Muhammad bin Dhabit has just left us after receiving treatment for his eye. It goes like this: Muhammad fumbles around outside the tent until we hear him and invite him in. He says, "How are you?"

We say, "Good. How are you?" He replies, "Very good."

We then say, "*Al Humdulallah,*" praise be to God. Then he sits down and "makes words" for half an hour or so until we ask him again how he is and then he gets down to business.

"Everything is fine, but I want some medicine for my eyes." Thereupon we squirt a zinc sulfate solution in his eyes, "make words" some more, and then he leaves.

The Emir needs a new hawk because Fellah was killed in a hunting accident. Fellah had caught a rabbit. When the saluki tried to get at the rabbit, the Emir kicked at the saluki, but missed and killed Fellah. It's a great tragedy. We've heard the story three times this evening from each of the three soldiers that have been here tonight for medicine.

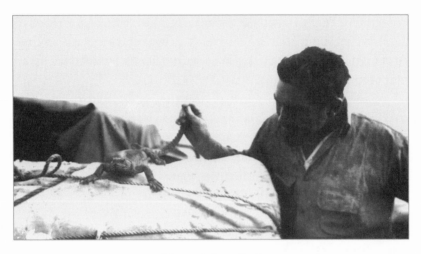

Max with a dhab

March 3, 1938
Camp Tarfa

After a dinner of creamed cauliflower, pumpkin, tomatoes and cucumbers I should be at peace with the world, except that the cars didn't bring the right parts for the station wagon so we're sending it back to Casoc.

Tomorrow we go out on a four-day trip to find a new site for our base camp. Max is coming soon, and we are going to set out with five cars to try to reach Longitude 55 east. The guides say it is all sand, but we want to see for ourselves.

Our cook tent is quite a zoo. In one corner is a box with the hen setting on the eagle eggs we found the other day; she is covered with a straw basket. Then we have a young rabbit in another box to which the dhab is tied by a string. A dhab is a big desert lizard. We're sending the rabbit up to the Steineke girls tomorrow before it can die or escape. He's a cute fellow, tan-colored, strong and unafraid.

This is a great place. Abdullah, the mechanic sent to fix the station wagon, is Indian. Mahomet Ali, one of the drivers who brought him down, is a Somali who speaks both Indian and Arabic. Abdullah speaks Indian, English and some Arabic, so Jerry gives his orders to Abdullah in English; he passes them on in Indian to Mahomet Ali, who in turn passes them on in Arabic to the rest of the fellows. Although everyone speaks Arabic to some degree, this system leaves fewer chances for misunderstanding.

Long-suffering Abdullah was a gentle and competent mechanic, who was generally sent down to repair the problems we couldn't fix. When he finished his work, a great fuss invariably preceded his departure. Abdullah would say, "Sahib, Shauby has stolen my crescent wrench (or whatever tool Shauby had his eye on at the moment) and won't give it back."

Shauby would reply, " Stole his wrench? Am I to blame if he is careless with his tools and loses them in the sand?"

There were many variations on this theme. Eventually Abdullah had to depart without his lost tool, and some days later, as Shauby and I worked on a repair in which that wrench would be handy, the wrench would appear.

I would say, "Where did this come from?"

Shauby would say, " We've always had it."

"I've never seen it before."

"Well, I had it put away."

"I think you stole it from Abdullah."

"You mean the time he fixed the lorry?"

"No, I mean the time he fixed the transmission."

"Oh, that time. That was the time he lost his screwdriver, not a wrench."

I would then tell Shauby that I knew he stole it from Abdullah and I didn't want to hear of him doing that again, secretly happy that we had the tool. Like Shauby, I regarded Dhahran as a vast storehouse of tools from which Abdullah could easily replace his loss. However, this was not the case. With the disappointment at the lack of success in finding oil, the storehouse had been greatly depleted, so Abdullah probably got a dressing down from his foreman for being so careless with his tools.

Apparently, there are many slaves in Arabia, particularly in the Nejd, the central region, and in the Hejaz on the western coast. According to Salih, the cook, they are brought across the Red Sea from Africa. I am starting to find out all kinds of things now that I can speak a little Arabic for myself. Abdullah keeps urging me to hurry up and learn more quickly. After three months I already know more of the language than most of the people at Casoc, but I can't get too swelled up about it because it is always this way. The geologists have to learn quickly in order to talk to anyone but their partner.

l-r. Salih bin Qumra, Khamis, unknown, Muhd. bin Dhabit, Tom and Abdullah, "the pint-size soldier," at Ain Tarfa. In the foreground is a portable camel trough.

The oasis of al-Ruksa, an island of date palms in a sea of dunes

Chapter 6
"In Search of Jiwa"

March 14, 1938
Camp Tarfa

Two letters from you when we returned yesterday made me thank Heaven for you. It is very fine to have a wife who has letters waiting upon your return from the desert; of course, this is desert, too, but it has come to seem like home.

To your grandfather's question, no, we haven't had any snow. We've only had rain once, and the district we were in last week hasn't had any rain in two years! A drought year in North Dakota would be a gift from Heaven here. When I told the soldiers about all the snow in Canada, they were properly impressed. Shauby, from the Hejaz where there are fairly high mountains, has seen snow often. Khamis described seeing some "white stuff" on the tents, which I presume was frost, twice in his life. He said that he didn't like that kind of weather. The *gurbas*, water sacks made of hide, were "very strong" in the morning and had to be put in the fire before the water "walked," melted.

The only dogs in the desert are the lean, greyhound-looking salukis. The Arabs consider dogs unclean but don't class the saluki as a dog. They are beautiful animals when fattened up a bit, but the average one in the desert is a bag of bones. The British explorer Major Cheesman received one as a gift from a Murra shaikh when he visited Jabrin. He took it back to England, entered it in a dog race and won first prize.

This language is going to get the better of me. The saluki is not a dog, but a saluki. Now I find that there are a hundred or more words for camel, none of them synonymous. The books say that *jamal* is the word for camel, but to the desert Arab, it is the word for only one kind of camel.

The Bedu measure distances in so many days by camel, specifying the kind of camel. A fast-riding camel day is about 60 miles while a pack camel day is about 20 miles. These camels are hardy beasts. In the winter, if there is enough rain for grass and vegetation to sprout, a camel doesn't need to drink at all, even if it is a riding camel, *thelul*, that is being driven hard. However in the summer, when it is hot and the pasturage scarce, the camel must drink water every three days. The cows give milk 11 months of the year in quantities varying from two to six gallons a day, depending on the season.

Because there is no pasturage fit for a horse, there aren't any horses at all in these parts. In the old days, less than 20 years ago, the shaikhs used to keep some horses specifically for fighting. On a military expedition, each horse would be assigned a cow camel, *naga*, to keep it fed with camel milk. In case of defeat, the shaikh could mount the horse and outrun the victors mounted on camels. Among some tribes, it was the custom to mount a young girl on a white horse and have her carry a banner into battle with the tribesmen rallying about her as if she were an Arabian Joan of Arc.

On the fifth, we set forth on another trip to the southeast, not to reach Jiwa, but to find just one well of drinkable water somewhere to the east that we could use as a base for the big trip to Jiwa. We loaded *Abu Sita* with water and gasoline and took it 90 miles south on an elegant road, a well-traveled camel trail, to this well. From the truck we loaded the cars with all of the water and gas they could carry and headed east.

It was a long day with a hot south wind blowing all day. We went through dunes most of the way. The sedan was stuck a dozen times and the pickup trucks even more often. Jerry claims that in a few years Arabian geologists will grow specialized flippers for digging sand from under cars and strong backs for pushing them. We camped that night in a small valley that was cool and quiet, but there were no campfire conversations as we all went to sleep directly after dinner.

The next day was a repeat of the first, except there was a cool wind from the north and we didn't get stuck quite so often. Going east, we traveled through a belt of large dunes scattered helter-skelter in rolling sands. The vegetation astonishes me, not only because of its quantity in a land that counts two or three inches of rain a wet year, but also because of its variety. One kind of plant will be abundant in one locality and completely absent in another place only a short distance away. Several kinds of plants will grow together in one region, not far away a couple of varieties will be absent, and then, farther away, the original combination of plants will be found again. If there was some dirt, it wouldn't be so puzzling, but it's all sand with rocks sticking through here and there. We go into great ecstasy over the rocks to impress the guides that outcrops are our prime object in life.

Eastward the only change in the sand is its color. A thin top layer of coarse sand gives it a red hue that becomes redder the farther east we travel. It is a welcome relief from the glare of white sand in the afternoon sun.

Thus far, which wasn't very far as this country isn't built for traveling in straight lines, we had been mapping as we went. The second night we sat around the fire with the soldiers and pried information out of Salim Abu Ar-Ru'us. We were now in his home range where he has lived all of his life. He said two days east by *thelul* there was a well of sweet water. He thought we could get to it by nightfall if we drove straight and didn't stop to map.

The country we are now in consists of strips of rolling dunes separated by belts of dunes called *uruq* (*irq*, singular), meaning roots, which they resemble. A typical *irq* will stretch for miles in a north-south direction with a hard-packed, gentle, west slope and a steep, soft, east slope. They are usually about 50 feet high and a quarter of a mile wide. We cruise along the length of an *irq* until we find a likely looking place to cross. We send someone ahead on foot to test the sand, then race the cars up the west slope and speed down the east slope, hoping to find hard sand before bogging down. The system works fine, and the east slopes are more fun than a roller coaster.

After a morning of *irq* riding we came into a region where all the vegetation was completely dried up. There was evidence of former encampments among the scattered camel dung, but Salim told us that it hadn't rained there for two years, so the Bedu had all gone east. We continued up and down and east until one of the pickups ran out of gas. We had calculated that the gas would last much longer, so this really stopped us.

We couldn't go any further on the gas we had; we hadn't found a well of any kind and we were surrounded by hundreds of dunes that all looked more or less alike. As we were driving along slowly trying "to make an idea," Salim casually said that there was a *khor*, salt-water well, about two miles away. At the least we wanted to find water for filling the radiators, so we ducked in and around the dunes, and two miles later we popped around a monstrous dune. There in its cup was the well beside a small, flat-topped hill.

The well was called Abu Gabr, Father of Graves. On top of the hill were the graves of a Bedu woman and child who died of starvation when their camels ran away from them. No one knew how many years ago that this happened. Salim says 20 years ago, but 10 and 20 are favorite numbers. The well was filled with sand, but Salim knew another *khor* about two hours away that had been used only several months ago.

Sometimes Jerry drives me up a tree, if there were any trees around here. We set out for the other well, but Jerry wanted to traverse, i.e. make plots with the compass and measure the distances with the car's odometer and map our road to the other *khor*. He said, "If we don't find it, we will at least know where this one is and how to get back to it."

This reasoning made no sense at all to me. If Salim could find the first well, he could find the second well, and, failing that, he could certainly find Abu Gabr again. However, Jerry is the senior geologist, so we started out traversing until he threw off the odometer by going around a dune. From there on we drove back and forth so much that there was no more talk of traversing.

Then Jerry began to wonder what kind of camel Salim had because we had already traveled nine miles by the odometer. Finally we drove up a small sand hill and looked down at the two shafts of Abu Jumbia, Father of the Dagger. It is so named because two Bedu had a fight there that ended in one being stabbed. I asked Salim if the man was killed in this fight. "No," he said, "it only went about this far into him," marking off three inches on the blade of his own *jumbia*.

Khor Abu Jumbia

Near the well we climbed a dune, and Salim immediately pointed out a dune near Khor Abu Gabr, about six straight miles away. I was astonished by Salim's knowledge of the country and asked Khamis how he did it. He replied, "He has lived here since he was a little boy. He has a good heart and a good head. Some men forget, but Salim is a correct man, and when one lives in a place all the time, winter and summer, he must know the place or he dies."

This place of Salim's is about the size of the state of North Dakota, and he seems to know every dune as though it were his brother. Abdul Hadi dug out Abu Jumbia which was 15 feet deep and filled with about seven feet of sand. The water was very salty and smelled considerably, but it would do for radiator water. We split an empty gasoline drum and covered the well to keep the sand out.

We were pessimistic about going west over the *uruq* as we would have to climb the steep, soft-packed slopes, but it was easier than we expected. We'd cruise along, spot a likely place and wind across and up a relatively gentle slope with the car going full speed in low gear in case we should hit a patch of soft sand. Usually the top of the dunes and the *uruq* are hard and flat, so you can zip up a slope and stop at the summit to look around for a way down. The trip home was pretty easy. We were stuck only twice going through the place where we had stuck a dozen times before, and both times we were out in 10 minutes. We twisted in and out under the direction of Abdul Hadi, who I suspect has made this westward trip in a hurry before, returning from raids on the Awamir and Manasir.

The diplomacy around the campfire is wonderful. In songs and stories about raids or battles with one of the tribes represented, the opponents are always called simply "robbers." Having no Manasir among us, the Manasir come in for more than their fair share of defeats in battle and discomfiture in raids.

March 30, 1938
Camp Tarfa

We've been in camp two days, inking the maps and experimenting with the sextant that we prevailed on Max to send down. You have a stubborn husband. Everyone said the sextant had been tried and wouldn't work and was impractical, but I couldn't see why. If it could be used every day on thousands of boats all over the world, it should be easy to use on perfectly quiet dry land. It's no cinch, but after two days of practice we are getting good results.

When we go east on our big trip every time we stop to make camp, we can simply shoot the stars, moon, sun or whichever is most convenient and plot our position on the map to within a couple miles of accuracy.

Before using the sextant, we used a heavy, bulky transit for making our astronomical observations. Though the transit was much more accurate and it normally stayed in adjustment, we gave it such a jolting in our travels that we had to test it for adjustment every time. This meant that we had to use at least an hour of daylight so we could adjust it before sundown.

The sextant, on the other hand, nearly always required adjustment; however that was quickly accomplished in daylight or at night. The light, compact sextant gave us an accuracy sufficient for our purposes and enabled us to take more astronomical observations than the transit. For example, we frequently took observations on the sun at noon for latitude, something we would not have taken the time to do with the transit.

Max is due tomorrow with Floyd Meeker, Casoc's chief mechanic. The four of us traveling in five cars will try to reach the eastern boundary of the concession at 55 degrees Longitude east. We have stockpiled water and gasoline 100 miles south of here; we will go there, refuel, head east to Khor Abu Jumbia for radiator water and then on to the fresh-water well at Shillah. Beyond Ain Shillah, no one knows what to expect though we hope to find this place Jiwa, if there is such a place.

We've already gone as far east as Jiwa is shown on the maps we have, but they aren't worth a damn. Somebody sat in an office, brought a Bedouin in, asked him the names of the places and then wrote them on the map, scattering them about so as not to leave too many blanks and thus produce an effect pleasing to the eye.

Rabbit for dinner tonight. Khamis shot three, and we always get one because it's Jerry's shotgun. Chicken dinner last night, and we are having two ducks and a chicken tomorrow night in honor of our guests, Max and Floyd. The poor ducks, their webbed feet have gone unused for months.

April 1, 1938
Camp Tarfa

Max and Floyd arrived last night, and feasting on ducks and chicken we made our plans for finding Jiwa. The next morning we set forth in five cars: the sedan ahead with Max and Jerry and the three guides; the three pickups with drivers Shauby, Ibrahim and Mahomet Ali, Salih, the cook, and Hamud, the fourth soldier. Floyd and I brought up the rear in the Marmon Harrington.

The first day and a half went so smoothly that Jerry and I began to wonder if we had exaggerated our description of the difficulties involved in crossing the *uruq*. That afternoon the guides decided to take a shortcut, but Abdul Hadi guessed wrong, and before long we were into plenty of *uruq* with dunes and soft sand. It was one long series of pushing out one stuck car after another while the guides trotted ahead of us picking out a trail of firm sand. About an hour before sunset, we got out of the mess and into a *hauta*, the rolling, easy-driving sand strip between two *uruq*, that led to our destination, an old camp site from our last trip.

The next day about 10 o'clock we climbed an enormous *irq* that stretched for miles in either direction to see if we could cross it. The soldiers immediately spotted several camels grazing a couple of miles away, and shortly thereafter their owner appeared. To our astonishment, he got out a white rag, tied it to his rifle and approached, waving the flag of truce. The first person we had met in this desert after a month of traveling surrendered to us.

Salim and Abdul Hadi went out to meet him without their rifles. It turned out that he was a member of the Manahil tribe. He had thought that we were raiders and far too numerous to resist. He gave the soldiers some camel milk and wanted to present us with a gift camel. We thanked him profusely, but explained that we were in a hurry and couldn't accept such a generous gift. In fact these "gift" camels usually end up costing about twice as much as if you bought one outright.

By noon we arrived at the fresh-water well, Ain Shillah, the first drinking water since Tarfa, 180 miles away. Seven Bedu men with their families and a large herd of camels were there when we arrived. Three of the men were Manasir, and four of them Awamir, Salim's tribe. He greeted the former with a formal handshake, but engaged in some cordial nose-rubbing with his tribe mates. They were strong, healthy-looking men and looked to be much more fit than the town Arabs I had seen. Though they had stripped to the waist to clean out the well, they, like Abdul Hadi, still wore their cartridge belts.

The well was in the cup of an enormous dune, 190 feet high. Close by was a low rock mesa; we drove over and parked behind it, out of sight of the well, so as not to frighten the camels. After our lunch, we had coffee and tea with the soldiers. All the Bedu were there stuffing themselves with dates. They were highly amused at our account of the surrendering Manahil we had met that morning and couldn't understand why he should have been afraid. Floyd's explanation rings truest – maybe he hadn't raised all the camels he had, and his guilty conscience got the better of him. I don't know the penalty for camel rustling, but in a country where a man's camel can be the only difference between life and death, I imagine it's similar to the fate of a cattle rustler in the old West.

Though these Bedouin had never seen a car before, they were typically blasé about it and seemed most interested in the station wagon's leather upholstery, which they patted and rubbed affectionately. They gathered all the tin cans we had emptied for lunch and asked if they could keep them. One little boy wanted to know what had been in the sardine can. Jerry told him that it was fish, and the boy said, "Fish? I don't know fish. Only dates, milk and camels."

The dunes at Ain Shillah

We went a few miles east of Ain Shillah and made camp. According to Salim Abu Ar-Ru'us, we were only a day's journey by *thelul* from Arrada, the westernmost village of the Jiwa area. He said that we could only make it about half way with our vehicles, but the road didn't look difficult to us, so we set out the next day, hoping he was wrong.

As we went further east, the dunes got bigger and bigger. The Bedu at Ain Shillah had said there was a *hauta* running to Jiwa. Knowing the *hauta* to be a friendly, rolling sand-strip between two *uruq*, we continued on in high spirits. Then we found the *hauta*. It was in proportion to the towering dunes on either side. The "friendly, rolling sand-strip" in between the *uruq* was covered with sand ridges and dunes as big as anything we had ever encountered in our westward journey.

We made 12 miles by noon and stopped to climb a nearby sand peak. Abdul Hadi pointed out Qa'adah al-Arrada, a tremendous sand mountain, barely visible in the blue haze of the afternoon. A *qa'adah* is not a dune, but a huge sand pile made of dunes heaped upon dunes. This one is the landmark for the village of Arrada, which lies at the qa'adah's base. Our forward progress wasn't exactly barred, but the steep sand slope in front of us didn't show any breaks where we could come back or up or over it. Had we wanted to keep going east into Oman, we could have made it, but we had to return the way we came. Stymied, we plotted our position, then turned back a distance and made camp.

The next morning we returned to Ain Shillah and then headed northeast to see if we could go around the sand. About lunchtime we met a lone Bedouin tending a half-dozen camels. He was a Murra like Abdul Hadi, and the two greeted each other like old friends and immediately began a long conversation about all the tribal news.

The soldiers took advantage of this lunch break to make some bread in the approved Bedouin fashion. It's done like this: they build a big fire, allow it to burn out, and then scrape the loose sand and ashes back to make a hole a few inches deep. A flat cake a foot wide and three inches thick, made of coarse brown flour and water, is placed in the hole and covered with hot sand and coals. When it is ready, they scrape back the sand and coals, retrieve the loaf and beat it with a green stick to knock off some of the sand.

They break it up in a pan, sprinkle it with sugar, add a little water, pour ghee, a kind of clarified butter, all over it and knead the result vigorously. It tasted pretty good, though the ghee tasted a bit old. That night we camped near Ain Muhibbi, an interesting place only because its true location is 100 miles away from its position on the maps we have.

A lot of dew in the morning made the sand firm and easy to drive. We left camp just after sunrise and traveled light and fast in the sedan and the empty station wagon. By noon, we were 25 kilometers out, and the sand had stopped us again. We sat on a high dune and had lunch while we looked east; it was obvious that the cars could go no further. We asked Salim how the sand was beyond Jiwa, and he replied, "For two days by *thelul* it is very difficult, then it is like this."

On our way back I climbed up a large dune to measure its height with our barometer/altimeter. Max took the car around to the bottom, while Khamis and Salim waited for me about half way up the dune at a sort of narrow ledge in the sand. At this place it appeared that the sand below was at a slightly steeper angle than the sand above. When I finished the measurement, all three of us ran down the lower slope, and the sand rumbled underfoot, which is usual enough.

After we reached the bottom, it kept on roaring, a deep note that sounded, as we remarked at the time, like a fleet of distant airplanes. We were delighted to actually hear singing sand, and timed the song. It lasted more than nine minutes, much longer than is recorded in any books we have read. These may well be the biggest dunes in the world, and I'm sure none of these writers has ever seen such monsters. This singing dune was 250 feet high.

The great dune at Ain Muhibbi

On our way back to camp, we detoured to see Ain Muhibbi and measured its dune at 300 feet, the highest we have found. We visited a number of outcrops on the way home and were surprised to find so many in this ocean of sand. Nearly every large dune had bedrock exposed in its cup. Apparently the wind swirls around the big dunes and scoops out the sand on the leeward side with more force than it would generate on a smaller dune.

That night we sat around the fire with the soldiers and their guest, an Awamir Bedu. He was a most unusual fellow. Though Khamis admits that often times he can't understand the Awamir dialect, even I could understand this man's Arabic. In the course of the conversation, we told him about the singing sands we had heard the day before. We nearly dropped our coffee cups when he replied that he had heard it before and didn't we think that it sounded like an airplane!

He explained that he had seen and heard airplanes fly over when he had been near the coast. The Imperial Airways route to India apparently follows the coast.

Called on for a story that night, Salim Abu Ar-Ru'us told of how 50 years ago the Shaikh of Qatar came with an army as numerous as the sands of the desert, as he ran sand through his fingers. Starting with Arrada in the west, they destroyed all of the villages of Jiwa. Each village has only one stone building, a fort; the rest of the dwellings are made of palm mats. The Shaikh simply burned the towns, beseiged the forts one at a time, and starved out the defenders and killed them.

We were horrified by this tale of wanton slaughter, but Salim explained that the Jiwans had killed the Shaikh's first son and had brought this trouble on their own heads. Abdul Hadi, a former tax collector himself, told us that the people of Jiwa were like rabbits, attacked by the hawk from above and the wolf from below; they pay a palm tree tax to the Shaikh of Abu Dhabi and a camel tax to Ibn Saud.

Finally, the Awamir Bedu said that the women of Jiwa went around unveiled and were rather promiscuous. Mahomet Ali, the Somali driver, said he'd never heard of such a thing in Arabia. Where he came, from women would lose their heads for such behavior. "Where were their husbands?" he asked.

"Pearl diving," replied the Awamir. That was it for our illusions about the lost civilization of Jiwa. Each spring the Jiwan men trek to the coast and spend the summer pearl diving with the boats from Oman. In the fall, the women, children and old men return to pick up the men and the rice, cloth, sugar, tea and coffee they need to supplement their diet of dates and camel milk.

It is strange and somehow appropriate that the inhabitants of the greatest sand region in the world spend four months a year diving for pearls in the cool waters of the Arabian Gulf.

Rising at 4:30 and off before sunrise, we drove all of five kilometers before we reached a point where there was no place to go but forward, down steep slopes of soft sand that none of our cars could ever climb up again. We decided to leave the cars, walk as far as we could before lunch, then return and call it quits. The four of us Americans started off with Khamis and Abdul Hadi. In the clear morning air we could see not only Qa'adah Al-Arrada, but dozens of other qa'adahs stretching off to the east and south like mountain ranges.

After we began to walk, Abdul Hadi remembered there was a garden nearby, al-Ruksa. In the summer the Bedu come there to pick the dates. Pointing into a vast ocean of dunes that all looked alike, Abdul Hadi said it was about six miles away.

"Could you find it?" we asked.

"Of course," he replied, "I was there once, 15 years ago."

We set off towards al-Ruksa, and sure enough, in about six miles we came over the crest of a sand ridge, and below us was a neat little oasis that covered about two acres. As it is wintertime, there were neither dates nor people to be found, but we had reached the outer edge of Jiwa.

After lunch, we took a nap under the palms and then started home. We Americans were pleased that we had successfully negotiated such a long walk until we realized that Abdul Hadi and Khamis had covered twice as much ground by zigzagging around to poke every bush they could find in their search for rabbits.

Among the palms of al-Ruksa

April 4, 1938
Camp Tarfa

Driving home the other day, the soldiers spotted a patch of locusts about 20 feet square. I suggested that we take some for the ducks and chickens to eat, and the men fell on the insects with great enthusiasm. They would shoo a bunch of the hoppers into a bush, gather them up in handfuls and put them in a gunnysack. A snake under one bush interrupted the proceedings until they killed it. I took movies of this procedure, and Shauby obliged me by eating a few locusts on camera. We left when we had half a sack full.

Back in camp, Muhammad brought over the chickens and the two remaining ducks for the feast. When we tossed them the locusts, the chickens ran away, and only one duck was game for locust. He'd waddle around with his bill thrust out an inch off the ground, eat a few, go have a drink, eat some more and then have another drink. After sunset he was still poking around for locusts. Later, I understood the soldier's enthusiasm in gathering them when they asked for some (the rest) of the locusts. They explained that locust is good for the stomach. According to Salih, they boil them, dry them in the sun, pound them in a mortar and make a sort of locust mush. I think I'll stick to oatmeal.

The lorry is broken down five miles from here. Our final journey will be delayed because we need the lorry to carry gas and water to our jumping-off point.

No, my darling, I don't even hear music on the radio; no, that isn't quite right. I do hear music on the radio, but I don't listen to it often because it makes me lonely, more desperately lonely for you than anything else, so I try to avoid it.

Grand Forks – April 11, 1938

One week from today is our anniversary; just think, darling, one half a year gone since that hectic November. It seems like a hundred years, and I wish that it were one and I were with you for once and for all. It's such a horrible feeling to see other women with babies they don't want and me without any.

One of the girls in the office announced her marriage today. She's been married since 1935, a well-kept secret.

Darling, I love you so much! What are you doing for relaxation? Any pretty girls? I worry about you continually and sometimes think I should have been smart and married a less handsome man – almost forgot, the beard does detract a great deal. Just plan on shaving it quite a while in advance of my arrival.

I do hope to hear from you tomorrow. Please write me soon and often, and take awfully good care of yourself.

Murra tribesmen watering their camels at Khor Mijhud

Chapter 7
"Into the Rubʿ al-Khali"

May 5, 1938
Selwa

With all four small cars, the lorry and all the gas and water we could carry, we went south 150 miles to the place where we had stored some water left over from our Jiwa trip. The plan was to make a few short trips to locate some nearby wells that would at least furnish water for the cars, then to go as far south and east as our supplies and the sand would permit. In the end it was our supplies and not the sand that stopped us.

The next day we struck off 50 miles south to Khor Mebaʿuth. Four Murra, fellow tribesman of Abdul Hadi and old friends of Salim, were camped by the well with their camels. They invited us for coffee at the tent of the oldest Murra, a sharp-eyed, fierce-looking patriarch with a long beard. The tent, made of hand-woven sheep hair, was separated into two compartments by a curtain. The one on the right had a couple of camel saddles in it; the left-hand side was for the women, so I didn't see it.

The carpet-like walls of the tent, fastened to the roof by rope loops and then banked with sand, are adjustable to suit the weather at a moment's notice. In the winter the walls extend all the way around the tent. An opening that serves as the door is left on the leeward side. If the wind changes, the door is laced up and a new one opened on the opposite side. In the summer the walls are usually removed altogether to get the full benefit of any stray breeze.

Jerry and I, the guides and the old Murra crowded into the men's side of the tent. Salim and Abdul Hadi told him all about our travels. He was most impressed by our speed; distances that had always been three days by *thelul* were now one day by car. They talked and drank coffee for some time until the old man sang out, "*Allah Huwwa Akbar*, etc." that is, "God is the greatest. There is no God but God, and Muhammad is his prophet," which we easily recognized as it is an integral part of the call to prayer. Khamis seemed displeased and talked slowly and quietly, while Abdul Hadi and Salim watched us closely. All we could understand was Khamis saying, "Perhaps they have a God without words." Apparently we were being invited to make a confession of faith, and Khamis was angered that the King's guests should be pressed like this.

The talk of converting us to Islam died down, and someone brought in a big bowl of camel milk with three inches of foam on it. The host flicked the flies off the foam with a small stick while a woman's hand passed a small wooden bowl over the partition. It was filled and passed around until everyone was full.

Afterwards, while we were filling our drums at the well, six or seven youngsters stood about watching us, the boys naked as the day they were born and the girls in cotton dresses. During this procedure, one of the boys, about two years old, fell flat on his face in a puddle of water and camel dung. At that, his sister, about half a head taller than he, gathered him up in her arms and carried the lad off to the tent as he screamed bloody murder the whole way.

The next day we went to Khor Mijhud, a well 30 miles west of our camp. A couple of Murra were watering their camels when we arrived. These people live almost exclusively on camel milk. They are too far away from the towns to get rice or dates, and there is no fresh water for sheep and goats so they have very little meat. Yet, for all that, they looked much healthier than most of the Bedu we had seen, and Khamis assured me that "they are stronger than other Bedu."

Young Bedouin girl at Khor Mijhud

In the morning we set out with the sedan, two pickup trucks and the station wagon, food for six days, 240 gallons of gasoline and 135 gallons of water. We traveled all day over rolling, brush-covered desert without a hitch. The next morning we met four families of Murra at Khor Qara. One of the Bedu had a long, white beard and fairer skin than Jerry or I. Stocky and heavily built, his features were not at all the usual Arab type. After looking him over, Khamis came over to us with a big grin and said, "Do you suppose he is an engineer from America whose car broke down so he turned Bedu?" From then on, this Bedu named Hamid was "the engineer from America."

We filled our radiators and some empty gas drums with salty water and drove about five miles before the rear wheels of the station wagon quit working. We made camp and left the two drivers, Shauby and Ibrahim, to repair the wagon while Jerry and I went 30 miles to the southeast. The traveling was fine for the last 15 miles. According to Salim, it hadn't rained in this area for 10 years, so most of the vegetation had blown away, leaving only smooth, rolling red sand which we zipped over in good time.

On our return, Shauby told us that the station wagon's rear drive shaft was broken. We decided to leave the wagon with Ibrahim while the rest of us went south for two days. We would pick him up on the third day. Ibrahim wanted someone to stay with him to tell stories and pass the time, so Jerry and Abdul Hadi went back to Khor Qara to find him a companion. There was no one there except Hamid, "the engineer from America." Jerry told Hamid that although the company paid men who worked hard all day three-fourths of a rupee per day, because he was Abdul Hadi's friend, he would pay him a rupee a day to stay with Ibrahim. Hamid wanted two rupees a day, but quickly changed his mind when Jerry began to leave. This was Hamid's first car ride. Whenever the car would have a bit of hard going, Jerry would reach out the window, pound on the door and then honk the horn. Abdul Hadi explained to Hamid that Jerry was urging the "camel" on and that it sometimes made this peculiar noise.

We left Hamid with Ibrahim, went 50 miles south and made camp early so we could get a sextant reading from the sun. In the evening, we shot the moon and the stars. We failed to get a time signal at 9:30, so we laid on our cots to rest and slept through the 10:30 time signal from French Indochina. Luckily, I had set my watch by radio the night before, or all our work with the sextant would have been wasted. The *uruq* in this country ran southwest like a series of neat, parallel walls. The *hautas* in between were broad and easy to drive. We traveled east, crossing the *uruq* whenever we found an easy place, until they got so high and difficult to cross that we turned southwest and followed a *hauta* at 30 miles an hour. Whenever the *irq* on the west died out we crossed into the next *hauta* and continued in this manner until we were in the same *hauta* as our camp. We followed it northeast and arrived back before sunset.

The weather was hotter than hell. The sand is uncomfortably hot on the hands when digging out the wheels, and the metal parts of a car are too hot to push on without putting a *ghutra* around your hands. I don't know how the Arabs can walk barefoot in the sand. I asked Khamis, and he said that though they could, there wasn't an Arab that he knew who wouldn't rather wear sandals.

Late in the afternoon a wind came up from the north. By morning, a fine *shamaal* was howling as we made a big circle to the west and north back to the station wagon. What a country! Years ago this had been one of the principal pasturages of the Murra; now we could drive 15 miles without seeing a single living plant. Abdul Hadi pointed out to us scores of once drinkable wells that were now *khor*s because of the dropping water table. Without a *naga*, milk camel, to quench his thirst, a man would die quickly in this place.

After traveling 150 miles and now approaching the station wagon from the opposite direction by which we had left it, I stopped in a flat, featureless area that Khamis had never seen before and asked him to estimate the distance to the station wagon. He said about seven miles. I checked, and according to our map the distance was six miles!

We arrived to find Ibrahim very unhappy with his companion, Hamid. The first day, several of Hamid's friends visited and ate all the food we had left. Worse, they hadn't even brought any camel's milk in exchange. Shauby rolled on the ground as Ibrahim related his tale of woe. It struck him as particularly funny that Hamid's friends had all been "*mukhtal.*" In the Murra dialect, it means "hungry", but everywhere else in Arabia it means "crazy." Poor Ibrahim was sure that he was overwhelmed by lunatics.

That night around the campfire, Hamid, who looked like Santa Claus with his long, white beard and the fire light flickering on his fat, red cheeks, sat next to Jerry and regarded him solemnly for a long time. Finally he reached over, poked him in the arm, and said, "Ya Harrees, you have red eyes. Please, I would like some more money."

To tell a man he has red eyes is the ultimate compliment, but Jerry played dumb and got Khamis to interpret. Hamid was asking for more money than the rupee a day. It was not a must, but if Jerry wanted to give him more, he would be glad to accept. There was no harm in asking. Jerry then asked Hamid if the station wagon had gone out to get anything to eat while we were gone. He replied that no, the camel had stayed right where it was all the time. At this, the soldiers, without cracking so much as a smile, expressed great shock at Hamid's thoughtlessness. Didn't he know to feed the car? Three days without water was bad for it. They continued until Hamid became genuinely concerned. The soldiers enjoyed themselves immensely, and in the end Jerry did sweeten up Hamid's retainer.

Hamid, "the engineer from America" and Abdul Hadi bin Jithina

The next day the retreat from the Rub' al-Khali began. It was nearly a rout. We broke a front spring in the station wagon and another in one of the pickup trucks. After a bit, the station wagon's fan knocked a big chunk out of the radiator. We left the wagon with the two drivers and continued on in the lorry. The next morning, we were towing the station wagon with its front wheels in gear and driving when its fan sliced open the radiator again. It was another hot day,

109 degrees in the shade. That night Max radioed the good news that we should return to Selwa and wind up the season.

We visited with the soldiers for a couple of hours after we finished our radio work. It was a fine night with a big moon. Muhammad bin Murdhi told a woeful story of how he was unjustly arrested for attempted robbery in Bahrain. False witnesses testified against him. The police took all his clothes and belongings away, threw him in jail and beat him. Abdul Hadi furnished the funniest part of the story. All ears, he exclaimed, "And they threw you in jail and beat you?"

Whereupon Muhammad, the moon glistening on his clipped skull, threw up his hands and replied, "Don't say it."

He was just like an American who doesn't want to be reminded again of an unpleasant experience.

I told them about the fox and the sour grapes. Jerry related the story of the Trojan horse. I followed up with Achilles sulking in his tent because the other shaikhs of the Greeks wouldn't give him the girl he wanted and how his friend, Patroculus, then fought in Achilles' armor and saved the ships, but lost his life to Hector. Achilles was "very angry," so he killed Hector the next day and dragged him around the city walls by his heels. The stories were quite a success; we sure get our money's worth out of Homer and Aesop.

Our luck continued; five miles out of Camp Tarfa, Jerry's car broke a spring hanger, and he limped into camp after dark at three miles an hour. We spent the whole next day fixing cars and packing up. We had to take two fans apart and put selected pieces together to make a new fan for the station wagon.

On Easter Sunday, we sent the lorry off towing the station wagon on the smooth roundabout road to Selwa. Jerry, Salih bin Mijhud and I drove the two pickups and the sedan on the direct route to Selwa. Halfway to Selwa the front spring in the sedan broke. Our three spares were rear springs, so we left the car with three soldiers and went on to Selwa.

In the morning we went back for the sedan. While I put in the new spring, Jerry and Salih went back to Camp Tarfa for a couple of loads of empty gas drums. On the way back to Selwa, Jerry's pickup twisted off a rear axle. We were reaping a fine harvest from the beating we had given the cars in the last three months. Fortunately the lorry and the station wagon were in Selwa when we returned. It would have been the last straw if we'd had to search for them.

We finished our work at Selwa in two days. One assignment was to locate a well that was north of the border without crossing it. Salim Abu Ar-Ru'us said he knew where the well was, so we took him up on a ridge to a station we had mapped previously. Before us was a stretch of rolling, brush-covered desert with no apparent sign of a well. We set up the Brunton compass on its tripod and invited Salim to point out the well. Salim pointed the compass, and we drew a line on the map. We then moved to another station and repeated the process. Again he could see the country in which the well was located, but not the well itself. Just to be sure, we went to a third station and took another bearing. When we drew the third line, it intersected the other two lines in a point no larger than a pencil dot. This was especially remarkable because from the third station, he couldn't even see the country around the well.

It seemed too good to be true so we went to a fourth station nine miles away with a range of hills between us and the well. When we read the compass and drew the line, it intersected the other three perfectly. Salim certainly did know where that well was.

Sunday, April 24, 1938, we nailed up the storehouse at Selwa and returned to Dhahran. The next day Jerry and I and all the soldiers went to Dammam to visit the government representative. We told him in English how well they had worked with us and what good men they were. He translated into Arabic and told the Emir how pleased he was to get such a good report on them. Hussein beamed with delight. The same night there was a big dinner at the mess hall with everyone there, including the five or six wives in town. We were the guests of honor and made speeches about the Rub' al-Khali.

Leaving the Rubʿ al-Khali in April 1938

Right now we are surveying a site for the refinery. A gang of laborers is out behind the office starting on a big bunkhouse. It will be a year before the camp will have housing for more wives because much of the material and most of the furniture comes from the States. All the work is directed to building the refinery and laying a 45-mile-long pipeline to the nearest feasible tanker harbor at a place called Ras Tanura.

People are running about in all directions. Usually the geology office is quiet as a country churchyard, but now there are half a dozen air hammers going full blast outside and a horde of refinery people over from Bahrain studying our maps. All is in an uproar. The Rubʿ al-Khali was much easier on the nerves.

Grand Forks – April 22, 1939

I am so sorry that you hadn't received the letter I wrote from the hospital. It seems stupid to be telling you about my ailments when I feel so grand now.

It all happened the last week of February. I felt so jittery and miserable and had a constant backache. I went to the doctor feeling like a sissy. He examined me and found that a pelvic infection had set in, probably due to the miscarriage. If these infections are allowed to run rampant, they cause sterility. So, as I had hospital insurance, I went there for a week, and then Mother came and took me home. Our doctor in Dickinson sent me to bed for another week, and then I told you the rest. There, I guess I've told you the gory details. Don't worry; I'm getting well and fat, and I might make a satisfactory wife, though I doubt it; I still can't cook.

I've just heard "I'm in the Mood for You" on the radio. I believe that was the finale number of the Cotton Club show. Didn't we have fun in New York, darling? Have you any place to dance?

The motor launch **Calarabia** *enroute from Bahrain to al-Khobar*

Chapter 8
"North to the Neutral Zone"

May 17, 1938
Seismograph #2, 110 miles north of Dhahran

The last dance – Kass, I remember it so well. In your black dress you were the most beautiful wife in New York City. So you remember all those little things in our life – I do, too. You lying in the couch on the porch at Medora in your trousers and boots, hair tousled, sparkling eyes and a beautiful smile; and coming out of the shower, hair wet and your medals dangling out of your bathrobe. The feel of your hand when we knelt to be married. We have been together so little; if I continue collecting brain pictures of you at the same rate, I'll bust wide open in a year.

I was sort of wondering just how long it would be before my folks found out about our marriage. I cannot tell you Kath, how much I hate to hurt my mom, but on the other hand, I was, and I am, so madly in love with you that nothing else matters as much as that you are my wife.

While we do a small mapping job in the northern desert, we are staying in a seismograph camp and have the comforts of modern civilization. The camp's core is five steel trailers all hooked together and moved about by tractor. One of them has bunks for six men; two are used for offices and radio, one contains the generator and one is for the kitchen. The kitchen trailer has an enormous frigidaire that is built in from wall-to-wall. A large lean-to tent attached to the side of the trailer serves as the mess hall. They have drilled a water well nearby and installed an electric pump to bring water to the camp, so there is running water and showers – in other words total luxury.

There is much more grass in the north than in the Rub' al Khali; hence, more Bedu, more camels, more sheep and goats and more game. I shot my first gazelle the other day. I thought it was a buck, as it had horns, but it was a doe. Apparently all gazelle have horns. At least it was a long shot at top speed from a moving car. I'm told the usual method is to chase the gazelle until it tires and lies down, then shoot it.

Two days later we scared up a young gazelle, chased him onto a *sabkha* and circled him a couple of times while he tired. I chased him on foot and finally caught the little guy with a flying tackle. Shauby has taken charge of him and feeds him twice a day from the soldiers' milk goats. We are going to give him to the Steineke girls. Sometimes I wonder if Mrs. Steineke doesn't grow somewhat tired of pets. The time Max brought home the *damusas*, small sand lizards, from his trip with us to Jiwa, the girls nearly broke up a bridge party by showing them to the guests. I believe they even offered to let some of the ladies play with them.

May 5, 1938
Dhahran

I have just been to Bahrain on the *Calarabia*, the company's motor launch. It was my first ride on the craft, which makes the run every two weeks on the day off. It does the trip in an hour and a quarter, whereas the *dhow* trip is three hours but more interesting. Jammed inside the *Calarabia*, it is hard to see anything for all the spray it throws up.

Right now we are working on the final maps and the field report of our year's work. I've been spending the last few days on the names. We have a guide pronounce the name for an interpreter, who writes it in Arabic and tells us its meaning, if any. Then we write the name in English which is the hard part. Jerry and I bickered back and forth over the spelling of a list of words before finally calling in Bob Philips, who knows little Arabic, to pronounce them. Despite our best efforts, he got 90 per cent of them wrong. Henceforth, I don't pay any attention to the English spelling. It doesn't make any difference how the names are pronounced in San Francisco, and here they can find someone to read the original Arabic.

Dr. Nomland has been due here for about three weeks. Last we heard he was in Egypt – just his way, no advance notice; he simply drops in. Max tells about one time in Columbia when he didn't know Doc was coming, and Doc had to cool his heels for two weeks waiting for Max to come out of the jungle.

Max, Marian, Tom, the gazelle, and Maxine

Grand Forks – May 17, 1938

Has it ever seemed strange to you that we probably know less of each other than most of our friends and yet infinitely more? Like how sweet and solicitous you are when I am sick and how mad you can get when I smoke. Life goes on in spite of all that, and some day we will probably be so sick of each other that we will wish there were something new about us just to keep life from being dull. But right now nothing is dull, especially not the way I love you. Please, please love me always, and pray that we will be together in the next six months. It just has to be, darling, or I swear I'll join the circus and break my neck – maybe.

Goodnight my love, I just must get a letter from you tomorrow, or I'll be very, very unhappy.

June 26, 1938
Dhahran

Our trip north was a success. All the geologists went up to the seismograph camp with Doc Nomland and Max Thornberg and his 9 year-old son, Russ, who visited from Bahrain. After two days, it was decided that Max Steineke, the two Thornbergs, Norm Meadows and I should go on a two-day reconnaissance trip up the coast as far as the Kuwait border. It was a sort of picnic for us geologists, but for Max Thornberg, it was a big trip into an unknown desert.

We had lunch the first day on a rock hill that rose out of the water's edge about a hundred feet. From the top we saw hundreds of fish in the clear blue water, as well as many stingrays. That night we camped close to the beach, just south of the Kuwait Neutral Zone.

The wind dropped just before sunset, while the humidity rose. We looked as if we were in a Turkish bath. In the morning, we used the Steineke system on the grapenuts: add powdered milk and sugar to the grapenuts, mix well and add water to taste. We continued north until we came to a long, river-like arm of the sea, beyond which we were assured was the land of the Shaikh of Kuwait. We turned back and went inland to find a flowing, salt-water well called Ain al-Abd, Well of the Slave.

The day before, an old Bedu with a loud voice gave us directions to this place as follows: "God bless you, I will tell you where it is. Look this way, put the *sabkha* on your right, leave two sand hills on your left and you will see a large *jabal*. It is in line with the *jabal* and this side of it, not far." Notice the directions. When you are learning Arabic and only understand a few words they are most confusing.

If you ask, "Do I go to the right of the *jabal*?"

He will probably reply, "Leave it on your left." You hear the word "left," don't recognize the other words, so you go to the left and the Bedu wonders what is the matter with you.

We went looking for Ain al-Abd until the pickup truck broke a spring. The two Maxes and I went ahead in the sedan while Norm replaced the spring. The first Bedu we met was wary of us and ran off as fast as he could. The second was mounted on a camel, and I approached him on foot. This was my first attempt to talk to a Bedu without Khamis along to explain what my Arabic was supposed to mean. Being the mounted man, he was supposed to greet me first, but I didn't know this and opened with a loud *Salaam Aleikum*.

After we exchanged greetings, we got down to business, and I asked him where Ain al-Abd was. He didn't understand me until after repeating the question several times I managed to pronounce the "ain" with the right sound in my throat. He replied, "Ain al-Abd?" as if to say, "Why in the hell didn't you say so in the first place?"

While he circled about on his camel, he pointed out the well and Max tried to take the bearing with the compass, but it was difficult. A camel is driven by a rope around its neck, combined with taps on the neck with a long stick. This camel wouldn't stand still, and the rider was tapping it first one way and then the other. In the maneuvering, a white, enamel pot fell off his head. I hadn't noticed it before; I guess it was on his head because it was a convenient place to carry it. I made a mistake by picking it up and giving it back to him.

He made one more gesture to the well and then rode off. Had I been more clever, I wouldn't have returned the pot to him until I finished questioning him.

In the evening we were back at the seismograph camp drinking ice water. To my surprise, I found everyone called Max Thornberg, "Mr. Thornberg," while he was Max to me. I'd heard of Max Thornberg so I'd called him "Max," just like we call everyone else by first names. As it turns out, Mr. Thornberg is a vice president of Caltex, the subsidiary company controlling Bapco, and is quite likely to become a director of the California company. So, you see, I should rise in the profession, hobnobbing with the big shots and calling them by their Christian names.

Medora - June 13, 1938

Having just returned from a harrowing trip, every muscle and bone in my body has been loudly protesting. Saturday morning Bud *(Kathleen's younger brother)* and I left with our packhorse and equipment in an effort to find two horses. We camped at a perfect place with a bubbling spring in a grove of trees. We each had a roll bed and down quilts, which kept us almost too warm. That night for supper we had corn fritters that were not very good looking, as we only had a sharp knife with which to turn them, and Bud's coffee which was truly delicious. Before retiring, we had quite a struggle hobbling the horses, and then we had to kill a rattler. We got three during the trip. When we went to bed, the moon was coming up a clear gold. It was so calm and beautiful, you would have loved it.

The next morning about six, we packed up everything and started off over some really rough country. I've never seen it more lovely; the grass was high and the hills all green instead of brown, almost too good to be true. We parked our packhorse on a hill and started off. After riding about ten or fifteen miles, we found our two horses and had one hell of a time catching them. Fortunately we had them cornered between a fence and a high gumbo hill.

Absolutely starving, we returned to the spring around four o'clock. We built a fire and cooked almost everything we had left – mostly beans and bacon. About five, we started home and arrived at nine. I was so stiff that when I got off Don I could barely walk. It was a wonderful trip, our only regret was that we didn't bag a prairie chicken. We encountered about five coveys but Bud could never approach close enough to shoot one.

Darling, you can't know how lonely it is without you; it would be so good to have you with me, and yet I know that it is better for you to be where you are. Life is not going well here. The recession is much worse than the Depression, and we here in the Middle West are considered to be better off than in other portions of the nation for the coming year.

This morning I had the grandest time cleaning and raking around the ranch. We had the most beautiful rain, and then it cleared off. If you could only see the thousands of red roses; they are indescribably lovely and fragrant.

*Kathleen at
The Buddy Ranch
1938*

July 10, 1938
Dhahran

Well No. 4 is almost down to the pay zone. They were ready to start testing it, only to be delayed for weeks because of the lack of a device called a "packer." Someone slipped up, and the one on hand is half an inch too large. They are trying to get one sent by air from London. Much depends on it as literally millions of dollars worth of construction is hanging fire awaiting the results of these tests.

The news is betwixt and between. You remember Doc Nomland told me I might get married, but not to ask him to bring my wife over. Later, of course, I found out that the statement was made because of the lack of housing here and that the company policy is not to take the wives of new men on foreign jobs until they've been with the company for a year. However, this last doesn't apply too strongly to the geology department. Max told me he would do all he could to get you over here, so I had him tell Doc of my change in status. Doc was not at all surprised and said that while the company was under no obligation by agreement, he would bring you over as soon as possible. When that is could be anyone's guess. The building program calls for a large number of duplexes, but no one knows when they will be built.

This letter is three days late because of a horrible accident we had four days ago. The fast gasoline launch, *Calarabia*, exploded, burned and sank half way to Bahrain. Aboard were Al Carpenter, the captain, four Arab sailors and Charlie and Mrs. Herring. She was going over to the hospital with a suspected case of appendicitis. It was a windy day, so the water was rough and choppy.

The explosion occurred amidships in the engine room. Al and three of the sailors were in the wheelhouse, so they weren't hurt. They threw out the anchor and went overboard. The Herrings, one sailor and all of the life preservers were in the after cabin where the fire raged. She could not swim and would not jump over; she just clung to Charlie until the Arab sailor pushed both of them into the water.

Al and the others clung to the anchor rope and gathered wreckage to float on. They gave the Herrings a large hatch cover. She was badly burned and either unconscious or dead. Charlie wouldn't abandon her to come with the others. Though the wind was from the northwest, the current carried them off northeast. Finally, the anchor rope burned through and the hulk drifted downwind with Al and the sailors swimming after it. Captain Eid, the ranking Arab sailor, probably saved Al's life. He had managed to get together a steel compressed air tank, a fire extinguisher and a piece of life preserver for Al to float on.

All this happened about 10:30 in the morning. It was 6 at night before we were sure the *Calarabia* hadn't arrived at Bahrain. The next morning two boats set out, while cars drove down the coast to look out from high dunes. Everyone assumed that there had been some engine trouble and the boat was drifting. By noon, one of the boats picked up Al and two of the sailors; the other man had slipped under early in the morning. It must have been terrible clinging to that steel tank all day long in the blazing sun. Al probably couldn't have hung on much longer. That afternoon all of our boats were out, and a RAF plane joined the search.

The next day, four of us went down the coast to Oqair to spread the word of a reward for the bodies and drove back along the beach looking, but one of our ships had already found the bodies of the Herrings. Charlie was fully dressed and even had a fountain pen still in his pocket. They were fine people. You might remember that Charlie was with me at the Crown Prince's reception the first day I arrived here. When Mrs. Herring died, it is probable that Charlie didn't struggle much longer. The Arab who tried to get him to come with Al and the others said that Charlie told him, "My wife finished; I finished too."

Local Leave in Kashmir

Normally the geologists would return from the field about the end of May, make their maps, write up a report of the year's work and present their conclusions. When all this was finished, they took what was called a "local leave." Usually they went to Lebanon on the Mediterranean, where, because of the mountains, the climate was good. Beirut had plenty of restaurants and nightclubs, and there were dentists who could be trusted. However, Max thought we ought to go to Kashmir for our vacation. It was reputed to be a nice enough place, but Max was more interested in the geology of the area and wanted us to investigate for him. His offer to increase our expense money and lengthen our leave if we went there convinced us that Kashmir was the place to visit.

Jerry and I started on our report in Dhahran. As the junior geologist, my responsibilities were to draw the geographical map, write up the physical data we had collected, such as the composition of particular rock sections we had found, describe the flora and fauna we encountered and relate any physiographic details, such as roads or sweet wells, that would be useful for any further geological exploration in the areas. My final chore was to create a glossary of Arabic place names, so that future geologists could correctly pronounce these names to their guides.

I began with the map and immediately ran into a problem. When someone draws a map, he portrays a curved surface on a flat piece of paper. When long distances are involved, the mapmaker must have some system to make allowance for the earth's curvature. There are a variety of systems to do this. The cartographer who had come out in the early days and had since returned to the States had chosen a system called Alber's Conical Equal Area Projection. This is a fine projection, except that the co-ordinates for longitude and latitude had not been calculated for the latitudes in which we had worked. Before I could begin my work, I had to refresh my long-neglected knowledge of calculus and develop my own projection table.

As senior geologist, Jerry's part of the report was to describe the geology we had encountered and superimpose the geological map on the geographical base map I had made. I was finished in six weeks, but Jerry wasn't finished with the geology. Max suggested that we complete the report on our vacation, so we took a trunk full of maps and notes and left Bahrain by British India boat en route to Karachi.

From Karachi, we made our way up to Kashmir. After a week in a hotel, we still hadn't progressed much on the report, so Jerry thought we ought to move to a houseboat on the lake, which undoubtedly would provide us a better working environment. We rented the Miss America, a wonderful houseboat with two bedrooms, a dining room and parlor for four dollars a day, including food, cook and houseboy. We had a great vacation in Kashmir, but when it came time to leave, the report still wasn't finished. We returned to Karachi and spent the last two days of vacation on our hands and knees drawing colored lines on the map spread out on the tile floor of our humid hotel room.

Aboard the Miss America *on Dal Lake, Nagin Bagh, Kashmir*

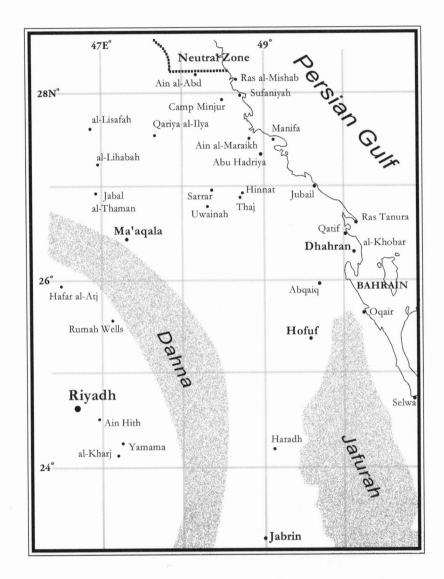

Northeastern Saudi Arabia, from the Neutral Zone to Jabrin

The walls of Riyadh in 1937,
photograph by Max Steineke (Saudi Aramco)

Chapter 9
"Riyadh and King Abdul Aziz ibn Saud"

September 20, 1938
Riyadh

From the capital of Arabia, the chief town of the Nejd, the center of the Wahhabis, and a tent just north of His Majesty's palace, I send you greetings. This is a real believe-it-or-not stunt, so this letter may or may not reach you. Anyway, if it arrives, you will have a letter from Riyadh. There have been fewer than four dozen Europeans here, and I don't believe that many of them sent letters out.

Located in a valley named Wadi Hanifa, Riyadh has many palm gardens irrigated by water drawn by donkeys from 100 foot-deep wells. As the donkey walks down an incline leading from the well, he draws a weighted goatskin full of water to the top of the well. There the water bag empties itself into a trough, and the animal walks back up the incline, lowering the goatskin for another load. Usually the four to six camels, oxen, or donkeys work under the guidance of a small boy. The water is used to irrigate the two main crops, date palms and alfalfa. All night long the pulleys of the wells creak. It sounds like distant factory whistles.

Dick Bramkamp, the paleontologist, and I are here to locate a water well to be drilled for the government and then scout the geology around Riyadh. The King asked for someone to examine his palace and design an electrical system for it, so we've brought Liston Hills, a young electrical engineer, with us. Liston is the lucky one, as he has to survey the entire palace – harem and all, to see what the power requirements are.

Day before yesterday we went about 60 miles down the *wadi* with Shaikh Abdullah Sulaiman, the Minister of Finance, to look at some land he wanted to irrigate. We arrived at this place about nine and had quite a breakfast: crisp whole wheat bread in great, thin sheets, watermelon and muskmelon cut and piled in huge stacks, *leban* – butter milk from goat's milk, camel milk in bowls, and dates with butter. I've never eaten dates like these before. They were big, fat, golden-yellow ones fresh from the palm; dipped in butter they were delicious. After breakfast, the servants brought in big bowls, pitchers of water, soap and towels. We washed and then freshened up with rose water.

Afterwards we went out to the three wells. Some wells! They were great pits with straight walls, 70 to 100 feet in diameter. The clear, blue water was about 20 feet below the surface and deep. The Shaikh claims to have lowered a big rock on nearly 700 feet of rope without touching bottom. He wants to irrigate from these pits with pumps. It is quite feasible, as there is much flat bottomland in the valley floor, but the trouble is they have no power, and the cost of fuel oil will be terrific.

Back at Shaikh Abdullah's garden, we sat in the *mejlis* and had tea and coffee while lunch was prepared. The *mejlis* is made of mud walls about six feet high, open to the north and covered about six feet from the top of the walls with palm fronds. It makes a cool and sensible shelter for these parts.

The lunch was a whopper. First, the servants spread a big, white cloth on the carpets and then brought in three huge trays of rice and bread on which were piled whole sheep, complete to the head, and a variety of roasted fowl. The rice was flavored with spices and colored light yellow with saffron. Mixed with it was a sort of whole-wheat mush, which made it easy to roll everything into balls. There were bowls of wheat porridge, dates, *leban*, milk, bread and fruit. We ate while the servants stood behind fanning us. One fellow tore apart the birds for the guests and placed the best parts on the rice pile in front of us. After we washed our hands, there was more tea, this time green and black; arranged in two rows with alternating colors, it was a good effect, as the tea is always served in small glass cups.

So we prosper in Riyadh. Though the afternoon is very hot, the nights and mornings are cool and pleasant. We are up every morning at 5:30, and the last few days I've been so weary from climbing hills I'm in bed at 8:00.

Shaikh Abdullah Sulaiman, center, with the American diplomat, Armin Meyer. Standing to the left is Sheikh Yusef Yassin, the Saudi Protocol Minister – 1945

Shaikh Abdullah Sulaiman was a bright, intelligent, enthusiastic man, lithe and skinny, but full of energy and ideas. Though his title was Minister of Finance, he was really what we would call the "Grand Vizier." He was the King's minister in every function of the government except for foreign affairs, defense and the government of the provinces. A Najdi from the Qasim, he was with the King from the earliest years and went through the very difficult years of the Depression with the Kingdom's treasury in a tin trunk.

When the money came in from taxes and so on, it went into the trunk until the King decided to spend it. When the King gave someone a chit *for 100 riyals, Abdullah would redeem the* chit. *This would go on as long as there was money in the trunk; if the money ran out, Abdullah would make himself scarce.*

Abdullah was the driving force behind the development of agriculture in the kingdom, especially in al-Kharj. He was always looking at new ways to further develop new crops or new breeds of livestock. He was a remarkable man, who had the absolute confidence of the King.

Medora – August 1, 1938

It gets unerringly lonely without you, and somehow my letters can't tell you how much I miss you. This has been a perfect summer, and my family has been grand to me, but I'll soon have to do something. I hate to think of casework; I know I need only two or three rodeos to drive out this uneasy feeling. I have never thought before of the terrific adjustment that I'll have to make some day; to suddenly change a life you've built for 20 years isn't easy. And I'll never see an arena or a bronco that I won't ache to be in the middle of it all. I don't get like this often. I need you so much, darling, and I always will. Have patience and pray that we may soon be together. Love me forever, as I love you.

September 26, 1938
Dhahran

The radio has just finished with the latest war news from Czechoslovakia. It sounds black indeed. I imagine that by the first of October we shall see if one side backs down, or if there will be war.

Here the situation is looking up. The company is going for Arabia in a big way. Another well came in satisfactorily last week. They've started building duplexes, and new men are coming in all the time. We have more than 200 Americans now.

The geological division is going to be expanded from one field party (Jerry and me), a seismograph crew and three other men to four field parties, two seismograph crews, a gravity meter team and two drilling outfits. The men and equipment are to arrive in November. The company is not only speeding up the work here, but the development of the whole concession. The best part is that many of the men are new with the company, as I am, but I have more service time. The houses are allotted according to position and length of service. In 1937, the black year when it looked as if the Arabian venture would be a flop, they only sent over seven men, so there aren't too many ahead of me on the housing list.

The European developments might make this the last airmail for awhile. The radio is now a popular institution. The news is broadcast every hour during the evenings. Heretofore, we usually listened to only one broadcast, but these days we try to get all the information we can. It seems incredible that Hitler will risk a war, considering the present economic condition of Germany, yet unless Czechoslovakia accedes to his demands, he must start a war to save face at home. If Italy stays out of it or enters on the side of Britain, we won't be affected at all. If Italy sides with Germany, the air mail service to England, along with most commerce through the Mediterranean, will cease. Our mail and supplies will then have to come via the Pacific. I think you and my folks do not fully realize the geographical remoteness of this place, so do not worry about me in case the dogfight begins by the time you receive this letter.

Before we left Riyadh, we donned our white suits, *ghutras* and *bishts*, the dark, flowing cloak, and went to see the King with Shaikh Abdullah and Najib Salih, his assistant and interpreter. We walked into the new, mud-brick palace, along whitewashed corridors and up a flight of stairs lined with guards. The meeting room was a large L-shaped affair, with the King sitting at the elbow, facing towards the longer side. Along the walls were assorted davenports, chesterfields, benches and what-have-you. The King is a big, good-looking fellow. We greeted him and sat on the davenport to his right. The walls were distinguished by enormous mirrors painted with flowers, intricate designs and Arabic inscriptions. In addition to several ceiling fans, there was a *punkah* directly in front of the King.

A *punkah* is a sort of stiff mattress hung from the ceiling by ropes and swung back and forth by a boy who pulls a rope attached to its lower side. The King explained that he liked the breeze of the *punkah* better than that of the fans. "It was cooler," he said.

Walt agreed that it undoubtedly mixed the air up most thoroughly. We had a cup of tea to sip while Walt, who speaks excellent Arabic, conversed with His Majesty and invited him over to see his oil wells. The King asked a few questions, and after half an hour we all trooped out again. The mirrors were the wobbly kind with wrinkles on the glass.

I enjoyed meeting the King; he was quite a tough character in his time. He took Riyadh with 30 men, attacking the garrison of 80 soldiers with six men. They killed the governor and drove the rest under cover, while the balance of his men came over the wall and took the defenders from the rear.

Our return to Dhahran was uneventful, though we took a different route. My .22 rifle arrived just before we left for Riyadh. The size of the bullets amused the soldiers, but the first day we saw any game birds I got five hits out of six shots, and they were much impressed.

When we left Riyadh, we were asked to provide guides for two busloads of drivers from the Hejaz who were being sent to Dhahran. As there were so few cars in the Eastern Province, there weren't any available drivers. We were now getting cars faster than we could train drivers, so we imported these drivers from the other side of the Peninsula. We decided that Hussein would start out with the drivers, and the rest of us would leave later in the day and catch up with them along the way.

The problem was that the road branched in two or three places, and we needed to know if we were following the right bus on the right road. This was solved because the buses were equipped with high-pressure tires and were forever getting stuck in the sand. As we drove, we would come on spots where the bus had become stuck; this was evident by the number of footprints where everyone had left the bus. Khamis would then get out and look around until he found Hussein's footprints, and we knew that we were on the right road. On one occasion when he couldn't find Hussein's footprints, we went back to the other fork and proceeded to follow the proper road.

October 4, 1938
Dhahran

Tomorrow Bill Seale and I are going out to the desert. He is a newly arrived engineer who is going to do some high-powered surveying in the north. When Jerry comes back from Bahrain, he and I will start on the geology using Bill's survey points for our maps.

I was looking at the new duplexes today. They're going up slowly, as most of the labor force is working on the pipeline, the docks and the new wells being drilled. Also the design is new; they've changed the plumbing plans three times already, and the materials are very slow in arriving. Many of our supplies are shipped by Hansa boats, a German line operating from New York to the East, and they have been delayed by the recent war scare. Plus, the company must accommodate all the big shots' housing before they get around to the young squirts like myself. There is some hope, though; the oil wells are proving to be even better than expected; in fact, they are exceptional.

Since we returned from Riyadh, I've been busy getting ready to go into the field. To complicate matters, the lack of supplies remains a chronic problem. Cars are especially difficult to obtain and keep. We are sending most of our food and heavy supplies ahead by boat because we can't requisition a truck. The wind is clocklike compared to the local boats.

When the three new geological parties arrive, Jerry and I will be split up. He will run a couple of crews in the north because he knows the geology of that area better than anyone else. I will have a party to work south of Hofuf to Jabrin and possibly across the great wasteland of Abu Bahr to the Tuwaiq Mountains. Abu Bahr has barely been examined, and I'm anxious to explore it.

Medora – August 13, 1938

Last night, a most embarrassing occurrence came about. We gave a barbecue for the county supervisors; afterwards the boys rode out on a few broncos, and we were sitting on the side hill east of the corrals in small groups. About six feet from me was a friend of yours, Mr. Jenkins (which I learned later); next to him, an informative friend, Mrs. Short. When she found out he was from Linton, she asked if he knew you and said she'd met you last summer. Whereupon he launched into a lengthy life history of you, your merits, your love affairs, your family, your vacation in India, your beard – your everything except your wife. I was so completely jittery before the two had finished the conversation that I could scarcely see. Later I introduced myself as your wife, and he asked me to give you his best regards.

Jerry, Shauby, a rijm *and I*

Chapter 10
"Camp Minjur, Shauby's Troubles and the Wolf"

October 13, 1938
Ain al-Muraikh

Bill Seale and I are camped near the above well, which you will not find on any maps outside of the company offices. Ain al-Muraikh is two holes in the sand near a ruined mud mosque that belongs to the Awasm tribe. Jerry is now back from the hospital in Bahrain, but Max won't let him into the field until he finishes that eternal report of ours. Max is annoyed, but it is becoming to be kind of a joke. He says Jerry is trying to write it so that he'll get an A.

Our camp is a regular tent city with our tent, a dining tent, a big tent for the four soldiers and three small tents for the cooks, drivers and laborers. Driving home tonight along the *sabkha*, we ran into a flight of *qata* birds and stopped to shoot them for dinner. Bill left his pickup truck to come in the sedan with me. We bagged three of the birds. They are a sort of grouse and are quite delicious.

When we returned to Bill's pickup, it was gone. One of the laborers had driven it in, for which he was promptly fired. We can't afford to have a scarce, $1500 truck bumped about by a 40-cent-a-day laborer who had never driven before. In Dhahran, a couple of weeks ago, one guy hopped into a truck, put it in gear and crashed into the camp's portable kitchen. The Chinese cook was somewhat astonished by the huge gas stove jumping three feet away from the wall.

The desert is so quiet tonight; there is only the rasping breath of the Coleman light and the faint voices of the Arabs talking around the campfire. Now that the weather is turning cool, there are many birds coming down from the north. One variety, a kind of marten, is nearly tame and will come in and fly around the tent. Bill put one in a box last night, intending to make a cage and keep him, but the poor creature was dead in the morning.

I had a lively discussion with Salih, the cook, at dinner tonight. Like most of the mainland Arabs, he belongs to the Sunni sect, the largest group of Moslems. In the coastal towns, Hofuf, and on Bahrain are a great many Shi'a, members of the other principal division of Islam. According to Salih, only Sunnis are true Moslems. Since all sects make the pilgrimage to Mecca at the same time, you can well imagine what fertile ground for friction the pilgrimage provides.

The moon was full two days ago. In two weeks when it is new again, Ramadhan begins. For a month Moslems will fast all day, no food or water from sunrise to sunset. They eat and talk most of the night, a combination that hardly fits in with the work schedule of an oil company. During Ramadhan there are more accidents, especially around the drilling rigs. Cal Ross, Casoc's chief carpenter, told me that last year one of his men was caught eating during the day. The police took him to Qatif and beat him heavily. A Bahraini, he went back to the island as soon as he was able to walk again.

Bismarck, North Dakota – September 4, 1938

Congratulate me, darling. Before my 21st birthday I have received the position of *interviewer* for the Public Welfare Board of North Dakota, with an office in the Capitol on the 14th floor. Oh, what I would give to be keeping house for you this winter instead of myself. I'd give ten years of my life to just have your arms around me; it's so awful loving you like this.

October 22, 1938
Ain al Muraikh

The Emir sent over to ask us to coffee. It was a pleasant session in which I did most of the talking, describing modern instruments of warfare and discussing the wars in China and Spain. After the second round we started to go, but the Emir asked us to stay and motioned one of the drivers, Ibrahim, to leave. He began, "There has been some very bad business here. This afternoon when I was sleeping, your houseboy came and told me, 'Come! The cook and the two drivers are doing something bad.' I told him to go away; I didn't want to hear any gossip, but he said, 'You must come; the government will want to know this.' So I went. It was very bad. I took it away from them, but neither the company nor the government will like this." He pointed towards a corner of the tent.

I had visions of them drinking whiskey smuggled from Bahrain and was quite relieved not to see a bottle of Scotch, but only a couple of five-gallon gasoline tins, one with a sort of chimney on it and the other with a couple of small pipes projecting from it. I told him that I didn't know what it was, so one of the soldiers brought it over and put one of the tins on top of the other. "It is for making liquor," said the Emir. "Perhaps you don't know what liquor is (I didn't know the Arabic word for it), but it is very bad for Arabs."

They had a young still, the kind we use in school laboratories for making distilled water. Where the technology came from I don't know, but the bottom tin was full of fermented date mash. I was amazed.

The Emir didn't know what to do, nor did I. He explained that if only the soldiers and I knew about it he would destroy the apparatus and nothing more would be done. But the houseboy would tell everyone, and if the government found out, his failure to report it would put him in hot water. So Khamis and I left here at nine, drove to Dhahran, and awoke Max at one in the morning. He said that it was a government affair that the Emir should handle as he saw fit. To keep from getting involved myself, I left about 2:30 and arrived at sunrise.

At 8:30 Max confirmed the decision by radio, and I passed it on to the Emir. He was very unhappy. This is the sixth year he has worked with Salih and Shauby. He said he would put in a good word for them and try to get them off as lightly as possible. Salih is the best desert cook in the country, and Shauby is the master of all our Arab mechanics. Ibrahim is a driver and, being a Hejazi, probably the instigator of this scheme. A few years ago, a bootlegger in Qatif died from the beating he received in jail. Since then, fines have become popular, especially for those working for the company. I hope they get off with fines and at the worst a light touch of the rod. In the meantime, the houseboy is cooking for us, but all the cars need greasing and I'll have to do it myself.

The day after our night trip all I wanted to do was get some sleep, but, just as I was about to go to bed, Booger Arnold arrived from the seismographic camp. It was a day off and he came over to hunt gazelle. We had lunch, and since we can't work during mid-day when the heat waves ruin our surveying, I went to bed. An hour later Dick Kerr and Jim Garry woke me up. They were reconnoitering roads for the seismograph team. I watched them eat lunch and went back to bed with the temperature about 110 and my prickly heat in full blossom. That night, after a half-hour's cranking on the radio's generator failed to make it run, I was in a fine mood to bite a bear.

Yesterday Khamis and I laid out a road to the seismograph camp by dragging a chain to leave a trail for the tractor. We had been using their tractor to make roads for our work and were going to send it straight back to the seismo camp, dragging a road between us as it went. It went about four miles and was quite motionless when I went to pick up the crew that evening. "It just stopped," the driver said.

Most of the morning was gone before I had cleaned the sand out of the carburetor and got the tractor running. I came back and the damned radio generator still wouldn't run. In addition, my nose was running like mad and my prickly heat was doing remarkably well, I thought I had beat the cold but was mistaken. Khamis says I got it because I worked on the tractor this morning without my *ghutra*. He says he doesn't know if it is true or not, but that is what the Arabs say, and this is the season for colds if you go bareheaded. Maybe they're right; they've been here a long time.

This afternoon I sat and stared at the generator for a long time. It is cranked by winding a rope around the flywheel and pulling on it, like an outboard motor. I finally had an idea; I jacked up the rear of a pickup, started the engine, put it in gear, pressed the generator's flywheel against the rear wheel, and it ran beautifully. It even did so again tonight for the radio schedule, at least long enough for us to transmit the important messages before it gave up the ghost again. Sometime soon, maybe, I'll have time to do some engineering or geology, or whatever it is I'm being paid for.

Orders from San Francisco are that the drilling is to take precedence over everything else. The new cars are slow in arriving, and there aren't any mechanics to spare for the field. Dick Kerr is at his wit's end, his seismograph crew has a fleet of cars and trucks and not one mechanic. Most of the crew can do the work, but you can't keep them working and servicing cars at the same time. I hope the government doesn't decide to keep old Shauby in jail.

Tomorrow or the next night, when the new moon appears, Ramadhan begins and lasts a month.

October 31, 1938
Ain al-Muraikh

Today I am quite content, especially if I get a letter from you tomorrow. It has been awhile since one arrived. During the late war scare, the Imperial Airways planes were called back, and they now have half as many mail schedules as before.

The day before yesterday, Shauby, Salih and Ibrahim were released from jail and came back to work. It seems that the Emir of Jubail, not wishing to have them flogged to death, reported that they were found drinking wine only, with no mention of their manufacturing activities, so the law tanned their hides a bit for appearance's sake and let them off.

The other day, Khamis and I went up to the boundary of the Kuwait Neutral Zone to look for Ain al-Abd. This was the same well I was looking for when I met the Bedu with the porcelain pot on his head. We went straight from here, going from *jabal* to *jabal* and from sand hill to sand hill. At last, Khamis said, "There it is; those bushes are our destination."

The bushes were about 10 miles away, so I asked him, "Are those bushes near the well?" He replied that they were right at the well, so we drove over to them and the well was right there.

It was a big well, bubbling with sulfur gas. It sounded like an airplane and smelled worse than rotten eggs. A beautiful, clear, blue stream flows away from it to the coast 40 miles away. Lots of little minnows in the stream reminded me of happier lands, but the water is so salty and bitter the camels won't even drink it.

After we left the well, Khamis said he had never been there before. I asked him if that were the case, how did he know where it was? Pointing to a couple of sand hills twelve miles away, he said, "Do you see that hill over there? Do you see that one over there? One day I was on the first hill and a man told me that Ain al-Abd was this side of the other sand hill."

It is simple. You have someone point out a sand hill about 15 miles away and then you return some years later and recognize a round, low, sand hill by approaching it from the opposite side and, of course, anyone would know where the well was.

Ain al-Abd, a significant landmark on the border of the Saudi-Kuwait Neutral Zone

On another occasion in the following field season, Max came up to visit us on his way to Hafar al-Batin, which was about 125 kilometers from our camp over flat terrain that was mostly gravel and grassy plain. He wanted to make a straight "road" there that others could follow. To do this, he was going to lay out a compass direction and then, with his three cars following in each other's tracks, they would lay down this road.

Max brought along Shauby as his mechanic and Khamis as his guide. Jerry was as nervous as a cat on a hot tin roof when he heard that Shauby was coming. He gathered up all the tools and put them in a metal box that he hid under his bed, which was a reasonable precaution with Shauby in the area.

The night before they left, we mapped a straight line to Hafar al-Batin and estimated the distance. The next morning we went to the take-off point with Max, set up the Brunton compass and then asked Khamis to point it straight to Hafer al-Batin. Khamis wiggled the compass a bit, backed off, sighted down it two or three times, adjusted it once more, and finally said, "I think that's it."

The bearing that we read off the compass was one degree different than what we had calculated the night before, and it was quite likely that Khamis was right and our map was wrong.

Last week we were driving on a nice, smooth *sabkha* when we spotted a wolf. We chased him as he ran for the sand at the *sabkha's* edge, where there were bushy hummocks about chest high. It was quite a race. Just as I slammed on the brakes to prevent breaking all the springs on these huge sand bumps, Khamis let him have it with the shotgun. I jumped out and hit the beast with one .22 bullet as he ducked over a ridge. The laborers with us thought this was great, as they would never think of wasting a bullet on a running animal.

We finished our work at a nearby *jabal* and returned to continue the hunt. A Bedouin who had shown up started following the wolf's tracks, which were distinguished by one leg that was dragging. Then the laborers took turns running in front of the car. They are all Bedu and have no trouble at all in tracking a wolf or gazelle across ground that is churned up with countless sheep and camel tracks. After two or three miles, we caught up with the wolf on a flat stretch of sand.

With only three legs, he ran like a gazelle and gave us quite a chase, but finally Khamis hit him again with the shotgun. By the time I had stopped the car, we were about 100 yards past him; he was back on his feet. I shot him in the head with the .22 and then again when he tried to trot off once more. When we drove up, he was still alive. All the Arabs hollered at me not to get out of the car until we shot him again. I shot him again, and then they all piled out with hammers and sticks just to be on the safe side.

After they poked the carcass to make sure the wolf was dead, they took turns kicking it and saying, "Oh, wolf! You like sheep, do you?" or "Eat our sheep, will you?"

A big brute the size of a large police dog, the wolf was nice and fat because the country is full of Bedu and their flocks. The men wanted to take out his eye teeth for medicinal purposes, but after a few minutes of hammering at his jaw to no avail, they loaded back in the car and we left. Khamis said that all the Bedu would be extremely happy when the news of the wolf's demise spread, as they like nothing better than killing a wolf. When you realize that the wolf is the only serious predator of their sheep and their sheep are often all they have, this attitude is easy to understand.

The Emir has a new hawk, which he and the soldiers train assiduously every afternoon. They have him outside the tent on his perch. A soldier stands off a few yards with a bit of meat or a bird's wing and keeps yelling, "Shelwah! Shelwah!" interspersed with a sort of war whoop that is effected by all good hawk trainers. Finally, the bird gets the idea and flies off to the food; there is a string tied to his leg. Shelwah was freshly caught in a trap as he came down from Persia to winter in Arabia. At first he was wild and didn't sleep or eat, but now he eats heartily and sleeps all the time with his head thrown back over his shoulder as if his neck were broken. The Emir says he uses his back as a pillow.

While I was in Dhahran last week seeing about our jailbirds, I had a look at the plans for the camp. The present houses are progressing slowly. Instead of the four drilling outfits that were proposed two months ago, there are four here now and two more on the way, all of which requires more and more laborers. However, the plans are good – a school, a hospital, a big clubhouse and a swimming pool to help you keep your figure.

Sometimes I'm optimistic and sometimes I'm not; everything is in an uproar in the camp. As Max says, coming out in the desert is like a rest cure. In addition to the Dhahran work, the test well at Abu Hadriya should be started within a month, and if it comes in with plenty of oil, there will be more rush and struggle to develop the new field. Nevertheless, there should be quite a few houses ready by next summer. The days are always long without you, Kass. I would give a great deal for just one long look at your brown eyes.

That was the first day I had spent in camp for some time. We've been bringing up the maps and laying the plan of attack. Jerry and I will work together here until the first of the year. I am glad of it. This is a tough area; the rocks are inconsistent, hard to recognize from place to place, and the outcrops are few and far between. There is no better man for this kind of work than Jerry. I will learn much and gain considerable experience by working with him.

It's nearly 11:00 and high time for bed since we arise with the sun. Some people ask, "What do you do with your time in Arabia?" We tell them we fix radios, take generators apart, repair cars, see that the camp has water, make sure there is enough gasoline, write reports on geology, servant's time and food expenditures, and keep radio schedules. In between, we work, and if there are no letters to write, we sleep. Good night.

Bismarck – September 21, 1938

Before starting to work, think I will dash off a few lines to you. It will be close to Christmas by the time you receive this, and I can scarcely believe it. I am sending your Christmas gift air mail, and I hope it will get there in time; if it doesn't please you, know that I love you just the same and all my love to you on our second Christmas. Let us not let a third one pass without being together. That seems to be the only thing in my mind at this time, despite the fact that times are increasingly worse, and all my days are filled with people complaining and tales of hard times and no money, children hungry and the need for medical care.

Was so glad to get your letters telling that Salih and the others were not beaten too hard. Must say I thought the one that ate the grasshoppers was too cute for words. The pictures were wonderful.

Do you honestly think I'll be able to come next summer? If I can't, I'll come anyway, or do something equally drastic. Good night, darling, afraid this letter hasn't been too cheerful, but I love you more each day and you must know that I want to be with you more than anything in the world. Write me often and love me much.

November 9, 1938
Camp Minjur

As if it weren't bad enough for one of us to be in love, Jerry has now fallen, smitten by one of the nurses in the Bahrain hospital. She's Irish, and her name is Molly. When the mail comes, we shuffle through it, dealing out letters to him like cards in a whist game. As for Jerry, it used to be that any old tablet was good enough for his letters. Last night he was rummaging about, carrying a tablet on which I had written four or five pages of computations. He explained that he was looking for a tablet. I told him to use the one he had, but he replied that it was sort of frowsy and rumpled. Shades of Shakespeare! I have noticed him copying poetry out of my anthology, which, being an English version, is sort of high-brow and doesn't have "The Shooting of Dan McGrew" or "The Face on the Barroom Floor."

He has his difficulties, including a rival in Bahrain. He is also the brunt of everyone's kidding. According to Max, Mrs. Steineke started kidding him the other evening as he was leaving their house. Jerry got flustered and backed all the way down the walk to the curb, jumped into Max's sedan and drove off, waving good bye and leaving his own yellow station wagon behind. Today, as we ate lunch, he asked me how one is supposed to behave in a Catholic church.

The night of an eclipse I had to stay up until 10:30 for the time signal, so I wandered about waiting for the event, which didn't begin until 12:30. Jerry woke up, and the cook made us some coffee. He and the houseboy were making a sort of mulligan stew for breakfast. They eat just before sunrise during the Ramadhan season. We kept calling the cook's attention to the moon, but he avoided looking at it. It was a fine eclipse; the moon was almost completely blackened. Nasir bin Jamban, our present guide, told us that after we went to bed, one of the laborers became terrified and woke him up. There was a great fuss and much praying before the man calmed down.

Nasir is the big hawk man. Immediately upon his arrival he took over the training of Hussein's new hawk, Shelwah. Last night, long after dark, we heard Nasir training him by emitting the shriek indispensable to the education of hawks and then yelling, "Shelwah! Shelwah! Shelwah!"

Finally I stepped out of the tent and called, "O, Nasir, have you an owl?" There was much laughter from the soldiers and no more training. This morning Nasir said he was angry with me for asking if he had an owl. "Well," I said, "it was dark, and no birds but owls can see at night."

Nasir replied, "Yes, but this is an ignorant hawk. Hussein has not been teaching him properly, so I must have school for him by day and by night." Night school for hawks!

Nasir is a born comedian. He says he has a good wife, but her head only comes up to his chest. Next time he wants a little stronger one. On the road home today, he kept us in convulsions by mocking an emir one of the field parties had a few years ago. This emir and his soldiers caused all sorts of trouble until finally Krug Henry, the chief geologist, wrote a letter of complaint to Saud bin Jiluwi, the governor of the province. The reply came that he would send a new emir and new soldiers, but he couldn't be bothered with the old ones – just cut their heads off on the spot. Nasir thought this was a great punch line. He then straightened up in the back seat, and, thumping his knee with his fist, imitated the old emir. "I am Khozam, the Emir. I want wood. I want water. I want this. I want that. I do not want this. I do not want that."

Time for the time signal. It isn't easy trying to hear a bunch of dots and dashes through the midst of a German band. Sometimes they have a soprano who makes it really difficult, as she usually hits a high note about the time I'm waiting for the minute beat.

The time signal was simple tonight. In addition to the German band, we heard a squeaky voice telling the world something in Spanish, an automatic code station and the aforementioned soprano hovering in the background. Fortunately, the German choir with its tenor soloist quit just before the signal began. It comes from French Indochina, so I shouldn't complain about all the interference, but it is hard on the nerves listening to a series of dots every second and straining to hear the dash that marks the minute.

Somewhere I read a line, " I shall love you until the sands of the desert grow cold." Don't believe it. I shall love you much longer than that.

November 18, 1938
Camp Minjur

It's a far cry from a snowy November day in Medora to a dusty, gray day at Minjur a year later. Remember how Father Roesler thought I was so nervous I wouldn't be able to put the ring on the right finger? And breakfast afterwards? I love you as much now as then. Love me always, Kass, and pray for me. A whole year seems so long, and yet it has passed quickly like a dream. May we have many, many anniversaries and all of them together.

Tomorrow, we are going west on a two-day trip to the gravel plains. Khamis has a new tent for his family, which is in the desert somewhere 200 miles west of here. We are going to deliver the tent and hunt on the way back. Booger Arnold, a hunting fiend from the seismograph team, is coming along. This area is supposed to be the best hunting ground in Arabia, full of gazelles and game birds.

At last we're beginning to get some mapping done and are starting to learn something of the twists and quirks of the geology in this area. All of this preliminary work has enabled us to go ahead on the details without much difficulty. This is a horrible country for an oil geologist, but it is excellent experience for me. As Jerry says, after this, anything will be easy.

Bismarck – December 12, 1938

Just was thrilled to have your letter of November 18th waiting for me tonight when I came home. I was sure that you said you expected I might be coming in the spring, but then perhaps it was an error; darling, if only it could be. I would only be too happy to come to you. America is crazier than ever. Everyone is doing the Lambeth Walk – trucks, shags and jitters. Last week an H.G. Wells program panicked the nation when the use of news flashes was inserted and people actually thought that men from Mars were invading our fair land with weird devices. It made headlines in all the papers.

I can't think of anything more wonderful than to be with you. I love you so much, and the last couple of weeks have been so lonely – day and night. I think of you and it is all a dream. You drinking your four-star Hennessy at the Cotton Club, telling me stories and looking so handsome. I wanted to cry on the spot.

The last night out in Manhattan, November 30, 1937

December 1, 1938
Camp Minjur

The hunting trip was a success. The first day we got nothing but *hubarrah*. The Emir's hawk, Shelwah, was in fine form. He would make a beeline for the *hubarrah*, pounce on him and down they'd flop together. Finally, Hussein sent him after a bird that was 200 yards away. They staged quite an aerial battle. Every time the hawk dived, the *hubarrah* would tuck in his head and Shelwah would sail on by and swoop around to strike again. At last, the *hubarrah* outmaneuvered him and lit out with Shelwah on his tail. They headed west about 500 feet going 60 miles an hour, and that was the last we saw of either of them. Poor Hussein, he had big plans for Shelwah.

Shooting *hubarrah* is quite an art. Even though they are big birds, they are fast once in the air. One of us stands in the back of the pickup as it approaches the birds from downwind; when they fly up the man in back gets his shot. We got six this way on the first day out.

We arrived at Khamis's tent late that afternoon. His two sons, Shabeeb, who is 12, and Abdullah, who is 6, came out to greet us. I asked Abdullah how he was and offered my hand. In a soft whisper, he said he was well and put out his left hand. Shabeeb quickly told him to use the other hand. Poor Abdullah was somewhat rattled with the simultaneous arrival of his father, two Americans and two cars.

In the evening we had dinner with Khamis. Booger, Salih the cook, Emir Hussein and I ate *hubarrah* on a great platter of rice. Khamis didn't eat, as the host never eats, but supervises the meal. The men were worried about Booger being able to ball up the rice and pop it in his mouth because he lost his right index finger in an accident, but he did just fine. They call him "the father of the missing finger."

Khamis's family was delighted with the new tent. They were camped about 40 miles from the nearest drinking water. About every 10 days, all of the Bedu in the area send their camels in together to load up on water. Soon, when the rain comes, they will move even farther from the wells and will only drink camel's milk. They will even boil their meat and rice in milk. The only water they'll need will be enough to make coffee and tea.

l-r. Shabeeb, Khamis and his daughters: Wothha and Shaikha
Photograph by J. W. "Soak" Hoover - 1936

Bismarck – December 18, 1938

Yesterday your letter of December 1st was waiting for me when I came home from work. Were it not for them I should not exist, my darling. Next week you and Jerry should be with Molly and I shall be with my family, bless them. My heart is full of things I want to say – how I want to hear you walk in the door and take me in your arms, how I want you and Michael and mostly how I just want to take the next boat and never sleep until I see you.

December 9, 1938
Camp Minjur

At last we have some rain, a little night before last, more last night, and quite a bit today. The Bedu measure rain by how far it soaks into the ground. Here the sand is wet to about six inches;

about 35 miles west they have had "rain to the elbow." The astonishing thing is that the dry grass and bushes have already begun to sprout. Green shoots here and there would make you think they'd always been nourished instead of having no moisture since last spring. Also there will now be lot of *faqa'a*, a desert truffle, which Jerry says is fine eating.

The men keep coming in. We were in Dhahran a few days ago, and 23 men arrived that day. We went to town because Jerry had to get another typhoid injection. You see, Molly Brogan, the nurse to whom he spends all his spare time writing, gave him one in Bahrain and gave him the syringe, needles, and two vials of vaccine for the other two shots. When the time was ripe, I volunteered to administer the injection. First off, I inquired about sterilization, but Jerry said, "Just wipe it off with alcohol."

After drawing the vaccine into the syringe, I had some trouble getting all of the air out of it. It is considered bad form to shoot air into the bloodstream because it might stop the heart. Next, after I poked the needle in, I withdrew the plunger to see if any blood appears – if it does, try again. Well, I didn't get any blood, but I drew plenty of air into the syringe. So I tried again and got more air. By the time I got all the air out, I'd lost over half the vaccine. I was willing to quit, as we couldn't get a tight fit between the needle and the syringe, but Jerry greased the syringe with analgesic balm, of all things, and insisted that I try again. I was doubtful about this whole operation and was much relieved when Jerry smashed the last vial of vaccine in trying to break the tip off. So he had to go in to get his shot.

We are trying to finish this area before Christmas. After Christmas, I will probably go out with a party of my own to the south, and Jerry will come back here with two new parties.

This afternoon we were out on a peninsula where there was a *barasti*, a hut made of palm fronds, in which three fishermen were living. Jerry and I had lunch while Khamis went over and made some coffee out of the rain and gathered information from them. After we'd eaten, he brought the coffee out to us in the car. The fishermen

A small **barasti** *made of poles thatched with palm fronds*

were friendly and insisted on giving us fresh fish. As we made ready to go, they said, "This is your place; anytime you come we are ready."

As we drove off, Khamis said, "Please God, this is not our place; we have another. They wanted me to bring the engineers inside for coffee, but I said, 'No, they are busy; we will take the coffee out to them.' It was smelly inside of fish, very bad; I do not think you would have liked it."

Looks like more rain in the west; we'll be wetter than North Dakota soon.

Bismarck – January15, 1939

Darling, can't we be together soon? Things just aren't the same as they should be without you. Such fun if you were here skating and dancing and riding. Tonight Mary Lou and I watched a plane landing. It was lovely coming onto the field through the dark – another thing that reminds me of you, and I don't know, just everything, weddings, mass, people, a lump in my throat and an empty mailbox. Darling, I'm just blue; I shall try hard to write a lovely happy letter next time. Good night, my dearest.

The camp at Ma'aqala

Chapter 11
"Ma'aqala"

January 13, 1939
Dhahran

Day before yesterday, we heard that a ship coming from San Francisco with much of our building materials aboard was lost at sea. Everything will have to be reordered, and the construction timetable is once again delayed by six months. There have been plenty of incidents like this, and they all contribute to the bedlam around this place. For instance, the number of cars has tripled since last summer, but last October when the tools and spare parts needed to maintain this fleet were to arrive, they couldn't be found and had to be reordered. Until they arrive, the garage is working day and night trying to keep the cars in the field.

Someone in San Francisco had the bright idea that since the four-wheel drive Marmon Harrington cars were so good in sand dunes, all of our cars should be Marmon Harringtons, even the new sedans for the geological parties. The hitch is that no one is working in sand country this year. The Marmon Harringtons ride very, very hard, and in the rough *dikakah* country of the north they are always breaking springs. Now there are no more spare springs in stock and the machine shop is making extra spring leaves that will have to do until more arrive.

The number of men has increased several times since the food order for the year was shipped, so we're short of countless items, such as fruit juices, the very staff of life for geologists in the desert. We never go hungry, as there is always plenty to eat, but just now the variety is a bit stunted.

I was in Bahrain last week buying mess outfits for the geological parties. Just before the boat left, I was called at the pier and asked to buy a complete outfit for 20 more men, the second seismograph party, which was ready to go out except for the lack of forks, spoons, pots and plates. Strangely enough, I managed to find nearly everything I needed. Alice Bush, who went shopping with me, said it was much different than when she and Mike first arrived here five years ago. They had to use wooden forks for four months until they could ship in some metal ones from the States.

January 23, 1939
Dhahran

I went back to Bahrain last week to buy cord for the tentmakers, medicine and palm mats for us. The doctor there is young and, hence, very scientific. He says that analgesic balm and Vick's Vapo-Rub are no good and only offer mere temporary relief. I admit this, but it keeps our patients happy and makes them think they are better, so I bought two dozen of each. Without them, I'd hardly be able to practice my quackery in the desert. Think how fine analgesic balm is – a pleasant but penetrating odor, it stings in cuts, and, when rubbed vigorously, it makes the skin burn. It is obviously a powerful remedy that is bound to do a man worlds of good. The doctor made up some evil-tasting cough syrup on the theory that it

Pre-engineering student, St. Mary's
College, Winona, Minnesota – 1927

B. S. Mining and Metallurgy,
University of North Dakota – 1931

Engineer and assistant manager, Bear Exploration & Radium,
Contact Lake, Northwest Terrirory, Canada – 1934

Passport picture – 1941

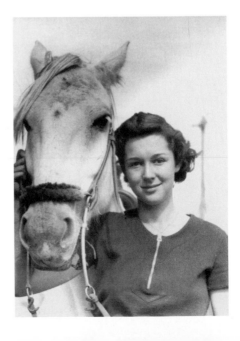

Kathleen at age 17 with Don,
her trick-riding horse – 1935

Lake Bemidji, Minnesota – Spring 1937

Tom and Kathleen at The Buddy Ranch,
Medora, North Dakota – September 1937

At Port Said, enroute to Jabal Dhahran – December 6, 1937

The tents of the Crown Prince Saud and the Shaikh
of Bahrain at al-Khobar – December 1937

Surveying the location of the well at Selwa – December 1937

Shillaif Camp, last camp before al-Ruksa – 1938

Children in Jubail, Casoc's original headquarters – 1937

A Bedouin watering his camels at Ain al-Akerish – 1938

The field party assembled for the trip to Jiwa – 1938

Khamis with the guide Muhammad
Ali Kathri at Anaizah
(J. W. Hoover) – April 30, 1935

The soldiers of Saud bin Jiluwi in attendance at his *mejlis* – 1938

Max Steineke – 1938

Johnny Thomas, Khamis and
a hubbarah, Ma'aqala – 1940

With Jerry Harriss at the
conclusion of the 1938 season

Enjoying the day off with a game of football and some light reading

Bedouin tents pitched outside the walls of Riyadh – 1939

The walls of the *Kut*, or citadel, at Hofuf – 1939

King Abdul Aziz with Shaikh Hamad bin Isa of Bahrain
May 1939

would discourage excessive demand, but his psychology may be wrong. Such a vile concoction must certainly be necessarily beneficial to any man, Arab or American.

Tonight, BBC News said that the Insurgents are within 15 miles of Barcelona; by the time you read this letter, the civil war may be over.

The last shipment is nearly all in the storerooms now, so I will be going into the desert in a few days. Drills, chisels, canteens, towels, sheets, coffee pots, drawing instruments, generators and what-have-you. First, I must get Dutch Schultz off, day after tomorrow I hope, and then I head out for the great blue.

Dutch's partner hasn't arrived yet; he's due in today or tomorrow. He'll have a warm reception, as he'll land in the afternoon and be popped out into the desert the next morning. Neither of them speaks any Arabic, and their cook can say a very good "good morning!" and that's it for his English. I don't envy them. However, we'll be close by, and they can learn with some discomfort, but no danger. Dutch's partner may be used to it, as he is supposed to have had a couple of weeks' experience in Afghanistan.

Boats are most unsatisfactory carriers. They carry much, but when the cargo has been shuffled and dealt, there always seems to be something missing. In one of our orders we got tools for 25 cars, but the crate containing the toolboxes was missing. I guess we should be happy to have the tools without the boxes, rather than the other way around.

The commissary ran out of butter for a few days until they could bring some over from Bahrain. There always seems to be an item or two to furnish the fellows with wisecracks at the expense of the chap in charge of the mess hall.

The other day Khamis and I were dragging the chain from Hinnat to Uwaina and stopped at this well for lunch. As we ate lunch, this fellow strolled up. He was with a caravan coming from Shagra, far in the interior, and going to Jubail for rice, tea, sugar, coffee and the like. Khamis pumped all of the relevant information possible out of him while he was eyeing our back bumper. Finally he asked, "What are you doing with that tail?"

Khamis replied, "Why, we're strangers here. We drag that along so we can find our way back and not get lost following some other track."

The Bedu asked, "Is that right?"

"Beyond doubt," answered Khamis.

Then the Bedu said, "You ought to have a guide here in the desert as you might get lost and die."

"Oh, no, we'll be all right; we're not going far, and we can find our way back," Khamis said with a lofty air, as if we were superior to the ordinary desert Bedouin and had no need for such a useless person as a guide.

In a purely professional way, Max's principal attribute was his tremendous intellectual honesty, combined with his willingness to stick his neck out by making interpretations and predictions based on whatever geological data was available at the moment. One of his favorite words was "embarrassed," and he was always talking about being "embarrassed," though I doubt that he was ever fundamentally embarrassed in the professional sense. As new data became available, he was perfectly willing to throw out the old hypotheses and develop new ones. He was not at all embarrassed to call a given structure an anticline on the basis of new information, even though he had said that it was a syncline the year before. He never could understand people who obstinately clung to old theories in the face of new facts.

In addition, he possessed a great amount of humility, some of which was possibly designed to encourage his young staff, but most of it because he genuinely sought help and ideas wherever he could find them. He would discuss his ideas with us young geologists as if he were seeking our advice. Part of this was Max just thinking out loud; nevertheless, it gave us a great sense of importance and confidence.

He certainly gave us our heads, and most of us responded by working our heads off to justify the confidence. As I remember, the instructions he gave to Ernie Berg and me at the beginning of 1939, when I first became a party chief, were as follows.

"You go out to Ma'aqala."

I asked, "Where's Ma'aqala?"

Max replied, "Oh, it's out there, 100 or 150 miles west of Jubail. We'll send a guide to find it for you. When I went through there two years ago, I didn't have time to look around. Something's happening there, and you find out what it is."

These were the totality of my instructions for five months of work.

February 7, 1939
Seismograph #2, 110 miles north of Dhahran

My new partner, Ernie Berg, and I left Dhahran last Wednesday morning with the lorry piled high, two pickup trucks and the sedan. We were delayed in Jubail for three hours, drinking coffee with various personages and waiting for the soldiers to say good bye. In the pouring rain, we made Dutch Schultz and Ken Parsons' camp just in time for dinner.

Next day we went on to Ma'aqala, a place about 200 miles west of Dhahran. We arrived just before sunset, but were lucky to find a fairly good campground; i.e. a flat, sandy place out of the rainwash on the south side of a hill near firewood. That is something of an order, as sand is scarce in this region. The country is low, rolling, rock hills, with most of the sand lying in gully beds that become torrents with the least rain. Our site is a good place on the north side of a low *wadi* that empties into a mud flat about a quarter of a mile to the west. It is now covered with green grass and many *sidr*, thorny, acacia trees, which make a green grove that is especially striking in Arabia.

Ernie and I are running a two-barometer traverse back from Ma'aqala to tie in with one of Bill Seale's survey stations. We read our barometers together, then I drive ahead for half an hour and stop and read mine. Ernie reads his and comes up, and we repeat the performance. In this way the chap behind is able to record any change in the barometric pressure while the chap ahead is traveling, and we can determine accurate elevations.

With Ernie Berg, the man who would
discover the largest oil field in the world

Ernie seems to be a good egg, I think we shall get along together. We had our radio set up and going the first night we were at Ma'aqala, though we started to unload and make camp only half an hour before sundown. The next day he was under the weather while I puttered about camp. Yesterday I had a terrific cold , the first in quite a while, but today we are both almost in the pink and ready to go.

I just shot a *hubarrah* near the road. Old Muhammad, the guide, is alive with excitement whenever he sees any game. He's of the Qahtan tribe of western Nejd, southwest of Riyadh. I think he is quite new to a car. Every time I put my window up or down he does likewise. Just now I opened my door and put my feet out on the running board as a more comfortable writing position, and he promptly followed suit.

Our new radio is fine. It has a built-in loudspeaker and the receiver is as good as any I've heard in Arabia. We've heard the news all of the past three nights, including discussions of Hitler's speech, F.D.R.'s secret talk to the Senate military affairs committee, and the announcement of the occupation of all Catalonia by the Insurgents.

Right now Muhammad and I are waiting for Ernie to show up with his barometer. Muhammad is somewhat mystified by me stopping within plain sight of the seismo camp, instead of going on in as any normal person would do.

February 13, 1939
Ma'aqala

The weather is making conversation. Night before last the thermometer went down to 26 degrees. About four in the morning, I gave up the struggle and arose from my bed of ice, lit the stove, warmed up and put on my sweater and socks before going back to bed. Ernie held out longer, but he was up before daybreak doing the same. In the morning all of the goatskins of water were frozen solid, as were the cars. Ernie keeps repeating a sentence from a letter his brother wrote him, "I know you are suffering from the terrific heat, but it will be a good experience for you."

About this time you will be looking forward to spring. By the time this reaches you, the winds of March will be tossing about your black locks.

I was sorry to hear of Pope Pius's death, not only because of the troubled state of Europe, but because he was a good man and a great pope. The radio announcer started out, "For those few of our listeners who have not been near a radio or a newspaper for the last 12 hours, we regret to announce ..."

At present, we have two big problems: water for the soldiers, and the King's brother, Muhammad bin Abdul Rahman, who is camped about 20 miles northwest of us. The water comes from *dahls*, sinkholes in the limestone that vary from a foot to 10 feet in diameter. Unfortunately they are not full of water as reported. The one with the most water has the dirtiest water; it is more thin mud than water. The biggest one requires crawling through 100 yards of winding tunnel and dragging the water out in *gurbas*. Our eight *gurbas* won't last more than a couple of weeks hauling water for 11 men.

Bedu are everywhere in this country, mostly from tribes outside of this district, who either do not know or will not tell us which *dahls* have the water. There must be hundreds of these sinkholes scattered around. At first we were leery about driving into one unaware, but now we've found out where and how to look for them. Khamis is sending us some more information about water-filled *dahls* through Jerry. Our new guide is good, but he's handicapped by having only a general idea of this region from talking with Bedu and from his own trips through here with camel caravans going into the interior.

Muhammad bin Abdul Rahman lives out in the desert all winter and goes into Riyadh for the summer. He has the reputation of being hot-headed and according to the cook, "the King does not say no to him." We have steered clear of his camp, though the soldiers took a hawk up to him as a present.

Tonight a carload of his men visited our soldiers and put the bum on me for gasoline. I told them that we only have enough for our work and that I have no orders from the company to give anyone gasoline; then I gave them five gallons. It is something they would love to turn into a habit, as they have a small fleet of cars and most of their gas is brought in by camel.

The country is fairly alive with game to the south and east of here where the royal brother has not been hunting. We've seen *hubarrah, kirwan, qattat* (about twice the size of a *qata*), and *hajjel,* a kind of rock grouse slightly smaller than a prairie chicken. A gazelle came within 400 yards of us when we were measuring a baseline on the gravel plain south of camp, but I had left the rifle home for the first time since we've been out here.

Bismarck – February 14, 1939

See by the paper here that it was 29 degrees below zero last night. The other day, one of the public welfare statisticians made a pointed remark indicating how nice it would be to be in Arabia.

Later a more pointed question, "How would you like to be in Arabia this morning?"

I replied, "I would like to be in Arabia every morning, Mr. Hempl." You see, I'm more or less the freak of the 15th floor. When all other conversation dies, people can reflect on my fate – Did he leave her in the lurch waiting at the altar, or didn't he? All good, clean fun, though.

February 26, 1939
Ma'aqala

The mail goes in tomorrow morning, and despite all my good intentions, I am writing this at the last minute. We took half a day off to write letters to send with the car to Casoc. By the time we had finished our calculations and instrument adjustments, the half-day and most of the evening were gone.

The work has been going more slowly than we had expected, though we are now finished with the worst of it. We've been surveying in a base network for our map. We go around and build *rijms*, rock cairns, for our stations and make them the points for the base map. We place them on the most prominent points so that wherever we go in the area, we can see at least two of them and thus locate ourselves with precision. In shooting over the rock surfaces, the heat waves are always troublesome, even on cold days. About nine o'clock the horizon begins to shimmy, and by lunchtime, all but the closest landmarks are indistinguishable. We take our long shots in the early morning and late afternoon and do the shorter ones at midday.

I have heard nothing of the housing situation of late. The few houses that were ready have been occupied by officials connected with the producing department, sent over from the States. The effect of the Abu Hadriya well is problematical. Shortly they should know if it is going to be an oil well. If it is, they may suspend construction of accommodations for families at Dhahran to begin construction for further drilling and production at Abu Hadriya. The two hardly can be carried on simultaneously because of the shortage of labor.

If Abu Hadriya is a dry hole, it will have a tremendous adverse effect on the concession as a whole. It would infinitely decrease the chances of finding oil in some other places that we think are good prospects, and the company will take it slowly for awhile until we can find something else. It's all up in the air, as usual.

A couple of weeks ago when we first arrived, the soldiers bought a couple of sheep from some Bedu who wanted Maria Theresa dollars instead of Saudi Arab riyals. Both coins are worth the same, but the Maria Theresa dollars are bigger than an U.S. silver dollar. The riyal is only the size of our 50-cent piece. First struck in the 1780's by the Austrian Empress Maria Theresa, they are still coined and exported for use all over the East; here they are called "French money."

One morning last week, the Emir wanted to have one of the drivers take him out in a pickup to buy a sheep from a Bedouin, so I told him that I had some "French money" and asked if he wanted some. I managed to make out "six or seven" from his reply and gave him seven of the dollars. He didn't give me any riyals in return, but I did not press the point at the time. That night at coffee, the soldiers had two new sheep, one of which was pointed out as mine. I admired it duly.

I've had no time for study, but I am learning Arabic from these new men, as they do not speak the "*sahib* Arabic" of Khamis and Hussein, but lay it all out in feminine and plural adjectives, feminine verbs and participles galore, until I am half swamped. Khamis and Hussein have been around us so long that they know that we only know a handful of the irregular plurals, and the masculine only of the adjectives and verbs. I just found out last fall that all words ending in "a" are feminine, that the feminine verb sounds like the second person singular, and all irregular plurals take the feminine. I had thought that when the soldiers said, "Al-jamal takuluh," they were saying, "The camels, you eat it," instead of "The camels eat it." It turns out that they were trying to speak simple Arabic for me, ala Max Steineke, whose verbs are all in the second person.

Muhammad bin Khursan, our new guide, is not as good as Khamis, but he is a competent guide and has a great sense of humor. He and all the rest of the soldiers get a big kick out of Ernie's Arabic and take an active interest in teaching him. Today he wanted to know the English reply when someone held a gun on you and threatened to shoot. He was fascinated when I showed him, "Hands up!"

Usually the Arabs sort of bargain. They say, "By my face, my rifle, and my camel;" i.e., I would like to be let off with my life, my rifle, and my camel. Whereupon the one behind the gun decides on how much to allow him.

Muhammad said that in the 1935 war with the Yemen, he saw something truly strange. It seems he came on four Yemenites who potted at him. One shot nicked him in the left shoulder, so he killed three of them with his "Mother of Five" repeating rifle, whereupon the fourth held his rifle before him with the muzzle in the ground. In Muhammad's words, "I let him go because I thought he wanted to surrender. I had not seen that before."

We have fine days and cold nights, several below freezing, but we eat and sleep regularly. As soon as we finish this preliminary survey, we will take off a day and use it for nothing but sleeping.

Bismarck – March 20, 1939

A major event in my life – a letter from you dated Feb 26th. The news sounded discouraging; seems they have us coming and going. No oil, no houses needed, oil and all houses needed for labor, but I shan't worry, nor do you; just love me always and that will be enough. I'm trying hard to grow up, and I think I will soon. Funny how you become conscious of adulthood so suddenly. Truly it has just been the last month or so I've realized that it seems as if I'm walking into a new world; everything has a different aspect altogether. If only I had you here to talk and talk.

Please write some silly letter, or send me something crazy, or baby me – just anything; it's so hard to grow up alone. I love you so much I can't think straight.

March 8, 1939
Ma'aqala

Today, I got what should be a dandy movie. It was a bitter day with a cold north wind, but we found a good place for lunch in one of the low grassy places. Muhammad made a fire for his coffee in the shelter of some big, green thorn bushes. After we ate, we came and drank coffee with him and talked for a quarter hour or so. Ernie and I have a new lunchtime game. One recites a verse or whatever he knows of a poem, and the other names it and the author. No holds barred, I got him with "Tannenbaum" in German, which I then translated for Muhammad. The second verse goes:

"Oh, maiden, how false is thy pledge
You swore to be true to me in my good fortune
But now that I am poor you leave me."
"Yes, it is the same with us," Muhammad said.

Then as I was in the midst of learning the first four lines of an interminable poem, a rider came by on a camel. To Muhammad's shouts, he hobbled his camel well away from the car and came up. He was an old man, wrinkled and ragged and dirty. Muhammad set out his dates and poured him some coffee. He came from the north, very far, and was going over there not far from our lunch site. I took a movie of him and Muhammad eating and drinking as they sat on the green grass with the smoldering fire between them.

Presently, a flock of 200 sheep came into the meadow with two youngsters driving them. One lad was about 9, the other 5 or 6 years old. Muhammad asked if they had any milk, and the old man replied by telling the oldest boy to bring milk. Off he went to return leading a goat, which Muhammad milked on the spot while I took movies of the milking, Muhammad drinking his milk and the two kids and their grandfather wolfing down the box of cookies we gave them. We were invited to have lunch at their "house" and stay for dinner, too, but we declined with thanks.

We are popular. Day before yesterday, a Bedu came dashing up on a camel, dismounted and came over with the usual salutations. Usually, they do not say much to us, but gossip with Muhammad.

After the greetings, I told him we did not understand Arabic well and to go see the soldier over there. But, no, he insisted I was a "correct man" and then put the bum on me for tobacco. Ernie gave him a cigarette that he sat down and smoked in nothing flat. Ernie said that now he knows why the Bedu say they "drink tobacco." As we prepared to go, he asked Ernie for another one. I advised Ernie against it; if the news should get around, he wouldn't be able to work at the plane table for the crowd.

As the plane table network of rock cairns or rijms *was being developed, I was appalled at Ernie's carelessness. He was not at all perturbed by the cigarette ashes he dropped all over the plane table paper. It was the messiest plane table job I had ever seen. I kept my mouth shut until we were ready to put it to the test and find out in a jiffy where we were by connecting three or four lines that were supposed to cross at the point we were working. I was sure they wouldn't connect and was ready to read him the riot act. To my astonishment, the intersection of the lines used to determine our position was flawless. A sharp pencil point was about the measure of total deviation from a hundred per cent perfection.*

Yesterday, I was much flattered. Ernie had the plane table set up on top of a hill, and I was working about a kilometer away pounding on rocks. I could see three Bedu approaching in haste; they were too fast for me, as they arrived before I could finish and get away. After the preliminary *salaams,* they stood around silent until I finished writing my notes; I could see that they were waiting to say something. At last, I finished, and said for the second time, "How are you?"

"Very good," they replied, " O'Shaikh, come to coffee with us." It took me back, as I had expected they wanted something, such as tobacco or a ride someplace. After profuse thanks, I explained to them that I was busy. It must have struck them as silly, as I was obviously doing nothing but pounding rocks with a hammer and, at intervals, holding up a pointed stick for another American to observe. They wandered off near Ernie to gossip with Abu Nasir.

When I joined Ernie, he and I looked over the results and decided it would be a good thing to go look at the rocks in a *dahl* we knew to be close by. This particular *dahl* has a dirty name in Arabic; the Arabs do not have our inhibitions in naming places. It was shown on the map as "Tayyib al-ism;" i.e. "a good name," a little Arab joke that is particularly funny if the surveyor doesn't know much Arabic and writes down, "Tayyib al-ism." The British War Office maps have several "Tayyib al-ism" places on them.

I walked over to where the four of them were sitting in the sand and asked them if they knew where the *dahl* was, naming it by its correct name. A smile flickered all around, a tribute to them, rather than to my Arabic, as I have a difficult time talking with many Bedu who don't understand my accent.

"No," said Abu Nasir, " they are not of this dirt. They are from Aflaj," a province south of Riyadh, "and the Wadi," Wadi Dawasir far to the south on the soutwestern corner of the Rub' al-Khali. So I asked about a couple of towns they knew and then said, "You are from the country of the *wudhaihi*." They looked at one another and muttered, "*ajeeb*," wonderful, and were all smiles. The *wudhaihi* is the Arabian oryx, which none of us, including Khamis and the soldiers, have ever seen. In response to their questions, as I swaggered off, I heard Abu Nasir say, "Ah, yes, he knows many things. He has not been there, but he knows about it."

The other day Muhammad bin Khursan was showing Ernie how he'd approach if he were a robber. He put his *ghutra* over his face and crouched behind a rock with his rifle. Ernie told him, in his brand-new Arabic, "You're no soldier. You're a wolf in a sheep's skin."

Muhammad thought that was hilarious, and now he's been three days learning "wolf in sheep's clothing" in English so he can tell Dick Bramkamp that "Sahib Berg is a wolf in sheep's clothing." He has a terrible time with "wolf," the "l" and the "f" together, and more difficulty with "sheep's clothing," the "p's cl" makes four consonants together. It is theoretically impossible to have more than two consonants together that are not separated by a vowel in Arabic. Besides, there are no nasal sounds comparable to the "ng" in "clothing".

*Muhammad bin Khursan,
the Qahtani guide at
Ma'aqala*

He is very interested in everything and is forever asking questions. He is very anxious to learn to drive, so I have promised to let him try tomorrow at lunchtime. He wanted to know what kind of clothes the people wore in New York, which we had told him was the biggest city in the world. Then he asked what they would do if he went there with his Arab clothes. "Would they kill me?"

He is intrigued at the absence of divorce amongst certain people in America. "If I took a wife, could I ever let her go?" he asked.

"No, Muhammad, not until you or she is dead."

"Even if she was old and wrinkled and no good?"

"Not even then," I said.

He has had three wives, but has only one at present. I asked him what happened to the old ones. He replied that someone else had married them. So I persisted, "What if no one else took them?"

"But someone would," he answered.

"But if no one did, if they were old and wrinkled?"

"Well," said Muhammad, "then their kin would take them in. God is kind."

He is coming with us to America when we return. We assured him that he could get a wife there, but if he tried to divorce her, the government would catch him and kill him. He says that he will get around this difficulty by bringing her back to Arabia. If she is not satisfactory, he will divorce her here.

He cannot quite grasp the idea of farms and farmers; that is, the idea of people not living in a town, and yet living in one place all the time. All agriculture here is, of course, carried on only around the towns, where water is plentiful. He wanted to know about camels in America. When informed that there were few or none and people paid money to see them, he wanted to know if we had grass. On hearing that there was plenty of grass, he said the camels would eat it, and we could buy one in Bahrain for 100 rupees, about $37, to take home to show our fathers. So expect me to walk in, hissing and whirring at a camel on a leash behind me.

That winter it rained all the time, so the dahls were full of water, and we had no problem filling the gurbas. *The meadows, those places that had clay soil in them, were green with new plants. If they had bushes on them they were called* raudhahs, *but if they were grass meadows they were called* faidhas. *The country was dotted with rainwater pools everywhere. One day Ernie had been off on some errand and was driving alone when he came up and over a rise to find half a dozen Bedouin women bathing in a large pool. To his utter astonishment, they were all stark naked. When they saw Ernie, they put their hands over their faces and ran away like mad.*

March 19, 1939
Ma'aqala

We have to send a car in tomorrow. Our soldier's cook has some sort of abscess on his finger; we have been treating it via radio instructions from Dhahran, but it hasn't responded well. Today his whole hand is swollen, and the doctor has ordered us to send him into the Jabal.

We have what looks at present like a pretty fair oil prospect. Dick Bramkamp corroborated our results and extended the closure in a way we could not have done without him. We are still working on it, as the mapping is by no means complete; if and when any oil is found, we will share in the glory. The actual discovery, of course, is Max's work, as is everything else here except Dhahran. He seems to have the faculty of picking out significant areas at a glance. Often he sends us out saying, "Well, I'd kind of like to have you map such and such an area. There are some dips, and I saw such and such rocks and maybe you'll find something. Then when you get through there, you ought to go up here and maybe you ought to go down there. But you'll know what to do."

So we go out to investigate a place that doesn't look like much, scout around to get our bearings, and finally turn up with a map and nice contours. Then he becomes excited and enthusiastic about "your find." I guess that's why people like to work for him. To see Max with his shirt hanging out, worrying about *gurbas*, radiator cement, drums of water and cans of beans, he looks like a bewildered farmer, but he certainly has the grand touch when it comes to geology and geologists.

Jerry has about the toughest area being worked this year. There are few outcrops, and they all look alike, so Max has had to be kind of stubborn to keep him at it because no one here but Jerry could do it at all.

Tomorrow we are getting the third driver, other than Mahomet Ali, we've had since we've been out here. The first was a wild man who couldn't get along with anyone. On the only trip he made to the seismograph camp, he netted a hole in the gas tank and a large hole in a new tire.

The next was a dopey-looking guy who had been here two days when the fellows caught him stealing food from the kitchen. Before I could send him in, he wrote a note making indecent suggestions to the houseboy, who spit on him and turned the note over to the Emir. The soldiers cut themselves some springy branches and gave the driver a preliminary beating. He left here yesterday on his way to the Jubail jail. Mahomet Ali says, "A crazy one goes, and a crazy one comes. Sahib, it would be better if you had a laborer to help me put cement on the *rijms*. I would rather do all the driving alone than have such 'friends'."

Last week a Bedouin came to have coffee with the soldiers and told them of some Dawsary camped nearby who had caught a stray, tame hawk. The next day, the Emir, Muhammad bin Khursan, and one of the drivers went over to see if it were Shelwah. There were about 20 untamed Dawsary who not only refused to show our men the hawk, but also ordered them away and struck the Emir. There was some pointing of guns until our forces retreated before the superior numbers. The Emir sort of lost face, though he hardly could have resisted under the circumstances. He sent a letter to Jubail that probably will bring some of Bin Jiluwi's men down upon those luckless Dawsary.

The days roll by quickly when there is so much to do and not much time to think. We are off in the morning immediately after breakfast. At noon Muhammad often entertains us with some story, such as today's, of how he, with 50 men, captured a fort in the Yemen Campaign. Sometimes I think he is a bit careless with numbers. Before the actual capture of the fort, he, with 15 of the 50 men, ambushed 500 of the enemy and drove them off in confusion.

After lunch we work some more and try to get back before sundown so Ernie can ink the map in sunlight. After supper we go over the notes, draw the contours and put the geology on the map, run the radio, get the time signal, listen to the news, feed the rabbit and go to bed.

We have a new rabbit now. The first thrived on milk from an eyedropper and grew big and strong, as he needed to be to withstand the Steineke kids. Dick took him in the other day, and the same afternoon Bin Khursan brought us another. This one is slightly older and refuses a milk diet. He must be eating the grass in the box, as his ability to kick and squirm does not seem to be diminishing.

April 9, 1939
Ma'aqala, 3:30am

As you see by the date and time, I have been out carousing again and taking in all of the Ma'aqala night life. Yesterday evening I had planned to write you at leisure and have a letter ready to go with the lorry in the morning, but fate stepped in. Von Hornlein, a gravity-meter surveyor who has been here about a week, hadn't arrived before dinner. We were lolling about, halfway through the meal, when Ernie noticed it getting dark and no Von. So we set out with a couple of soldiers, Ernie on the road and I on a hill with Bin Khursan. When we arrived at our stations, it was pitch dark and there was no sign of Von. After an hour of waiting, we started driving in the direction we'd last seen him in the afternoon. In less than a mile, we met his soldier and driver, who he had sent into camp. The driver had stuck the car about five in the afternoon, and they couldn't get it out. Furthermore, they weren't sure where Von was.

Muhammad and I drove until we saw headlights. We headed towards them, but about a half mile away, I stuck the car in a mudhole. They were Ernie's lights. When our lights quit moving, he came over and pulled my sedan out of the mud. We set a compass course and started out, only to have Ernie's car bog down in the mud. I pulled him out, then managed to get my car stuck again a half mile away.

Finally, we reached dry ground and after 10 miles, by the grace of God and the light of his stars, found Von's last station. We backtracked and found him well stuck. There was much slopping and digging of mushy sand before we started home. About a mile before camp, Von's Marmon Harrington bogged down again. There was more digging, swearing, and pushing as clouds came down from the north to blot out the starlight by which we were driving. Muhammad bin Khursan found one of our survey stations, from which he could see a light put on a high *jabal* near camp by our Somali driver. We arrived back in camp about an hour ago.

The Damon Runyon Collection arrived today with the mail from the Jabal. I kiss you for it, Kath. Remember when we sat on your porch and read about Zinser Fritz and Emerald Em?

Yesterday, Walt Hoag, Floyd Ohliger and one of the Casoc directors, a Mr. Russell, stopped overnight on the way to Riyadh. Ernie and I took great joy in showing Russell our child that we hope to see decorated with oil derricks in a year or two. Ernie is itching to see some of the boys he came over with, so he can say, "Well, now, I told Russ; we all called him 'Russ'," and "Well, Russ asked me..."

When Russell first arrived in camp we introduced him to everybody. When he met Bin Khursan, they shook hands and then Muhammad tapped him on the chest and said, "*Inta* (you are) wolf in sheep's clothing," which provoked a gale of laughter from us, but bewildered Russell. He didn't recognize that Muhammad was talking English to him.

Our oil well, my sole contribution to the discovery of oil in Saudi Arabia, was eventually drilled and resulted in a dry hole. By all rights, it was a classic geological formation for an oil reservoir, but then that is why the life of an oil wildcatter is so tough. However, in the next season, Ernie's success in finding oil was to change dramatically.

April 14, 1939
Ma'aqala

Your letter with the picture arrived; 'tis fine, and I crave more. Why I even liked the dress. I'd like it better if I could see it in person, with you inside of it.

This is going to be another short letter because the kerosene is gone out of the stove, the tent is getting chilly and I still have to write a letter to Max.

The last few days have been filled up, as usual. Dick Bramkamp came out and we made a 150-mile trip across the Dahna, the big strip of sand lying west of us, to a place called Hafar al-Atj. It was a fine trip with good weather and sleeping under the stars, but we didn't find any rocks poking through the sand as we had hoped.

We returned yesterday and spent today working on the south of our area, where we found some rocks that shouldn't have been there. It doesn't spoil the structure, but it messes up our map and the oil possibilities aren't quite as good. The structure is considerably more complicated than we thought, and we'll have to do much more work on it.

The gravity-meter crew of 10 Americans and a dozen Arabs are camped just across the way. I've been doing duty as interpreter, trying to straighten out the mess they have gotten themselves into by having two Arabs who are from a "better" tribe than the rest. They demand different (better) food and their own cook.

April 27, 1939
Ma'aqala

While you are gawking at the bridges of San Francisco, I'm exhausted from entertaining royalty in the deep desert.

First off, we had a couple of cars wheel up with a load of soldiers and camp about a mile away on Raudhah Ma'aqala. A *raudhah* is a low meadow with many thorny acacia trees in which much rainwater gathers. We had coffee with the visitors when they came up to chat with our soldiers. They were the advance guard for the King and were here to keep the Bedu from using up all the water in Ma'aqala.

The next evening, a great calvacade of cars appeared on the plains to the southwest, their lights looked like a moving city. They roared in and set up camp across the *raudhah*. There was much excitement in camp until Bill Lenahan, the company's Jeddah representative, appeared. Instead of the King, it was Shaikh Abdullah Sulaiman, the Minister of Finance, with only 100 cars. Bill and three other Americans were in the party on their way to Dhahran to prepare the way for his Majesty's visit. One of the Americans was Anita Burleigh. Traveling with her husband, Bill, Lenahan's assistant in Jeddah, she is the first American woman ever to cross the Arabian Peninsula.

Lenahan took all of us, including Muhammad bin Khursan, over to meet Shaikh Abdullah. The Shaikh was sitting out in the dark on a big carpet. Ali Ali Reza, a bright fellow from a wealthy Hejazi family who evidently has been around in the world, acted as interpreter. The big, bad, bold Muhammad was as meek as a lamb, and the only words he squeezed in were that I understood Arabic perfectly – this in a weak, small voice. I denied the accusation, but made the mistake of doing so in Arabic. The Shaikh laughed and replied, "You have proved yourself wrong."

I met him in Riyadh last summer, he is an affable fellow who is the King's right-hand man. He is a lot more than just a Minister of Finance, Grand Vizier to the King would be a more appropriate title. He began bantering with Lenahan. He asked how long I had been here and then asked Bill why it was that he has been here five years and still can't speak Arabic. Bill replied that he had been so busy learning about life from Shaikh Abdullah that he hadn't had time to learn the language. Afterward, we talked to the other Americans in the party and invited them, Najib Salih, the Minister of Mines, and Shaikh Abdullah's secretary to breakfast. Bill went off to get Shaikh Abdullah's permission and came back with the news that he would allow them to come only if he might come also.

We stayed up half the night fixing up two tents to hold 15 guests and 12 of us. The guests were up before the sun and arrived at 6:30, after the Shaikh had seen all of his cars under way. Breakfast was a success, even though his Excellency ate only a little fruit and drank some coffee. He then pulled out a package of Lucky Strikes (after I had warned everyone not to smoke; I knew he smoked in private, but didn't know whether he would in front of us), lighted up and proceeded to rib Bill and Najib on their appetites.

The next morning, another army of cars and great clouds of dust swooped up from the southwest, with the King himself. As he was supposed to stay here for two days, we instructed the soldiers to request an audience with the King in the evening or the next day, and went to work as usual. Within an hour, three soldiers came out to round us up, as the King wished to see us immediately.

There was a frenzy of scurrying around and putting on of clean shirts. Ahmed, our cook, brought in a *bisht*, the long, dark Arabian cape, for me to wear. I told him that since we did not all have *bishts*, it would be better if none of wore them. "As you wish," said Ahmed with a look of disapproval.

I asked him, "What do you think?"

He replied, "As you wish," again.

So I said, "Not what I wish; what do you think about it?"

"Well, Sahib, it is bad for many people to go see the King and have no leader." So I wore the *bisht*.

We drew up about 50 yards away from the King's big reception tent and marched en masse between two lines of 100 soldiers armed with sub-machine guns. Shaikh Yusef Yassin, who speaks English about on a par with my Arabic, met us. We'd brought Hassan Al Jishi, an English-speaking rodman on the surveying crew, as our interpreter. In the handshaking with the King, Hassan got shuffled around, so I had to speak a few words directly to the king.

He grinned broadly and said, "*Mashallah!*" It is the will of God. This is an expression of wonderment and admiration, and I was quite flattered. We all sat along one wall with a row of dour-looking mugs, mostly ministers, I presume, across from us. The King was cordial, not at all condescending, but in Ernie's words, "I didn't hear any of the servants piping up with their nickle's worth."

He was interested in our radio, so I invited him to come and listen to it. He would be glad to; at five o'clock that afternoon, he would like to talk to Shaikh Abdullah, or anyone who could speak Arabic. This took the wind out of me, as five o'clock is the worst time for radio reception, and Shaikh Abdullah was at Abu Hadriya, so the conversation would have to be worked by rebroadcast from Dhahran. He also wanted us to have a look at his radio, which was easy, as there were a couple of experts on the gravity meter crew. After a couple of rounds of coffee, we left and worked the rest of the day getting ready.

I called up Charles Homewood at Dhahran and he got in touch with Abu Hadriya. I tried working them directly; they could hear us, but we couldn't hear them, so we arranged for Abu Hadriya to listen for us directly while the Jabal would rebroadcast the Shaikh to us. The system worked fine, with Claude Jared, the boss driller at Abu Hadriya, telling us we were coming in fine, ad infinitum.

Ernie, head of the housing committee, put four big tents together and spread out all of the available mats. In the center of the closed end, he raised a sort of dais of blankets and pillows. We put the radio on the King's right and another mess of blankets on his left for smaller fry.

At 5:30 the King arrived in the first car. We were disappointed that he didn't follow the usual custom in towns of sending a couple carloads of soldiers armed with machine guns ahead to surround the place, though we did have a soldier in the kitchen all afternoon supervising the coffee preparation. A usual custom, Ahmed tells us.

Your husband, attired in a *zaboon*, a long, gray robe buttoned under the chin, which he borrowed from one of the drivers, greeted the King in Arabic and accompanied him to his seat. About half way there, His Majesty turned around to introduce the Crown Prince Saud and I all but broke my neck getting back to greet him before we all sat down. The Crown Prince sat alone on the King's left, flanked by the sourpusses. We sat on his right side; I sat next to the radio with Hassan. After the usual pleasantries, I called up Charles Homewood at the Jabal, who called Claude. We were still "coming in fine."

I handed over the microphone to the King; that is, I wanted to hang on to it to work the button that cuts off the receiver when you are transmitting. It was somewhat awkward when the King won and put the microphone up to his ear. Hassan explained to him how it worked, and he started out with, "Abdullah, Abdullah." There was a vast silence.

We heard Claude, "You're coming in fine, but let me tune up a little better." More "Abdullah's" and more silence. I tried to have Hassan tell the King to make a little longer speech. The sweat began splashing on the carpet as it ran off the tip of my nose. Finally, Shaikh Abdullah came on, and the King replied. There was more silence. Then Charles said, "Claude, please have Shaikh Abdullah say something. Put him on the air."

Claude replied, " You're coming in all right, Charles." There was more imploring by Charles, and finally the Shaikh came on asking the King if he wanted anything.

"No, I have nothing. I just want to see how this works," followed by more silence and then Charles beseeching Claude with disgust in his voice. Nearing the breaking point, I broke in and had Homewood call it off and asked him to put on the government representative in Dhahran. The King had a good talk with him. He'd learned to work the button better than many Americans and seemed pleased at the end.

After a round of orange juice and coffee, we took him out to see the gravity meter. He clambered into the truck and had a look through the reading microscope, quite a job, as he is as tall as I, but much heavier of frame. He has gained weight since the cars have come and he doesn't ride a camel anymore. As he stepped down from the truck, he asked the Crown Prince if he wanted to look, but Saud laughed and said, "I'm no engineer."

After much handshaking, they departed. Ahmed says it was a great success. If it hadn't been, the King would have frowned and said little instead of laughing and talking as he did. Hassan Al-Jishi, our Qatifi interpreter, was skeptical, if not outright antagonistic, about the King before the visit; now he is the King's most ardent supporter. Abdul Aziz's personality is even more powerful than his sword.

The only hitch as far as I was concerned was that I didn't get any pictures. As the host, I could hardly run off to fetch my camera. However, the other fellows all have promised me prints and if the movies are good, I'll have duplicates made. Anyway, I have the distinction of being one of the few Americans to speak with King Abdul Aziz ibn Saud in his own language. The company is having a three-day celebration in Dhahran after the King inaugurates the first shipload of oil out of Ras Tanura, the terminal of the new pipeline.

Our structure looks good, though we keep finding more work to do on it until I despair of ever completing it. The gravity meter is getting results that corroborate ours predictions. A driller will be out here to start a water well within the week, and they may start drilling for oil before the summer is over.

We heard Hitler's speech to the Reichstag tonight; afterwards, a couple of British commentators took it apart. It should be a huge success inside Germany. As Von Hornlein says, "I can't think of anything nicer for Hitler than a good cerebral hemorrhage."

May 11, 1939
Ma'aqala

So you liked San Francisco? That makes everything okay; now I can hurry up and work to be a big shot in the California company so we can live there. Didn't you love the sea and the brown hills across the bay and the clean, washed faces of the houses? The only thing I didn't like about San Francisco was the newspapers, which are lousy, but a city like that doesn't need newspapers.

No, I have never eaten crabmeat chow mein, but then you've never tasted roast *dhab*. A *dhab* being a big yellow lizard – fat and right for roasting this time of year.

I don't know whether you'll ever come to Arabia. I have hopes, but sometimes I feel despair. Encouraging words I get, but nothing tangible. The whole trouble is that I came here on the understanding that I was single and should I marry, I would not be able to bring my wife along. Quite a few men came over with the promise that their wives would be sent when houses are available. I hear gossip of others who have completed their first contract here and are coming back only on the condition that their wives come with them, or soon after. The whole thing is up in the air as there are many factors involved, such as length of service, position in the company, and so on.

I do not have two years' service yet, but I am counted as a senior geologist, which puts me ahead of some others with longer service. On the other hand, it will be argued that as a geologist I will be gone much of the time. Even Max Steineke had trouble with that argument and went over the head of local management to San Francisco directly, which I can hardly do. In truth, I can't see how we can hope to be together before another year, as much as I dislike admitting it to you and myself.

A year from next December, my contract will be up. I do not know what I shall do then, or what the company will want. However, December is the middle of the field season, and they may want me to stay over until the following spring. In that case, I shall be in a position to bargain that you be brought over next year, say in June. The more I see and hear, the surer I am that it will be at least a year.

Bismarck – June 21, 1939

After two long weeks, your letter came this morning and I was so very happy to hear from you; the contents took the wind out of my sails for a while, but somehow I'll live through it. Before the summer is over, it shall most likely be the smaller worry in my life. Everything that is happening seems like a nightmare – would that it were.

This is an ultimatum, however; you are not going to sign a second contract on the promise that I can come in a little while. I don't care if you never get another job – three years was my bargain and not one minute longer.

Darling, I can't express the things inside; my mind whirls with thinking. I love you so much I am almost green. My mornings are disturbed, as is every minute in the day and night. When I interview stricken young men from Linton, I weaken at the thought that they may have played with you or gone to school with you. I'm jealous of every minute anyone else spends with you.

By August, your vow will be up, and you'll be able to smoke. Remember what an eternity that seemed to you once? Would it make you unhappy to know that I smoke every now and then? Mostly when I have a good case of the jitters. I don't do so well, though, because it makes my throat sore. My Old Age Assistance supervisor has advised some ten-cent cigarette called *Sensations;* I'm afraid of just that!

Must close, darling; I love you much and hope you'll write me more letters like the last one, only with better news. Don't let it worry you; I shall somehow manage to be very, very busy with my riding, swimming and smoking – just like a real dyed-in-the-wool career woman.

May 11, 1939 Ma'aqala – continued

Our trip west was fine except for one mishap. The first day out, our sedan poked the fan through the radiator, which delayed us for four hours while we took it off and soldered it up. Then off down the broad Wadi al-Atj to see a sight strange in Arabia, haycocks, neat little piles of bushes like shocked wheat, except they were rather few and far between. Here and there groups of three or four Arabs gathered up the sparse bushes in piles and loaded them on camels to twice the height of the beasts who plodded off to their destinations, in some cases 60 to 80 miles away.

The sand in the backcountry is the reddest I've ever seen; it practically glows in the red dawn. There are high, bold hills with real cliffs on them rising six to eight hundred feet above the plains on their westward faces.

Hauling hay in the Wadi al-Atj

We did not pass through many towns, but one, Marat, was as picturesque as you could wish. The earth is a reddish clay, and just outside the town is a high *jabal* that we climbed. We took pictures of the town spread out below us with its red-turreted walls, green gardens scattered over the plain, and the great pool in which they gather rainwater by a system of ditches. When we returned through town in the late afternoon, there were lots and lots of cows – for Arabia – coming out the gates. Khamis was astounded. They are used for drawing water from the wells in place of donkeys or camels, the usual motive power.

Here and there in the center of Nejd, you find low mud walls across the *wadis*. They are dams to hold the rain. In good years they plant wheat behind the dams after a downpour has been caught and soaked into the earth.

Marat as seen from Jabal Marat

Northwest of Riyadh, we went up a long canyon crossing over the Tuwaiq Mountains. It was much like the 10 Sheep Canyon going down the westside of the Big Horn Mountains in Wyoming. If you've never seen it, we shall go look at it sometime.

On the east side of the *wadi*, we passed down a long valley full of ruins of walled towns, forts and old watchtowers on the hilltops. Once this had been a great center of population, but the wells went dry. Recently the water has come back, and a few of the wells are being worked again to water the wheat fields. It was harvest time. They were cutting the grain with sickles and bringing it in to the threshing floors, where four or five little donkeys walk round and round a post, trampling out the kernels.

Near here is the town of Sudus, which I would have liked to visit, but we didn't have time. It is said on good authority that there are tablets or rocks there which have inscriptions in a language said to look like English; they may be Phoenician.

We steered clear of Riyadh this trip, as the King was still in Dhahran, and to visit it would have meant much ceremony with the little shots. We took in the big cave Bramkamp and I visited last September and went home making a couple of surprising geological discoveries on the way that didn't quite fit former ideas.

I guess the King's visit to Dhahran was a success as far as he was concerned, but a nightmare for Casoc. He left yesterday and is at Abu Hadriya today. Tomorrow we will sit in camp because we have no gasoline. Our lorry is at the seismograph camp, but they won't let it go to Abu Hadriya for gasoline until His Majesty departs. They are afraid it will be commandeered to haul government cars through the sand. The King, himself, is fine. The headaches come from all the hangers-on. Judging by the radio reports, which are cautious, business in Dhahran is just about at a standstill.

The site for the test oil well here has been selected to start as soon as we can drill a water supply. Tomorrow the head of transportation and three engineers, including Clark Gester, chief engineer for the California Company who is in Arabia on a visit, are coming out to look the place over with an eye to roads, camp buildings, and a pipeline to the coast when and if there is any oil.

The weather is hot – over 100 degrees every day, 112 degrees today – but it cools down to 70 at night. In about three weeks, we shall go in for the summer.

May 23, 1939
Ma'aqala

Today we had to make a radio schedule at 7:30, which cut off the best of the day. We've been in camp all day, as it was hardly worth going out. A mechanic arrived this afternoon, and we are going to take him up to Jerry's camp tomorrow.

Day before yesterday, the *shamaal* began. It's a daily wind out of the north that lasts 30 to 40 days. The nights are calm and cool, but the breeze of the morning grows to a midday gale that whips the tent fly so violently that it cracks like a gunshot. It is nearly as hot as before, but the wind makes it feel cooler than a week ago when the noon sun poured straight down on the still earth. The *shamaal* is bad for our work because, in addition to the mirage, the air becomes so filled by a haze of dust that at noon you can hardly see more than a couple of miles. Not quite as bad as North Dakota, but bad enough.

I am at a loss for something to write about, Kath. These last days have been about as monotonous as any I've had in Arabia. The heat makes me feel as if I don't want to do anything but sit at midday. It is actually better to work outside than to swelter in a tent.

Today, after a vain attempt to sleep, I read some Hilaire Belloc in an anthology of his that I bought in Bagdhad. You must read him if you have not done so already. He does everything so magnificently well: history, fiction, poetry, or criticism. Ernie and I have read several times his essay on "The Nordic Man," who is kind to animals in decreasing amounts until his kindness closes when he comes to insects. As for his "A Guide to the Boring," Ed Golaby, who is drilling the water well here, is a natural-born example. About the only defect in Ed's technique is that he does not mumble, a fault which may in charity be ascribed to a slight deafness. Then there is "Al-Rafsat," or "The Kicks," in which a devoted servant of Allah instructs his small nephews in the art of becoming rich by relying on the ignorance of rich and poor alike.

Ed has a fixation, an unshakable belief, that if you talk baby talk loudly to Arabs they will be sure to understand it because obviously American babies understand baby talk well. He has developed a weird vocabulary, or rather I should say, syntax, in dealing with Arabs. He'll say, "*Sheyl* the boardie, boys, and *hutt* the boardie over here," meaning,"Lift the board, boys, and put the board over here." Though no Arab could possibly understand a word he says, his crew has learned by example what he means and what ought to be done.

Ed wasn't the only one with a specialized vocabulary. Bill Seale's crew had worked with him long enough to know what was required; they pretty well knew what he was saying in English and he pretty well knew what they were saying in Arabic, with neither of them being really cognizant of the actual vocabulary.

This phenomenon of Americans and Arabs communicating in a patois that nobody else could comprehend produced all kinds of opportunities for misunderstanding.

My favorite story was that of two laborers waiting to start work. An American arrives and gives them instructions that consist of a few Arabic words and a lot of sign language. The newest employee of the lot starts to get up and go to work when his companion stops him and says, "Hold on a minute; he hasn't said 'goddammit' yet."

Later on, when scores of Americans were arriving and we couldn't orient people fast enough to keep them out of trouble, we had several problems with the phrase "godammit." There was more than one court case in which an Arab hauled an American into court, claiming that the American had "godammed" him.

Most of these cases were simply instances of an American working with an Arab, a wrench would slip and the American would say, "Godammit!"

The Arab who had been around long enough to know what the phrase meant, but not the context of American slang, would take it personally and charge the American in court.

Then we would have to explain to the judge that the American wasn't damning the worker, he was damning the wrench. This made absolutely no sense to the judge; what would be the point of trying to consign a wrench to eternal perdition? I'm sure that these charges were often dismissed only because the judge was willing to accept our explanation in spite of the fact that it defied common sense.

Ed also takes a dim view of the way we socialize with the soldiers and others and said that by God when he runs the camp there aren't going to be any people saying "good evening" to him.

No news from the Jabal except that all is still confusion after the King's visit. They sent a fleet of trucks to Riyadh with him, none of which have returned. The reactions to our request for another truck to haul water for Ed's well bordered on exasperation. We shall go in soon for the summer; it depends on the water well. We have to stay here and nurse Ed until he finishes.

Continuing after supper, the gale of an hour ago has died down to a fitful breeze, and the fierce old sun has sunk through the haze. With night, the land seems to live again after the torture of the day.

Bismarck – May 17, 1939

Do you realize that you have not written me for nigh onto three weeks? I am more than a little irked; I don't care if it is the fault of the Germans or the geology. Please write to me; I am very unhappy when you don't.

We need rain so badly; the dust storms are increasingly worse, and people are so discouraged. There is constant trouble with Farm Security as to whether clients should spend their soil conservation checks for living expenses. They have nothing.

Tomorrow we will have been married one year and a half. Had it been one hundred, the difference would have been barely perceptible. Here I am working myself into a mood to which I have no right. The bare truth remains that I have become more in love with you than ever, and it irritates me more than a little because it was bad enough before, and I try to convince myself that I don't deserve having it any worse.

Had an idea that I might work overtime tonight, but if I do, I won't start until I have finished this letter. The dust storm is so bad by now that the downtown buildings are scarcely visible. Every time the wind blows, I get meaner and meaner; in fact I have one of the worst dispositions you have ever conceived of. Maybe if I cried it would settle the dust and I would feel better.

May 27, 1939
Ma'aqala

We've just returned from a three-day reconnaissance trip with Jerry and Johnny Thomas. Up at four and now it's 10:15, so be charitable if this is a bit muddled.

Returned to find your book from San Francisco. I am delighted with it. That is, I haven't read it yet, but I have read of Maynard and once heard him speak. Thanks for the St. Anne medal, which I shall wear as soon as I can get a chain for it.

I dream of you continually, Kath. Seems I'm all right as long as there is plenty of work to drive me, but now, except for these last three days, we're sort of marking time waiting for Ed to strike water. Then the drillers will come out to get started on the oil well, and we go to the Jabal. Up before dawn to work until noon, come in at two for lunch and dawdle in the tent all afternoon trying to sleep. Then after the radio business is finished, sit a few minutes in the cool night before going to bed. These days are the hard ones. I shall see what the situation is when we go in to Dhahran.

May 30, 1939
Ma'aqala

This seems to be the night for letters. Ernie has just written one, and I just heard Abdul Latif, the houseboy, reading one to Salih. It was from Salih's father, written, I suppose, by a friend or a sort of public stenographer. Then, at this end, Salih has to find someone to read it to him.

The weather continues to be warm. Yesterday was the season's record temperature, 125 degrees in the shade, which is hot but, not as bad as you might think. We've been broken in by six weeks of 110-degree weather. As I write at eight in the evening, it is 92 degrees. We get up at four a.m. and work to noon. Then we take our cots down in a big *dahl* and sleep three or four hours in the cool, natural air-conditioning of the cave.

The Emir was just in to report on his trip to Jubail. He went in to buy more food for the soldiers and returned just this evening. The soldiers are not happy because orders were issued to leave them here for a month after we go in; that is, until the new camp is started. They don't like it because they've been in the desert since January. They want to go home; they are soldiers of the "engineers," and the other *sahibs* don't know and understand them like we do, and besides, the permanent camps are supposed to have Hejazi police, who are wholly useless except as a source of trouble. I have been doing everything possible to get them in when we go, had Jerry talk to Max, and last night Max said he was making arrangements to have them replaced.

Two days ago Ed struck water in his well. We are now marking time until the pipe for casing it and the pump arrive, and then we will go in for the summer. The water is excellent; it is truly as sweet as rain.

Yesterday was wasted by reason of an invitation to see the Crown Prince Saud. He was camped a few miles southwest of us. One of his men came up just as we were ready to leave and told us the Emir Saud would like to see us. Off we went. All my long pants are worn out; I have been wearing shorts lately, but I fished out a pair that had the seat gone and borrowed the cook's *bisht,* which covered them up.

The Prince had a camp of about a dozen tents, and our audience was much more informal than it was with the King. We sat in front of him on cushions slightly lower than the one on which he was sitting. A friendly man, he laughed often and was much interested in our well. We talked about some of the affairs in Europe while the coffee and tea were served. We committed a minor faux pas by not leaving as soon as we should have. The conversation lagged; I couldn't think of anything to say for the life of me as sweat poured off me inside that woolen *bisht*, so I finally broke out with the "by your leave" of parting. No difficulty like that with the King; he tells you when to go.

I got along fairly well with the Prince; he was easy to understand except, of course, for the words I didn't know; for instance, the Arabic for "air-conditioning." At first he brought in an interpreter whose English I couldn't understand; he knew a little less English than Ernie does Arabic, but after a couple of attempts, Saud waved him away, and we spoke directly.

Since he didn't volunteer, we didn't ask his business except to find out that he was going to Al-Lisafah, northwest of Ma'aqala. One of our drivers spent his time gossiping with the government drivers and found out that the Prince was going to look at a new well he is having dug at Al-Lisafah, to check on his camels and to settle a murder. In a dispute over water at Al-Lisafah between two tribes, the Ajman and the Subai'i, a Subai'i was killed about a week ago. The Prince will find out who is to blame. If the Subai'i, they will be fined in camels and sheep. If the Ajman, they will be fined likewise, but the relations of the dead man will have the choice of accepting "blood money" to the amount of three to five hundred dollars, or the life of the killer.

If they choose the latter, and the choice depends on many circumstances – the wealth of the family, the relations between the tribes and between the families of the murdered and murderer – the offender will be bound to a stake and shot by the nearest male relative of the deceased, preferably his oldest son. It is the strict application of the rule of "an eye for an eye, a tooth for a tooth."

Several years later in Qatif, a man slipped and fell out of a palm tree, landing on a man below and killing him. The man's widow claimed her blood rights and wanted this man executed for killing her husband. This was a difficult question for the qadhi, *the judge of the Islamic court, as the man was innocent because it had been an accident. After much thought, the* qadhi *ruled that the widow had the right to kill him*

*the same way her husband was killed. She could climb up a palm tree
and fall on this fellow or she could settle for her blood money. She settled
for the money.*

Glubb Pasha tells of once in Iraq when he held a conference
between two unfriendly tribes, both of whom were disarmed
beforehand. Midway in the talk a free-for-all broke out before the
police could intervene. They finally stopped the row and started
pairing off the combatants, a bloody nose against a black eye, etc.,
until at last there was one man left over. Before Glubb Pasha could
say a word, a couple of the policemen seized a fellow from the tribe
that was short one man, whacked him on the head, and the pairs
came out even. Everyone laughed, was quite satisfied, and the
conference resumed.

We were up at Jerry's camp at al-Lihabah and made a two-day
trip west from there to the Dahna and back here. There are about
200 Bedu tents at al-Lihabah; Ernie says he is going to write home
that he'd visited one of the summer watering places of the Bedu, a
spa as it were, and that people would have a much different picture
of it than the reality.

Camels drawing water at al-Lihabah

At al-Lihabah, there are two wells set in a low place with low
jabals around them. Each has a high mound of camel dung built up
around the mouth. The water is at a depth of 150 feet. The tents are
scattered about in the *wadi*. They are mostly black, with an
occasional, rare white one marking the abode of a shaikh of some
sort. The ground is as bare as a pool table, with the camels, sheep,
goats, donkeys and even some magnificent-looking horses grazing
on their way to and from the well.

In late afternoon the water drawing begins. Camels cluster at the top of the mound to be watered as a couple of the ungainly beasts walk back and forth, up and down the mound, drawing up the water in skin bags pulled by a grass rope over a crude pulley. All about are groups of camels waiting their turn, being kept together by small boys as tall as the knees of their charges. There are donkeys braying, innumerable dogs barking, sheep and camels bellowing, and a little extra hullabaloo each time a group of camels moves from the mouth of the well and another takes their places. With the vertical sun making the sands as hot as fire, it is a fine place to spend the summer. Most of the Bedu at al-Lihabah are Mutair, but there are a few Ajman.

Our trip westward was uneventful except that the first day I managed to provide us all with meat: *hubarrah* for us, a *kirwan* and a *dhab* for the Arabs. They saved the best part of the *dhab* for us, giving us the roasted tail the next morning; it was really pretty good, sort of stringy but with a flavor something like walnuts.

The wellhead at al-Lihabah

Dhahran in 1939, Well No. 7 is visible in the upper right

Chapter 12
"Jabal Dhahran and Disaster Strikes"

June 6, 1939
Jabal Dhahran

In camp at long last, I'm bathed, shaved and in an air-conditioned room that is doing away with my prickly heat. If my letters have seemed perfunctory at times, I can only plead that nearly everything seemed perfunctory these past few weeks. The work we did was mostly of that nature, merely covering ground with no hope of finding anything of interest and existing through the blistering afternoons. By the evening we had no energy to do much but sit in the cool, clear nights, happy for the relief from the sun. In here, the desert seems far away, as if in another land, and water and shade cease to be the chief preoccupations of life. Ernie is not in yet, having been left to nurse Ed Golaby, but he should arrive today, as a couple of carpenters went out yesterday.

There are so many new buildings, I hardly know the new part of the camp. The chances of a house for us seem as remote as ever. Half of the new duplexes are crowded to the eaves with new men.

One duplex and Max's house (his family left last week) have been turned into additional geological offices. I understand the hospital, which was to have been the next item on the program, is postponed until next winter in order to allow more offices to be built.

It is really quite an experience to work in a cool room, drink ice water and have bread at meals, to say nothing of tomatoes and other fresh vegetables.

Ernie finally came in this afternoon and knocked on the door of my room. I opened it, shook hands and said, "Hello, Ernie. Did you just get in?"

I'd been napping for about half an hour and had my glasses off. Ernie looked me over and finally asked, "Is Tom Barger around?" That was a little too much for me; I rolled on the bed while he gaped at me until finally he recognized the laugh. No wonder he'd had trouble, what with my beard gone and shaggy hair brought back to respectability.

I liked your poem, Kay; send me more and more. You know, sometimes after I have spent weeks, or maybe even months, on rocks and maps, my sense for poetry seems to become dulled. The old songs do not seem to have quite the ring and lilt that I remembered, and it takes a day or two for them to rouse me as they should. Hence, I have decided that one geologist in the family is quite enough, and I forbid you to dabble in it lest we become mentally unbalanced. One of the few poems that tarnishes little with disuse is *The Hound of Heaven*, "forever new, my blood races with the chase."

Of what I am doing there is little to write. Diddling about, getting orders out for stuff we'll need next season, and then I shall start writing my report. After that, vacation, where, I don't know, probably either India or Beirut in Syria. Those are about the only places available, except Persia, toward which I am attracted. If I have a long enough leave, I might go to Bombay and down the coast to Goa to visit the tomb of St. Francis in that remnant of the great Indian Empire of Portugal.

Bismarck – May 8, 1939

The most tragic thing has happened to me; I thought after all of this I was immune, but spring fever has set in and there isn't a thing I can do about it. I've fallen in love with a married man. I'm sure you won't object; he's marvelous looking, good to his mother and everything, but his wife doesn't exactly understand him and so I try to do my part. I think, after all, it's the only Christian thing to do, don't you?

The worst part of it is that I don't think it's an infatuation, something more than that, every day in the middle of work I get that dreamy look in my eyes and just gaze out the window. I can't even keep him from disturbing my sleep, and considering the length of time this affair has been going on, it's really terrible. If you have any good suggestions as to ways and means for curing this malady, I assure you that they shall be gratefully received. I'm not revealing his name; you might be prejudiced you know.

June 6, 1939
Jabal Dhahran

Later. Two more of your letters just caught up with me. We'd radioed in for them to stop our mail, but these had already been sent out and had to come back from Abu Hadriya.

I, too, seem to be plagued with a double life. I am in love with a married woman. When I get pictures of her, especially pictures taken in San Francisco, I tremble all over, and my heart pounds like mad. I shall dream of her and try to reach out to clasp her hand, but she won't be there.

When we went swimming this afternoon, I spent half the time wishing she were with me. I imagine I should like her hair all wet and dripping with ocean; that is, until I inhaled a great gob of Persian Gulf water and sneezed and sneezed. I am still sneezing. We made a mistake. We should have swum off a headland instead of in a bay, as the bay water is about a third saltier this time of year.

Do you know Jo Eel very well? She and I used to be chummy when we were sinister politicians at the university. The system was to make the opposition think we were going to double-cross them, and then, contrary to custom, to do as we had announced. It worked well, as it was unorthodox and wholly unexpected.

Ernie just told me that after I left Ma'aqala, the Crown Prince came through just as Ernie and Ed were unloading a truck at the well. The well was out of action at the moment, as they were preparing it for installation of a cement casing. Before closing the well, they had filled 35 drums with water for themselves and the cement.

When Prince Saud came up to them, Ed kept on working while Ernie went over to shake hands and talk with the Emir. Unfortunately, none of our soldiers were present to translate Ernie's Arabic into a language that Saud could understand. Ernie finally got Ed over to shake hands with Saud and then Ed returned to the rig. The Prince wanted to see the drilling rig operate, which would have been easy enough for Ed to do, but he refused to run it. To Ed, the Prince was just another Bedouin bothering him. Saud asked again to see the rig operate, but Ed wouldn't even listen to him, and the Crown Prince of Arabia walked away angry.

That night Ed put one of his laborers at the well as a watchman. In the morning, all 35 drums of water were empty; the poor watchman didn't have a chance against 40 soldiers. Since the well was closed down for the casing work, Ed had to send in the lorry for a load of water. Had Ed been civil, the Prince's men would have used a few barrels of water at most, and everyone would have been happy. Some Americans here forget whose country this is and that we are only here on the sufferance of Ibn Saud.

June 26, 1939
Dhahran

Every morning the *shamaal* comes up and fills the air with sand. Working in Max's house, we look out and are glad we're not in the desert.

I'm revising and redrawing a cross section of the rocks of eastern Arabia, a big job that I probably will not finish for another week. Then I have to write my report, which is barely started.

Mrs. Steineke and the kids should be in Italy or Switzerland by now, where they will await Max's arrival in August. In a letter to Max, Florence told about the train trip from Basra to Bagdhad. It is a hot and dusty ride. Little Maxine was fussing and fuming, so Florence tried to cheer her up by saying, "Maxine, you shouldn't make such a fuss. There aren't many people that get to go to Bagdhad."

Unimpressed Maxine replied, "Why, Mother? Do they all die on the way?"

Every day we knock off at five o'clock and play a couple of sets of tennis. The *shamaal* usually is still whining before giving up for the day, so often there's not much science in the game.

This morning I went with Jerry to have coffee with one of our soldiers from the Rub' al-Khali who now works here in the garage on night shift. In his *barasti,* we perched up on one of the three beds about four feet off the ground and made of boards. A small boy brought in a five-gallon can of water and set it on the floor, rinsed off his hands and dipped out a pan of water for the tea and coffee. Thus, we got in ahead of one of the three goats that strolled over and had a drink out of the same can. A year or so ago I would have been somewhat shaken, but they boil the tea and coffee thoroughly before serving.

You are always with me; maybe it would help if I took your pictures from the dresser, but I might grow fat and lazy if I didn't have you to worry about.

Bismarck – June 14, 1939

My last letter was quite a gloomy one, as I remember; I still felt that way on Sunday and so I decided to take nice, long walk for myself. Put on my breeches and a sweater and walked down by the river. I went miles and miles. Watched the little boys fish along the banks and then cut across Pioneer Parkland over the hills and meadows.

I was so tired that I finally found some lovely high grass and literally threw myself into it. It made a good soft mattress, and it was fun watching the clouds and chewing grass. I couldn't help but feel that perhaps a part of you was there beside me, too. When I finally came home, it was about five-thirty, and I was so tired I couldn't move.

We are having another rodeo on Saturday, and Sunday is the exhibition for the special train, then a rest until the Fourth of July. I am still quite incensed with the old urge, and as I have said before, you probably will spend a lifetime beating it out of me. Still it is a resource if all else fails; darling there are so many things I could do to support you. If only you would come home, I'd work really hard, too. We could be enjoying so many things together; being away from you only seems to make you closer. I try to keep very busy so that I won't think too much, and fortunately the days are sailing.

I think that we are going to have a big family reunion this summer. We haven't had one since Grandma died. I can see her yet; she always used to sit in a big easy chair that we took along especially for her, and like the real matriarch she was, we all loved her and feared her simultaneously.

July 8, 1939
Dhahran

This afternoon about 4:30, just after he had left to play tennis, Bert Beverly came dashing in, yelling, "Number 12 has gone up." We rushed out to the front porch to see Number 12 belching forth black smoke and flames. In 10 minutes the derrick collapsed, and the well became a huge torch pouring out great billows of thick, black smoke that half masked the 100-foot flames. It had been drilled and was just about ready to start producing oil. The drillers were starting to hook it up today when there were a couple of small explosions on the rig floor, and the well went up in flames. One of the two Americans on the crew was rather badly burned, and one Arab was caught in the cellar and killed; all of the other Arabs escaped without harm. The well is situated about half a mile east of the camp;

shadows of the ghostly red flare flicker and dance on our rooftops tonight.

No one seems to know just what to do about it, one difficulty being that the point from which the oil is escaping is not known. We have just returned from the well. All is hustle and bustle. The eight-inch line that was to carry the oil away is now pouring out water without much effect. Gangs of laborers are stepping about laying pipe for steam and water lines; welders' torches flame out in the darkness, trucks rumble about and tractors crawl around like great bugs.

Well No.12 within the first hour of the fire

Bahrain has a great deal of equipment for fighting oil well fires, but we are not supposed to send radio messages to Bahrain, so two boats have gone over and about every 10 minutes the radio operator calls Abu Hadriya in the hope that someone in Bahrain will be listening. "Hello HZF, HZA at Dhahran calling Abu Hadriya. Hello, John Hello, John. Number 12 producing well is on fire. We would like to have you send down all help and fire-fighting equipment available, as Bahrain is doing." There's never any reply from Abu

Hadriya, where the only equipment available can't be more than a couple of fire extinguishers.

We all took pictures. Bert Beverly is out in the kitchen developing his now, so that we can tell whether we are getting good ones or not.

The drilling crew had completed drilling Number 12 and was in the process of perforating the casing, the steel pipe which encases the hole and which is cemented in place. After the cementing, holes are punched into the casing to let the oil flow into well bore. This is usually done by a perforating gun, which fires steel-jacketed bullets through the casing and into the rock.

The perforating gun was at the floor of the drilling rig and about to be lowered when it discharged. The escaping gas from the hole caught fire, and within minutes the rig was melted done into a mass of steel girders. One of the Americans and one of the Arabs were so badly burned that they died shortly thereafter, and we were left with a wild oil well and not much with which to fight it.

Eventually a small number of competent and imaginative men managed to work in close enough to the fire to place a pipe over the main source of the flames and divert the oil out into the desert. To bring the well under control, we had all kinds of Rube Goldberg suggestions, but it was finally Bill Eltiste who designed a clamp for the pipe, John Black who made the clamp in the machine shop, and brave men like John Ames and Cal Ross who advanced into the inferno behind a curtain of water and put the clamp in position.

With the clamp in place, a hole was drilled into the well bore, mud was pumped in to close off the well and the fire was brought under control before the professional firefighters sent from the States had arrived.

I was so excited about the fire I nearly forgot some more news of the first magnitude. Since Jerry came in from the field, he has been on the island several times, including 10 days spent doing geological work for the Bahrain Petroleum Company. Last week he came back with the triumphant announcement; he is going to be married on Friday, and I'm the Best Man. Only a few of us know the date. Jerry is happy, as he will be going home as soon as his report is finished – this time he'll complete it in record time. They will probably honeymoon across the Pacific.

As to my vacation, I have made up my mind to go to Syria, and I can leave as soon as I finish. The company is giving us an amount necessary for transportation to and from Beirut and four dollars a day for expenses. I am also considering going over to Cyprus, which is only 10 hours by boat from Beirut. It is supposed to have a fine climate; a great many English retire there. Having a long and stormy history, Cyprus is also full of ruins. The boat fare, including meals and berth is about $11. Hotel rates vary from $1.50 to $2.50 per day; one swanky place goes up to $4 including all meals! So I guess it won't be expensive, the rates being even cheaper than in Beirut, where they run from $3 to $4 dollars per day.

Jerry and Molly are married by Fr. Lewis
in Bahrain

Bismarck – July 5, 1939

Darling, I went home on the bus Saturday afternoon, and Saturday evening we practiced our Quadrille, a square dance on horseback. We did that until about 11 o'clock, and then went over to Grandma's house and visited for an hour. Up the next day and off to mass and relatives. Cowboys started drifting in on Sunday, and Sunday evening we practiced our Quadrille again. It was a lot of fun but we, as well as the horses, were just dead afterwards.

Monday was the pageant and I rode my Grandmother's sidesaddle, had a very long black sidesaddle skirt and a shirtwaist blouse with a high neck. My hair was tied back with a black velvet ribbon and I wore a rather small, felt Stetson, which had belonged to the Madame De Mores and now belongs to me. It was too much for the sentimental male onlookers, they thought I looked fine and were all for starting a new vogue in riding habits by reverting to the old.

Kathleen as the Madame De Mores, namesake of Medora, with her brother, Bud, dressed as Tom Mix

It was fun but I am mightily stiff from it all. Bud was Tom Mix and looked very handsome and dashing in a green satin suit and his new white hat. He did a little wild shooting and his trick-riding act.

There was a dance in town on Monday night and we took all of the ranch dudes in for a while, but I couldn't last the evening and so went home a little after one. Some of the fellows took our hired girls out, got mad at them and made them walk home. Poor Bud was up half the night collecting men and girls.

Goodbye for now baby, write soon and often and be good in Syria. Drink lots of beer, I think its good for your letter writing.

*From Bagdhad to Beirut, traveling in luxury
aboard the Nairn Bus*

Local Leave in the Levant

The second of August, a half dozen of us took a boat from Bahrain to Basra. I had felt wonderful the night before, but the morning of the departure, I felt like the wrath of God. I had been horribly sick all night with a fever and was unable to keep down either food or water. When I got on the boat and lay in a bunk in the un-air-conditioned stateroom, I wondered whether a man could die by simply losing all fluids by perspiration and having none of them replaced. Fortunately, by the time we arrived in Basra a day and a half later, I was much recovered, so much so that a whole afternoon in an air-conditioned room in Basra almost brought me back to normal. From Basra, we went to Bagdhad by rail and then caught a Nairn Bus to Beirut. Nairn was an Australian who had started a bus line from the Persian Gulf to the Mediterranean. With the best equipment available at the time, the Nairn Line was a thriving business until it was superceded by the airplane.

Once in Beirut, we gloried in the comforts of a modern city for a few days and then went sightseeing. We traveled into the magnificent mountains to see the famous Cedars of Lebanon, those cedars which remained after the Turks and the Germans had chopped down most of them to fuel the Hejaz Railroad in World War One.

While I was in Beirut, I decided to see if I could buy a .22-caliber pistol to use on rabbits in the desert. I went into one store that looked promising and asked if they might have guns. They looked at me strangely and said that I should try the man down the street. I went to this man's store, and he told me that he didn't have any pistols and didn't I know that the private possession of pistols was strictly forbidden.

This conversation was in Arabic, and I thought I was doing a decent job of expressing myself, when the man asked me, "Are you Bedouin?"

I laughed and then explained that I was an American. "Oh, you are an American. Well, come into my back room," he said.

We went into the back room and he opened up a huge chest about five feet tall. There must have been 15 drawers of pistols in this chest. They were mainly Italian, Spanish and German weapons, all of them rather small pocket pistols. I thanked him, but explained that I didn't want to shoot any people – just rabbits.

I tried to arrange an overland trip to Palestine, but the only other fellow interested in going was one of those types who, after the customs has cleared his luggage, says, "Are you sure you don't want to see anything else?" instead of shutting his mouth and moving on before the customs man changes his mind. I was not about to negotiate the many roadblocks in a troubled Palestine with such a character in tow.

Eventually five of us took a boat from Beirut to Tel Aviv, Haifa and Cyprus. The streets of Haifa were swarming with British troops, which started my interest in the Arab/Jewish problem that had been brewing for some 20 years, but had no effect whatsoever on anyone's daily life in Saudi Arabia.

Another aspect of this problem was presented to me at an outdoor cafe on the Beirut waterfront. Most every evening we would go to this place, eat and drink and relax in the cool night air. After nine, most of the Lebanese would go home to leave us alone with an orchestra of Austrians who would play any request from jazz to opera, for a modest tip. We often would stay until midnight or later enjoying their music and came to know these people very well. They were Jews who had fled Austria after Hitler's occupation. I was a bit surprised to learn this because they were all blondes, and my impression was that Jewish people tended to be brunettes. Furthermore, they were all Lutherans, but by Nazi standards they were Jewish because one of their ancestors had been Jewish. For these poor people, the world was already turned upside down, and their only hope was to work their way to Shanghai, where stateless people were welcome, and try to start their lives over again. The dark cloud was forming over Europe; the night we boarded ship in Basra to return to Arabia, the Germans invaded Poland.

A British armored car patrols the streets of Haifa

A dhow sailing the waters of the Persian Gulf

Chapter 13
"War Breaks Out"

September 7, 1939
Bahrain

Back from vacation, I'm in the hospital on Bahrain with an infected foot, but they're letting me out in the morning. So far, work is going on in Arabia as usual. They have six month's food supply and another nine month's worth is on the way via the Pacific. Ibn Saud has expressed his sympathy for Britain, while remaining neutral, of course. I've heard that this MacDonald White Paper issued by the British has restricted Jewish immigration to Palestine and thus eliminated the major source of friction between the English and the Arabs.

I have no idea how long this letter will take to reach you. The air mail is still going through, as Italy is neutral, but the British have upped the rate on letters to England and imposed censorship on letters to India. We get much radio news, but little information as to how the situation is progressing. Some Englishmen I spoke to in Beirut before the fighting declared they wouldn't go home if the government backed down again before Hitler, so I guess they can return now.

Bismarck – July 10, 1939

Big news from Linton, Fr. Feehow called Fr. Mac and asked him to have me call him, which I did. He was most anxious that we both understand that he had not advised your mother that it was contrary to church regulations that we marry as we did. He told her the same as he told you, mainly that it was obviously a dangerous procedure.

About two months ago your mother again called on him and told him that we were married, requesting his advice. He suggested that she be thankful I was Catholic and not one to lead you astray. I understand that he built me up wonderfully, and he said that she was quite appeased when she left. In view of this, it seems silly to keep up any pretense that we are not married.

Your mother seems eager to know where we were married and by whom. Should you decide to tell her yourself, you might furnish all of the details. I'm sure that everything will work itself out. We seem to have a faculty for getting into terrible scrapes. Suppose we shall be trouble-shooters all of our lives, but we'll never be dull, darling; we mustn't.

September 14, 1939
Dhahran

We've been assembling our outfits to go into the desert, but our plans are sort of upset at the moment. A German boat with 700 tons of cargo failed to show up. Most of the materials were for building a gasoline plant here, but there were also a couple of hundred custom-built sand-worthy truck tires aboard. Right now there are no spares in camp, hence we're sort of stalling. Four geologists have been assigned to help on a survey between here and Bahrain Island for a week or so. I'm going to the island tomorrow to make the arrangements. We will work at night by hanging lanterns on our survey stations; you can see them 10 miles away. The seismograph crew also is being held up temporarily because they use a small armada of trucks.

All is quiet here, as befits a neutral country. Probably it isn't actually as safe as at home, but it's damn near. About the only real worry is the remote possibility that the well will be sabotaged. The country is so sparsely populated that everyone knows everyone else, a stranger would have a tough time wiggling in. Export of food from British possessions, i.e., India and Bahrain, has been prohibited, which is causing some rise in prices for rice, sugar, coffee and tea, but I have no doubt the embargo will soon be lifted, as the government and the British are too good friends to allow it to continue long. The English will go to great pains for Ibn Saud because of his control of the holy places of Islam.

All of our supplies are now coming via the Pacific, which is, of course, wide open. If worse comes to worst, they can ship goods from San Francisco on company tankers and take oil out on the return. Our chief lack is news. Not that there isn't any floating around, everyone broadcasts in everyone else's language these days – but most of it is sketchy or else distorted out of recognition. One bright side is that our money is worth more now. The rupee has been dropped from about 37 cents to 27 cents, so we get nearly a third more for our dollars.

I'd give plenty to know what the opinion is at home. Nearly everyone here is in favor of selling France and England all they want to buy, but against participation in the war. Personally I think Dutch Schultz has the best analysis. He thinks we should strike up a sort of balance sheet of the cost of our entering the war as against our neutrality. Then either stay out and keep out, or get in at the start before our friends get beaten down. Unfortunately, it is too much a matter of opinion and well nigh impossible to forecast the ultimate effect of either policy. I fear we shall diddle about until, at length, we are forced to enter under comparatively disadvantageous conditions.

The big enigma is Russia. If she does not enter, or at least remains nominally neutral, France and England should be able to beat Germany, even with Italy thrown in. But if Russia should actually enter the war on Germany's side – God help us! Germany could get all the materials she needs, and there'd be cannon fodder galore. It would also mean the end of Western civilization as we know it in everything that matters most – most of these things being bound up with Christianity.

From now on the mail probably will come in squirts and jumps, as Imperial Airways is anything but regular in its wartime schedules. I don't think they give a damn much about Bahrain mail when they're probably flooded with official correspondence to and from India, Singapore, Australia and New Zealand. The mail was off completely during the first few days, before Italy decided on neutrality.

Bismarck – September 5, 1939

War has been in progress almost a week, and I am so worried that I think I shall have to cable you; I simply must know whether you will come home if there is the slightest suggestion of conflict, even if you have to break your contract. I can't stand to think of the possibility that you might not be able to get home. Please take care of yourself at any cost.

October 1, 1939
Dhahran

All last week I was in Bahrain on a surveying job. We went out every day in a boat to the various stations and returned home about midnight, if at all. The last two days were spent in a howling *shamaal* having a look at a place called Hawar Island about 30 miles from Bahrain. Recently acquired in a new concession to the company, it's a barren chunk of desert about 10 miles long and a mile wide. The Shaikh of Bahrain keeps a garrison of 10 soldiers on it to see that the Shaikh of Qatar, who also claims it, doesn't try to occupy the place. Aside from the army that was lined up on the wharf to salute our arrival, the population consists of two "permanent" inhabitants; they spend the summers in Bahrain. All drinking water is imported. The mayor of the island, a youngster of about 60 with one eye, came with us as a guide.

He was astonishing; without him, we' d never have been able to circumnavigate the island. The old bird came aboard and asked the Captain, "How much water does it draw?"

The Captain replied by holding his hand across his chest, "This much."

"O.K. Let's go," said our guide. We went – in and out, twisting here and there in water that all looked equally shallow to me. About five in the afternoon, we finally were stuck on a sandbank for an hour until the tide rose a little. Then we whistled through a bunch of rocks and sailed for an hour and a half after dark in the light of the full moon before our ancient mariner found a suitable anchorage. It all looked alike to me. Eating was an adventure of sliding plates, rolling potatoes, and lurching chairs, all flavored with gusts of spray. The second day was even rougher, so we couldn't put in to shore to do any geology, but we had a good trip all in all. It begins to look as if I do not get seasick. I have never been sure as to how my stomach would behave in rough weather. It seems there's no way of telling until you try it out.

At last, Kath, there is something more or less definite about the possibility of you coming over. My contract is up a year from December, but I am not enthusiastic about going home in mid-winter. It can probably be arranged that if I should stay until the following June, you could come out next spring. The arrangement is that I would be assistant to Max and would work out of the camp here, so I would not be gone months on end as I am now.

We could meet in either India or Beirut, as circumstances permit. Max seems quite enthusiastic about the arrangement, as Clark Gester, chief geologist of the California Company, has suggested that he have an assistant. It probably would be something of a boost for me, and we would be able to spend our vacation at home in the late summer and fall.

Aside from the Bahrain business, there's little enough to write about. The date for our departure for the field is not set. Tomorrow we go to Jubail to do some more surveying. Within the week we may go on a long trip west of Ma'aqala, the same route as we followed last spring with Gester, Davies and Max. If this materializes, we go out in the field on our return, say in two weeks. If not, we leave sooner.

The war seems to be developing very slowly. There are no repercussions here, save in our mail service. We're not allowed to send any second-class mail or photographs without a special permit from the Chief Censor of India. In other words, we ain't allowed. However, I have a bit of a Christmas present for you that Walt Hoag is taking home to mail to you.

Russia seems to be the big question. How good a friend of Germany, and how much an enemy of England? The poor Poles are in for a tough time. Even if the Allies win, they'll have a tough time trying to restore the former Poland. We heard tonight that Al Smith had made a speech asking the people to back Roosevelt's foreign policy. 'Tis a long time since he's backed anything of Roosevelt's.

October 17, 1939
Dhahran

On the BBC after dinner, we heard the English account of the air raid today on the Firth of Forth. One item related that the number of radio licenses issued in the last month brought the number of English receiving sets to nine million. That puts the German propaganda behind the eight ball. The day after the declaration of war, the Germans confiscated all private sets. You can be sure that the English account of an event such as today's raid cannot be so far from the truth, as it was seen by the whole of Edinburgh, most of whom also heard or read an account of it.

On the other hand, the Germans can say what they wish in their English-language broadcasts without fear of disturbing their population or losing their confidence by misstatement of internal events. It looks as if both sides have been sparring for an opening, and it seems that the French and English hope that the blockade will pinch Germany enough to goad them into an attack on the Maginot Line. It certainly is a difficult problem. Both of them sit behind fortified lines that cannot possibly be taken without a tremendous expenditure of men and material, and certainly the proportionate increase in strength with the passage of time will be all in favor of the Allies. I hope the Allies are able to win without turning Europe into a heap of ruins. The dear Russians seem to be out to do as much grabbing as possible while the opportunity lasts.

Our trip went well except for the first day, when one of the drivers had a flat tire on a pickup and turned it over. It was the first serious accident I have seen in Arabia. None of the three men in it was more than scratched, but it delayed us a day while we ordered a new car from the Jabal. Army Armstrong enjoyed the trip to the fullest. It was the first time he had been out in the back country, and it is hard to say whether he enjoyed the rocks or the towns and the country most. Me, I am getting blasé, and it was just a lot of driving between looking at rocks.

The first, but unfortunately not the last, serious accident I was to ever see in Saudi Arabia

We are going out for the season in a week. My partner is a new man named Johnny Thomas, who got most of his experience in California. We will be south of Hofuf near the oasis of Jabrin. Four Europeans have been there and two more have seen it from the air, so Johnny and I will be the seventh and eighth.

When Max left, it was decided that Johnny Thomas and I would spend the field season exploring the area south of Jabrin into the Rub' al-Khali as far as we could go in the time allotted. We left Dhahran about 8 o'clock in the morning and arrived in Abqaiq at sunset. It seemed that we were stuck all the time. One of the truck drivers was absolutely hopeless, so I replaced him with Salih to Salih's great delight and to the other driver's great embarrassment and chagrin; everyone knows that a driver is much better than a cook. At sundown, after we'd laid out the camp for the night, it was discovered that we'd forgotten something back in Dhahran. So Khamis and I returned to Dhahran, retrieved whatever it was that we'd forgotten, and arrived back in Abqaiq about midnight. There was nothing at Abqaiq then except the place that marked the site on which the first exploratory well was to be drilled. Abqaiq, now Saudi Aramco's main producing center, is only 45 miles from Dhahran, but before the road was built, we were all day in getting there

I hear someone else listening to the propaganda. I'm anxious to see some American newspapers and magazines dating since the outbreak of war. The American press news is posted on the bulletin board every day, but it doesn't have any pertinent details or any expert speculations.

An abandoned Ikhwan settlement at Ain al-Ghuba,
one of the many wells that comprise the Jabrin oasis

Chapter 14
"Jabrin"

October 31, 1939
Jabrin

It is fall here. The Bedouin name for the season translates as
"The Time of Journeying." They've been gathered around the wells
all summer and now are moving out to their desert pastures. Would
it were also the time of journeying for us toward each other.

Johnny Thomas and I have journeyed 250 miles from Dhahran
and set up camp just west of the great oasis of Jabrin, a place famous
in Arabian legends. It was first visited by Major Cheesman in 1925,
then by Philby in 1931, and by two of our geologists, Tom Koch
and Art Brown, two years later. Most of Cheesman's book, *In
Unknown Arabia*, is devoted to his trip here. He was much
disappointed to find it nearly uninhabited, the date palms wild and
uncultivated and the place occupied by the Murra tribe only during
the summer, when they gather whatever dates nature furnishes them.
It is a desolate country except close by here. Most of the way from

Hofuf there's not even enough pasture for camels, which is the worst that can be said about any pasture. The nearest well to the north is 100 miles from here.

Jabrin was an ancient oasis. Scattered around the higher ground of the oases are hundreds of tumuli, or burial mounds, that are similar to the tumuli on Bahrain that have been dated as far back as 500 B.C.

Jabrin had the reputation of being extremely malarious. The Murra came to the oasis only in the spring, at the time for pollinating the dates, and in the late summer or early fall to harvest them. When we arrived, the palms were not well tended, and many of them had apparently been left to pollinate themselves. From bitter experience, the Murra had learned that if they stayed in the oasis during the spring or fall, they invariably came down with malaria. It wasn't until 10 years later that the first Aramco entomologist figured out that it was too hot for the mosquitoes to breed in the summer and too cold in the winter.

Johnny and I could see the mosquito larvae wiggling around in the wells. We knew that fish ate them, but didn't know how we could obtain any fish without a great deal of difficulty. However, there were lots of frogs in the Hofuf Oasis, so the next time one of our trucks went back to camp we gave Salih 10 riyals and asked him to order us 100 frogs. He thought we were touched, but the frogs were delivered, and we released them into the wells of Jabrin. We found out later that they had virtually no effect on the mosquito population, but they did survive. I went back several years later, and there were still frogs at the oasis.

We stopped at the oasis the other day to fill our water skins. Two women were by the well with two small boys, evidently twins. The little ones' faces were a mass of flies. There may be some advantages in the black masks the women wear. The soldiers laughed and joked with the women. Muhammad bin Humaid, our new guide, wanted to know if we would like to take one for a wife, as they were of his tribe. We declined with thanks. The women asked us not to take too much water, as there was little to spare, but the soldiers told them not to worry as it was Ramadhan (no drinking during the daytime) and, besides, we would be there only five minutes and they would be there for days.

Johnny took a good picture of them. The women were watching Muhammad and I while the two boys watched Johnny coming up behind. When he was in position, Muhammad pointed at him and said, "He wants you." Whereupon, they both turned around and Johnny snapped them. It's against the rules to take pictures of the women. Strange ruling. Unless there are some shadows, they look like shapeless lumps of black in a picture.

We were two days driving to Hofuf: Ken Parsons, Ernie Berg, Johnny and I. Ken and Ernie had made camp about six miles west of the town. It was only 100 miles from Dhahran, but the two Autocar trucks were slow; we were making a road for the tractor and drag to follow, and only Salih, our cook, and I had had any experience driving in the sand. The third day we spent looking at the town and setting up Ken and Ernie's camp. In the evening we had an audience with the much feared and respected provincial governor, Saud bin Jiluwi. As Ernie says, it was a battle of words.

We sat at the end of a long chamber, Johnny and I on either side of his chair, and Ken and Ernie beside me along the wall. A couple of minutes after we sat down, he came in. All the soldiers, including ours, were at the far end of the room, almost out of earshot. After the usual greetings, we sat a while. Then I told him we liked the town of Hofuf and that none of us had seen it before. He said, "Yes, it is a good town," and we sat some more.

Then he said, "Let the coffee come," and all of the soldiers shouted "Coffee!" and it came. Some more sitting; we had tea and I told him Mr. Parsons thought this would be a better country for work than farther north, where he'd worked last year. He replied, "*Enshallah*," and we sat. The only animated bit of talk was about the Rub' al-Khali; we agreed that it wasn't really "empty."

It was a big night. After the Bin Jiluwi affair, we went to the house of Ahmed, Ken and Ernie's cook, ours last year, who fed us a delicious dinner. There was onion soup into which we squeezed lemons, a wheat mush, great chunks of barbecued sheep on big platters of rice, a kind of custard, string beans, dates, Arab bread, a vegetable called "lady fingers," I believe, and canned pineapple. Then we went to the house of Salih, our cook, for coffee and tea. Finally Khamis and I went to the Customs house to see about food for the soldiers and had more coffee. During Ramadhan, most of the business, except in the bazaar itself, is done after sundown.

November 10, 1939
Jabrin

Tomorrow is *Id al-Fitr*, the feast that marks the end of the month of fasting. From now on, the Ramadhan season will be worse and worse for some years to come. The Arabs have a calendar of 12 lunar months, each of which begins with the new moon, so their year is about 10 days shorter than ours, and the months move up through the seasons that much each year. Next year Ramadhan will start October first, so in a few years it'll come in the middle of the summer.

Winter is coming on us. It's down to 58 degrees in the mornings before sunrise, so we wear flannel shirts to breakfast. About eight, it warms up, but doesn't get above 95 at noon.

Our new guide, Muhammad bin Humaid, is an elderly, half-toothless Murra, the tribe of this region, who was with Philby on his Rub' al-Khali trip eight years ago. His guiding is quite laconic; mostly he just points, but otherwise he is garrulous and is always talking with Khamis in the back seat. I imagine he's quite a gossip, though I can hardly understand him, even when he's doing his best to convey some information to me.

In the stories he tells Khamis, he is always changing his voice to mimic the characters. Every time we pass a camel, he calls to Johnny and me to join in and yells "Farroh-yee-a!" followed by a sort of Indian war whoop. The other day, he and Khamis were sleeping while we had lunch. After lunch I bellowed out a couple of camel calls that woke them. As they came to the car, Muhammad looked all around and finally asked Khamis, "Where are the camels?"

Khamis grinned and said, "You're the camel." The old boy was slightly indignant at such a scurvy trick.

Muhammad had been with Shaikh Abdullah Philby when he visited Jabrin, so we were anxious to meet him. Toward the southwest side of Jabrin, there are three small, conical hills near a well called Uthabitiyah. On Philby's map, these hills are labeled Forayd al-Uthabitiyah. *Forayd* means little prominences, so we were sure that there was a more specific name for them. We asked everyone we met the names of these hills, and they all insisted that these hills had no name.

So when Muhammad arrived, I asked the name of these hills. He said that they didn't have any name. "But," I said, "you were with Shaikh Philby when he was here, and he has the name Forayd al-Uthabitiyah written on the map."

"Oh," said Muhammad, "I wasn't with Shaikh Abdullah when he entered Jabrin; I was with the baggage camels that day. Ahmed was guiding him that day. Shaikh Abdullah was a very hot man. We would be traveling along, and he would say, 'What is the name of that plant there?' I would tell him its name. We would go on for awhile and he would say, 'What is the name of this plant?' I would say 'So and so, like the one we saw before.' He would get angry and say, 'It is not the same plant.' I would tell him that this one is alive and the other was dead. He had to know both names.

"So when Shaikh Abdullah asked the name of those hills, Ahmed told him Forayd al-Uthabitiyah. It is not a bad name for those hills; Shaikh Abdullah writes it down, and there are no hard feelings, no hot words and no trouble."

Khamis ran into a similar problem two years ago, when he was guiding Philby back to Riyadh via Ma'aqala. They came upon a large hill with a *rijm* on it, and Philby asked Khamis for its name. Khamis told him that it had no name. Philby got angry with him and said, "What do you mean it has no name? It has a *rijm* on it. Bedu don't build *rijms* on a hill unless it is an important hill, a hill with a name."

Khamis replied, "This hill doesn't have a name. As for the *rijm*, I built it myself when I was working with the geologists."

Do not worry about me. I am as safe, if not safer, than I would be at home. There are no traffic accidents over here. The chief worry right now is that we have only two kinds of fruit juice, orange and grapefruit, and we won't get any other flavors in for a month. Both politically and geographically, we're quite secure. As Americans in a neutral Arab country, we are safely out of the grasp of the dictators.

Now that their schedules are adjusted to the war conditions, nearly as many ships arrive from America as before the war. Mail service is poorer, but I imagine as much delay is caused by censorship as it is by transport difficulties. Some of the men have quit and gone back to the States; almost without exception they were dissatisfied here from the start and only too glad to have an excuse to go home. On the other hand, some wives are due this month. Four wives, who were in London at the outbreak of war and were sent back to New York, are coming across the Pacific. The new hospital, which was postponed last spring, has been rushed to completion, and some real, live, single, female American nurses are being sent over to run it. There is much speculation about them. They should have a great reception.

Infections are the great Arabian malady. When he was a newcomer last fall, Johnny said he thought Jerry and I were a bit "touched" with our talk of infections. Now he finds that he is susceptible, too. I have no trouble with cuts, but skinned patches – ah, the bugs fairly eat them up. I've been using Dick Kerr's remedy, which consists of daubing iodine on them several times a day. It seems to have worked well on the half dozen scratches I collected incidental to loading cars and moving into the field. We each carry a small bottle of iodine in a wooden case in our pockets. In a country so healthy otherwise, it is funny there should be so much infection of small wounds. It may be from the flies, just common, ordinary houseflies, of which there are multitudes at certain times of the year. Last fall, out of a crew of seven men on the well at Abu Hadriya, three were in the hospital at once with infected hands. The Doc always gives you hell when you come in with a full-blown infection and has a routine treatment for it.

At Jabal al-Thaman, which we called "Sugar Loaf" – 1939
l-r. Jerry Harriss, Sennet, Tom, Khamis, Muhd. bin Khursan, Ernie Berg, Johnny Thomas and Mahomet Ali, a driver

Anita Burleigh, the first American woman to ever cross the Arabian peninsula, with her husband Bill at Ma'aqala – 1939

The seismograph camp near Ma'aqala – 1939

Hafar al-Atj – 1939

Sarrar, the abandoned capital city of the Ajman tribe

Khamis bin Rimthan
Sarrar - 1939

A *sidr* tree on the Hadhafa plain, west of Laila - 1940

Muhammad bin Mansur, center, shot this vulture near Laila – 1940

Khashem Ferdan in Wadi Dawasir, looking south – 1940
Note the car in the lower right.

l-r. Khamis, Ernie Berg, Walt Grumm, Johhny Thomas and a soldier – 1939

The village of al-Hanish in the Sulaiyl oasis, looking south – 1940

Khamis, at left, and the soldiers of bin Mansur on the trip to
Wadi Dawasir – 1940

l-r. Ted Yackel, Tom, Dick Bramkamp, John McLiverty, Max Steineke, Don Holm, Charlie Phillips - *front:* Fred Waldron, Sam Hobbs, Dick and Phyllis Kerr, Lloyd Owens, Bill Short, Ernie Berg and Bob Fleharty – 1946

With Abdullah Philby
Riyadh – 1950's

King Faisal at a reception during his visit to New York City – 1966

With Shaikh Zaki Yamani – 1968

Greeting King Saud at Riyadh – 1960's

At the San Francisco Zoo, *l-r.* Prince Faisal, Prince Khalid
and James Mac Pherson, V. P. Casoc – 1943

l-r. Spike Spurlock, Tom, F. A. "Fred" Davies, Norman Hardy,
Bill Burleigh, Roy Lebkicher and Dick Bramkamp – 1950's

Tom and Kathleen with their six children, son-in-law and
two grandchildren (B.H. Moody) Dhahran – 1968

Dressed for the Marine Ball at the U. S. Consulate in Dhahran, Saudi Arabia
November 18, 1967, their thirtieth wedding anniversary (S. A. Amin)

Bismarck – October 5, 1939

You can't know how wonderful it was to hear from you at long last. I almost wept when I read what your father had written you about our marriage. In a way I'm furious at him for telling Fay Hunter that you hadn't married me and that "it," evidently the rumor of our marriage, was a frame-up.

Tell your father that if he is interested in the Ray family tree, I'll be glad to discuss it with him. I'd love to learn about your family tree; you never told me about it. Perhaps your father is an SAR (Son of the American Revolution) and we would have a strong bond of relationship since, if I had the $25 membership fee, I could be a DAR (Daughter of the American Revolution).

November 10, 1939 - Jabrin – continued

I can't tell you all the details about my family, on account of I don't know them myself. Dad was always sort of vague about his forebearers. Most of them were Pennsylvania Dutch who came from Pennsylvania to Minnesota a couple of generations ago. However, one of his grandmothers did smoke a pipe.

On the other side, they were all Irish. One of my great-grandmothers eloped in Ireland with my great-grandfather and came to the States; he being shanty Irish and she being brick-house Irish. One of her brothers died in New York searching for her. Another lived in the South. She was at Des Moines, Iowa, when she heard from this brother, but the Civil War broke out just before she went to see him. He was killed in the war. Romantic, what?

There were also probably some horse thieves not mentioned in the chronicles. I understand one of my great-grandfathers was a devil on wheels. Part of the family denies the allegation, but my Mom holds out for him being one of the orneriest men of his time. One of my great-uncles made a small fortune by hard work and thrift. Another uncle spent most of his time bumming off the successful one. And so it goes. I get lost in the family councils as to who is related to whom.

Sooner than expected, we're sending a car to the Jabal. Our Emir had a cut over his eye, not bad, but it was full of dirt, so we're sending him to the Doc before it has a chance to get infected.

We'll be sending another car in about a week so you can expect another letter from me in a week to 10 days after this one.

November 18, 1939
Jabrin

All kings, and all their favorites
All glory of honors, beauties, wits,
The sun itself, which makes time, as they pass,
  Is elder by a year now than it was
When thou and I first one another saw.
All other things to their destination draw,
Only our love hath no decay;
This no tomorrow hath, nor yesterday,
Running it never runs from us away,
But truly keeps his first, last, everlasting day.

"Anniversary" - John Donne

November 19, 1939
Camp Jabrin

Yesterday we came in from a three-day spike trip about 40 miles to the east. We were going to make it a sort of vacation. The first two nights we got into camp an hour after sundown; the third night we were "early," about five o'clock, and then were up until after 10, tugging, yanking, and hammering on two flat tires. These tremendously oversized sand tires are the devil to fix when they're new. In the Jabal they have a big press that shoves them off the rim by main force.

A spike trip was designed to cover a great deal of area in a brief amount of time. Deploying from our base camp, we would travel lightly in two or three cars and stay out three to six days. We carried two tents with us, but seldom erected them. Johnny and I slept on cots, and the soldiers slept on the ground with their heads covered as usual to ward off the "night air."

These trips were always interesting, in that we only worked from dawn to dusk. As we didn't usually put up the tents, we didn't have any light, because the gas lanterns wouldn't stay lit in the wind. So we sat around the fire at night, talked with the soldiers, practiced our Arabic and exchanged stories about America and Arabia.

The tent we occasionally used while on a spike trip

This country, for all the oases round about, is nearly deserted. In addition to Jabrin, there are numerous palm groves about 40 miles east of here where we had our spike camp. There hasn't been any rain for at least two years, if not longer. We continually drive across old car tracks made by Tom Koch and Art Brown in 1933.

It was a fairly good trip, though we shivered and shook in the mornings when it was down to 50 degrees with a north wind eddying about us. Johnny has made a great contribution to Arabian geology. He sleeps with his shirt under the pillow so it's warm in the morning. Of course, one might sleep with it on, but we still wear pajamas. We, like the British colonialists who always dressed for dinner, always wear pajamas when we're sleeping outside on our cots.

The soldiers are beating a drum somewhere in camp that sounds suspiciously like a dishpan. It is funny that you hear so little music of any kind in this country. The natives of this part of Arabia don't seem to have any music except for the shrill, raucous, mournful Bedu songs. The poetry of the songs is good, but I can hardly recognize a poem I know when it is sung. The rhythm of the drumming is much like that of the Indians, or even more like African tom-toms. In this dead land, one almost loses the thought of music. Even the poetry attracts me only by the sound and rhythm. It must be good poetry to do this, lacking as I do all understanding of the subtlety and associations that are the very life of an English poem.

In camp we have a 12 by 14-foot sidewall tent made in Egypt for Krug Henry, the former chief geologist, who left here two years ago. It is lined inside with dark blue cloth that reduces the bugs and has mosquito netting sewn into the sidewalls, which can be rolled up. The doors in the ends can be rolled up or secured over with a heavy canvas fly, so it is warm at night and can be made cool in the daytime and still be reasonably free from flies. It is a big improvement on the big English army tents we've been using. However, if there are no flies, or one doesn't care if there are, nothing beats the tents we have designed to work like the Bedouin tents.

It is interesting to hear Khamis's reaction to our account of the revision of the Neutrality Act. "Yes," he says, "it is much better to keep the ships away from the war. Otherwise someone will sink a ship and then say, 'We didn't know it was an American ship,' or the ship's captain will say, 'I didn't know we weren't supposed to be there,' and, in either case, America will get into the war." Not a bad analysis.

The feast at the end of Ramadhan was quite an event; about half the fellows came around for epsom salts the next day. It took old Muhammad bin Humaid three days to recover from his gorging. He had been complaining before the feast that he couldn't eat as much as he used to and wanted some medicine to correct this problem. I told him not to eat so much. The Bedu seem to think that if a man can't eat half of a sheep at one sitting, his stomach is slipping badly.

Bismarck – October 26, 1939

I was so excited after getting your letter yesterday that I was completely good for nothing the rest of the day. I can't even let myself imagine that it will be possible. Do you realize that would only be six months? But listen, my friend, this is just another warning that if I can't go, you will trot yourself home very fast-like in December, whether you like winter or not. Honestly, I couldn't stand to wait any longer than that.

Almost forgot to say how wonderful it would be for you to be Max's assistant; that is something of a promotion, isn't it? I'm so proud of you, darling. Do you think that someday you will be chief geologist? They couldn't possibly draft you in case of war, could they? That will undoubtedly be my next worry. Be sure to tell them that you are married. See what an asset that will be for you?

Bismarck – November 17, 1939

Two letters I have gotten from you in the last two days, and tomorrow is our second anniversary. I have been so happy that I could scarcely contain myself.

About all of the household goods of which you were speaking, did you know that I have absolutely nothing in my hopeless chest besides a tablecloth? Aunt Florence gave me a silver chest with no silver and six sterling silver demitasse cups with no saucers. I'm afraid that you haven't a very domestic wife. Somehow or other I just can't go into raptures over hemming dishtowels and embroidering pillowcases. In spite of all that, I love you lots and can't wait to spend the rest of my life heckling you. Can you?

Write me millions of letters about you.

December 2, 1939
Camp Jabrin

Your letters were waiting for me when we returned from our six-day trip. Maybe I've missed a letter somewhere, because you didn't say you'd like to come over, though you did sort of say, "Whoopee! When do I start?" I am writing Max to tell him I'll stay over until the summer, providing you can come. Kath, it seems so long since I've seen you. Before, the year looked as if it would pass quickly until June. We'd go in at Christmas and then come out again and map desert and then come in and write and draw. Now that I know you're closer, the months will drag and drag.

Yes, assistant to Max would be something of a promotion, and yes, if I am good and study hard, I might be a chief geologist someday.

Our trip was without much incident, except that it is awfully cold getting up in the morning when the north wind is whistling through. Muhammad bin Humaid is still having trouble with his stomach. He says it puffs up on him. The day before we returned here, I gave him a big dose of castor oil. He said it worked fine, but after he ate a little supper, it was as bad as ever. While we were gone, a party of Bedu came through with four *wudhaihi* they had killed in the Rub' al-Khali and were taking up to Bin Jiluwi. The Bedu left a little meat and part of a leg and hoof. Muhammad busted up the leg bone, boiled it up with the hoof and then drank the broth. He says there is nothing like it for the stomach.

December 15, 1939
Camp Jabrin

We were out on another trip for more than a week. It was uneventful, except that we actually left the "explored" territory and crossed the Dahna, a great sand strip running the length of Arabia, further south than anyone before us. The evenings were somewhat enlivened by the performances of Nasir, who works around the camp and cooks for the soldiers. He is quite a comedian.

At the well from which we draw our water, he met a beautiful damsel named Damiya, who was camped there with her family. She is a Dawsariyah, the same tribe as Nasir, but how he knows she's beautiful is beyond me, as all the Bedu women are masked and muffled. Anyway, Nasir was entranced and received a great deal of kidding from the rest of the men in camp. Her father was dead, so Nasir made a tentative approach to her older brother.

Just as things were going well, Damiya's younger brother visited our camp one day and saw Nasir cooking. (Khamis told me this story.) Now, the occupation of cook is scorned by the proud Bedouin, who will cook for themselves on a raiding party, but would rather die than cook for a living. Nasir passed it off by saying that he was just substituting for the regular cook.

The next day he came to me to quit, with a long story about wanting to go visit his mother in Wadi Dawasir, 200 miles from here. So I sent him into the Jabal, but he forgot to take some government papers with him and wasn't allowed to quit. He came back, worked some more and is going in tomorrow to try to quit again. Damiya and family have gone out in the desert somewhere; he will come back here and wander around the sands until he finds her.

In our travels we found a short piece of what must have been a large camel road at one time. It was on ground so situated that the tracks would not be removed easily by wind or water. All were agreed that it was a great road and very old, since no traces of it showed in the softer or more eroded ground on either side. Khamis thinks that it was the main road between Jabrin and al-Kharj in those far dim days when both were great and Yamama, the chief town of the al-Kharj region, was the center of a Christian civilization in central Arabia. As the Arabs would say, "in the days of ignorance;" that is, before Muhammad.

We returned to Dhahran for a short Christmas break. One of the great delights of Christmas was that we received mail for the first time in more than a month, and then there was to be a big dance at Dhahran, where there were 250 men and 17 women. Out of pity for the women, we avoided the dance.

Bismarck – December 18, 1939

Merry Christmas.

Isn't this silly, writing a letter on a restaurant napkin? Had your letter today and just read it again for the fifth time. It was on our anniversary, and I love every line of it. Saturday I had your pictures from Mrs. Rector. The beer bottle one I like best; you look very boyish and much less like the professor. I hope you'll stay the beer-bottle type for a couple of years so we can catch up on our "lost youth."

Here's my beef stew, darling; will write more later – love you lots.

Bismarck – December 26, 1939

In spite of gallant efforts to work, it seems utterly useless. I sit and stare at my ring for hours at a time. It's so beautiful that it hurts. It came yesterday about an hour before I left home. I was so happy. It just climaxed the most wonderful Christmas I have ever had and how I wanted to share it with you.

Needless to say I love you a thousand fold more than two years ago. I didn't think it possible; it's probably because you are getting closer in time.

January 9, 1940
Camp Jabrin

Another hurried letter that has caught me unawares. We hadn't expected to send in a car for a couple of weeks, but Muhammad bin Humaid is sick again, and Dr. Dame orders us to send him in at once. Muhammad hasn't eaten anything for two or three days, yet his stomach is still swollen up to the size of a football. He's pretty old to be knocking about in the desert. The desert shaikh of the novels is a romantic figure as long as he's young and healthy; wealth helps too, but when age and failing health creep over him, he's about as abject and pitiable a figure as can be imagined.

Abu Hadriya is close to the pay zone now. In less than two weeks we should know whether it is an oil well, or just another expensive hole in the ground. Presumably it will have considerable effect on the future geological program, but just how, no one seems to know. Johnny had a letter from Jerry in which he says he expects to be back here in the spring. It may be that he is going to assist Max, in which case Max would hardly need me since Jerry would be here for three years, and I would stay only a year at most. Anyway, be of good heart, and we will wait to see what happens.

Soon after Abu Hadriya struck oil, there was definitely a major effect on all of Casoc. Though it eventually turned out to be a modestly producing well by Arabian standards, at most a hundred thousand barrels a day, the discovery at Abu Hadriya proved that there was more than one oil field in Saudi Arabia, and in San Francisco, Standard Oil of California began to expand its plans for 1940.

King Abdul Aziz ibn Saud leaves the well house at Abu Hadriya #1, as Crown Prince Saud watches

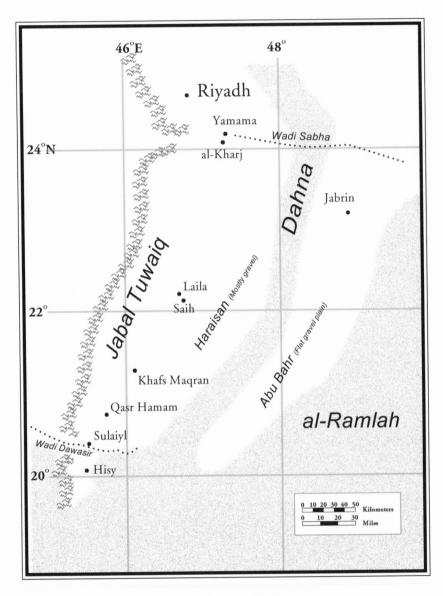

Jabrin to the Wadi Dawasir

Low jabals *west of the Dahna on the Haraisan Plateau; the darker* jabal *in the center is Jabal al-Amagher*

Chapter 15
"The Wudhaihi"

January 27, 1940
Near Jabrin

At present, we are about 90 miles southwest of Jabrin in the most God-forsaken country I have ever seen. This is the desert par excellence; compared to this wasteland, northern Arabia is a flowering garden. We are in between al-Ramlah, The Sand, and the Dahna; there is not much sand here, just an endless succession of utterly barren, low, flat-topped mesas, most of them less than 30 feet high. A few miles to the south begins the great gravel plain of Abu Bahr, "Father of the Sea," where we come to the tale.

Though it is so large that it is on many maps, until Philby crossed Abu Bahr in 1931, no European had ever seen it. I have just read a learned treatise in which a chap tries to prove that a "sea land" mentioned in certain Babylonian tablets must have been in eastern Arabia. He "shows" that the application of the name "sea" does not necessarily imply a direct connection with a real, wet sea. Then he quotes many descriptions of sand dunes such as "a sea of dunes" and "like a wave-tossed sea," and finally concludes that Abu Bahr, a prize example of desert land being named after the sea, must be a great sand area.

It isn't. Instead, it's as flat as a floor and twice as barren. Until we came, no car had ever been on it, and only three Europeans had seen it: Philby, who crossed the southern part of it, and Dick Kerr and Max Steineke, who saw the northern edge from a plane. Most of desert Arabia is criss-crossed with camel trails going to wells or pastures, but not Abu Bahr; it's devoid of signs of humanity. On the edge of the sands, the *wudhaihi*, the big long-horned oryx, still lives and struggles against civilization.

This morning we left our camp early and started south. Every 20 minutes we would stop the car, take its direction by compass, and mark on the dashboard the shadow of a piece of tape stuck on the windshield. As the sun moved, our direction changed, but we could average the beginning and end of each 20-minute segment. All the way we traveled 50 to 60 miles an hour over flat, gravel plain with hardly a bush and never a foxhole to worry about. About noon we ran into sand, and half an hour later we stopped because we were getting into the big dunes. Lines of green grass, about a yard wide, followed along the base of the south sides of the sand hills, which were otherwise as bare as eggs.

Shooting the sun at noon with the sextant

The south wind came up and filled the air full of sand. I had a helluva time shooting the sun at noon with the sextant to determine our latitude. In fact, Kass, I didn't look at all like the natty officer shooting the stars from the bridge in a cruise advertisement. We had the pickup in front of the sedan, sand belts against the wheels, and toolboxes piled up to keep the wind off me and the bowl of mercury that we use to simulate a horizon. I crouched alongside the sedan, with Johnny inside taking the time and keeping notes.

After the sun shooting, we had a quick lunch and started home. We'd not gone more than a half a dozen miles when Khamis sighted three *wudhaihi*. It was the only time I've ever seen him excited, and he was as excited as a small boy at his first circus. We lit out after them. They're about as big as small cows. There were two adults and a small one. We picked the one with the longest horns, more than two feet of straight spikes, and soon caught up with it. Johnny knocked it down with the shotgun; we left it for the soldiers in the pickup and started after the second oryx.

John hit it once with the shotgun, without much effect. Khamis emptied the .22 into the animal's hind quarters, and it stopped. Khamis shot it in the head with the .22, and the oryx fell down and then immediately got up and started off. Johnny held the wheel, and I shot the .22 and knocked the *wudhaihi* down again, only to have it get up and start off. My next shot, behind the ear, killed a very tough animal. This one was the bull; the one we shot first was a cow. We hadn't expected such horns on it.

The cow dropped all right, but when the soldiers arrived in the pickup, she arose and galloped off, then turned and charged the car, striking the spare tire on the side without damaging her horns. Muhammad bin Sennet shot her twice with his army rifle, but even then, the fellows weren't taking any chances. One soldier lowered a rope from the back of the pickup and raised the head up so another could cut the throat without descending from the car.

We went back, picked up the trail of the young one in the sand and caught up with him a couple of miles away. Khamis and Johnny stood on the running board, and after we followed him a bit, they jumped off and chased him on foot. John missed his dive, but Khamis gathered in an arm full of back legs and tripped him up. He is a cute little fellow and is doing right well at the time of writing. Johnny is the first American to shoot a *wudhaihi*, and we are of the few Europeans to get one; as far as I know, we are the only ones. I don't believe Philby ever shot one in his 20 years in Arabia and Doughty never even saw a wild one.

Back in Jabrin.

At home again. The country around here looks green and fertile after our trip to the southland. As Johnny remarked, "I didn't remember there were so many bushes here."

The news is coming in now, but I guess we haven't missed much during our absence. The Finns seem to be doing right well, as usual, and all is quiet on the western front. I would like to get the American news, which hasn't been coming in clearly this last month. It sounds as if big things are doing in Congress, especially, in regard to the Japanese treaty.

Remember the Bible I bought in New York before sailing? I have just started to read it a little at a time in the evening. It is very readable, and the proximity of the scenes of action makes it more interesting. These people have many of the Old Testament stories in their Koran. Khamis told me the story of Joseph by rapidly repeating to himself whole sections, which he must have learned from rote, and then resetting it in Arabic for me.

The funny thing to us is the perfect naturalness of the stories to the Arabs. A "well" to us means an old oaken bucket, or a wooden platform and a hand pump, but to them it is just an open hole from which water is drawn in a skin bucket, the same as in Joseph's time. His brothers pushed him in the well, and some of the soldiers of the King of Egypt came along and let down a *delloo*, skin bucket, to draw some water, and heard Joseph crying out. And so on it goes, just about like our story, even to the famine that brings Joseph's family to him after he has become King of Egypt.

An interesting variation has to do with the Queen of Egypt. She was enamored of Joseph, but he refused to have anything to do with her. However, there was much gossip about the Queen's behavior in offering herself to Joseph. So the Queen invited all the gossips to a great dinner, and, towards the end of the meal, she served melons and sharp knives to the guests. Just as they were about to cut their melons, she had Joseph appear in the doorway. A great gasp of astonishment went up from the guests, and, in their excitement, they slipped with their knives and each guest cut off a finger or two. The Queen said, "Well, what do you say now?" and they were all silent.

During this time, Max was coming out to see us, so Johnny and I drove to Ain Haradh, where Ernie and his partner were camped. Max would meet us there, and all five of us would drive back to Jabrin.

In the late afternoon at Ernie's camp, we discovered that he and his partner were no longer speaking. They were working separately, much like Walt Hoag and Jerry had done two years before. Ernie's partner was not the same gregarious type as Ernie and the rest of us, nor did he seem to have much enthusiasm for anything.

He ignored us as we concentrated on our discussion with Ernie about Wadi Sahba, which was the boundary between our work and theirs. The wadi *originated far in the interior on the back slope of the Tuwaiq Mountains, and for most of its length, it traveled due east in almost a straight line. However, in the vicinity of Haradh, the* wadi *bent south for a fair distance and then bent again and went east to eventually disappear in the low lands to the southwest of Qatar.*

The surface gave no clue to any particular reason as to why the wadi *should make this southward bend. We had discussed this with Ernie earlier in the year, and now he was investigating this bend on his own, as his partner wasn't interested and occupied himself mapping other areas in their territory.*

There were many small jabals *around Haradh with flat tops on them, what we would call a butte or a mesa. They were capped with a sandy limestone that seemed to be involved in much slumping, as the caps of the hills were not horizontal, but dipped in various directions that did not appear to fit any kind of pattern. Ernie thought that perhaps there might be some significance to the way in which these buttes dipped, so he meticulously had mapped a great many of them in the Haradh area.*

He then measured the slope and the direction of the slope of these jabals. As they were put on the map, it revealed that the tops of the jabals in general, with a few exceptions, sloped away from the center, which was near Ain Haradh, in a pattern that indicated an uplift that could account for the change in direction of Wadi Sahba.

Since a structural uplift like this is a prime indicator of an oil reservoir, Johnny and I were excited by Ernie's discovery and couldn't wait to see Max's reaction. Max arrived the next afternoon, and the first thing he did was pull out the maps. When he saw Ernie's map of these arrows all pointing away from the center near Haradh, he became as excited as we had been, and said to Ernie's partner, "How did you manage to find this?"

While Johnny and I watched him to see what he would say, the partner replied, "Well, we just map it as she comes, Max. Map it as she comes." Both of us bit our lips, as there was no mention of how this map had been drawn or who had discovered this phenomenon.

This was the first discovery of a structural uplift on what later became known as the Ghawar Field, probably the largest single oil field on earth. Its structural significance was confirmed a few months later when Max and Ernie went back to Hardh and found Eocene rock outcroppings at the center from which Ernie's arrows radiated.

Haradh was more than 200 miles south of Dhahran. With the discovery of oil at the much closer field in Abqaiq in 1940 and the advent of the war, which limited exploratory drilling, Haradh was not drilled until 1948. By then, most people had forgotten that Ernie Berg was the discoverer of the Ghawar Field.

February 4, 1940
Camp Jabrin

This truck business is getting annoying. It takes a day to make the trip one way, so, allowing two days in the Jabal, it should not require more than four days for the trip. The truck's been gone seven days now, and they still haven't sent it out of the Jabal. Butch, the *wudhaihi*, is getting awfully thin, as we are out of condensed milk and spinach. The soldiers scoured the nearby country to find a couple of large handfuls of dry grass. We hope to fatten him up on the alfalfa that we've ordered from the Jabal. We have a big box fixed up outside our tent for him, but he insists on sleeping in the doorway of the tent. About twice a night he gets all tangled up in his rope and sets up a squawk that sounds like a rubber-bulb automobile horn until one of us gets up and untangles him. I suppose he's good practice for our first child.

We were getting the American news for the first time in weeks when the station cut out completely in the middle of the broadcast and came on again for the last few sentences. Now they're playing "Someday Sweetheart."

Butch is doing much better on the alfalfa and milk that arrived on the truck last night. In fact, he's back in form and displaying an active interest in things. One of the soldiers came over for some eye medicine tonight and was the target of an enthusiastic, but ineffective butting. The little guy has been trying to eat his old loves: the rubber microphone cable and the canvas canteen straps. He's sort of dumb though; every night he makes a few scoops at the coconut matting in our tent before lying down and is always surprised that he isn't able to make a hole in it.

Johnny Thomas had an accordion that he usually played in the tent at night, but two or three weeks after we set up camp at Jabrin, he offered to play a concert for the soldiers. So after dinner, when we had finished our radio schedule with Dhahran, we went up to the soldiers' tent. After we had coffee and tea, Johnny pulled out the accordion to give us a serenade.

He tuned it up and tuned it up and then tuned it a little more until it was ready to go. He played a song that was popular at the time called "Moonlove," which was derived from some classical piece that I have long since forgotten. The soldiers were attentive to the recital and applauded after the performance.

So, I asked the soldiers, "How did you like the music of Mr. Thomas?"

"Well," they said, "it was pretty good music, but we really liked the first song much better."

Bismarck – January 4, 1940

Just think, our red-letter year. It's been a long time coming, hasn't it? Is there any chance I might see you sooner than December? Please let us have next summer together.

February 18, 1940
Camp Jabrin

On Valentine's Day I received three letters from you – all at once. As if that weren't enough, one of the letters had pictures in it, three pictures of you! As I have said before, pictures of you make me shiver and shake.

I'm coming home this August. Rather than have me stay for a few months over my contract, Max says that they would rather have me go home this summer and come back with you on a second contract. I will have at least two and a half months of vacation, and then I probably will be given some training in geophysics before being sent back. Further, Max says we can come back together across the Pacific. Many of the men coming back have been sent across the Atlantic, while their wives came across the Pacific. Anyway, from what Max told Johnny, it seems that I am in good favor with the company and they want me back again.

Max also told me that several men had approached him about transferring me into the Government Relations Department. He said that he would hate to lose me, but it was my own choice. I told him I wasn't interested, as I would be throwing away all the technical training and experience I've had. He agreed, and said that if I ever wanted to change, petroleum engineering or management would be more appropriate and offered much better possibilities for advancement. If I were a lawyer, it would be different, as the job would be good experience with great potential for promotion. As it is, I would be trading only on some knowledge of Arabic and the California Company's interest in Arabia.

It sure is our red-letter year, and it has been a long time coming. If God wills, the war will be over by the time we are ready to return, and we can make a leisurely sort of trip across the Pacific.

Johnny says, "Just think, next year I'll be able to sit and talk with my partner about plans for going home. Last year, I had to send Jerry across the Pacific, and now I have to get you across the Atlantic."

On Valentine's Day we took a day off; many more like it and we'll be wrecks. In the morning we set out with the best of intentions, but on our way to work we passed by a bunch of ruins we hadn't seen before. They are called "The House of the Mother of Ashes."

All around the ruins of a fairly large-sized building are piles of ashes three to six feet high. Philby thought it was a place that had burned down, but the ashes are too much for that. We stopped to look around and spent two hours gathering bits of glass, pottery, ostrich shells, copper, beads and charred bones. With such a hole out of the morning, we gave up the idea of work and returned to camp for some tools so we could dig up the biggest tumulus we could find. A tumulus is a pile of rocks used for a grave. There are hundreds

An unfinished tumulus three kilometers west of Jabrin

of them on Bahrain, where some archaeological work has been done, that have been ascribed to a date before 500 B.C. There are hundreds more here around Jabrin. We picked a big one with a ring of rocks around it in a circle about 50 feet across.

Well, it wasn't a question of just throwing out rocks; the wind of centuries had filled every nook and cranny with sand. So I shoveled, and Johnny shoveled, and Khamis shoveled, and I shoveled, and when we finally got down to bedrock, we had a hatful of fragments of bones and aching backs and not a single arrowhead or scrap of pottery or anything at all.

The next day we went east on a short spike trip and made camp on the edge of the great sands of the Jafurah. In the morning we found the sands were a fake at the point where we had touched them. After the first row of dunes, we traveled on gravel plains for 30 miles, then another 30 on rolling sand, and we were across. It was early in the day so we drove on 120 miles north to give Johnny a look at the famous storehouse at Selwa, the base for our attack on the Rub' al-Khali two years ago.

Here we are back in camp. Salih is going to Hofuf tomorrow to buy some food, so this letter will go up to Bill Seale's camp and on to the Jabal.

We looked at your pictures with a hand lens and find you are up until 11:20. Johnny says you will have to reform because everyone here goes to bed at 9:30 unless there are letters to write for a car going out in the morning. He also thinks you may reform me in such items as my sanitary toothbrush holder – a shaving kit in which the toothbrush rattles around with boxes of .22 shells, spare watch, sewing kit, glasses case, iodine vial and assorted junk. I claim I am too old to reform, but it may be an idle boast.

February 28, 1940
Abu Bahr

Since I last wrote you, nothing much happened in the first four days beyond a visit from our new neighbors, the triangulation (fancy name for high-powered surveying) party, Walt Grumm and Rudy Gierhart, who are now at Ken and Ernie's old camp site. On the fifth day, however, we set out for the south with all the cars.

Walt and Johnny were old friends. In late 1938 and early 1939, more men were coming into Arabia than could be absorbed in an orderly fashion. When Johnny arrived, he was put to work with Bill Seale on the triangulation survey. When Walt arrived, he somehow had been labeled a geologist and was sent to Max. Max didn't ask Walt if he were a geologist; he just assumed that he was and sent him into the field to work with Jerry.

Jerry finally discovered that Walt wasn't a geologist, he was a civil engineer. Johnny was the geologist, but he was working as a civil engineer. They were both overjoyed when this mix-up was discovered, and they each were returned to their own profession.

Just on the edge of the great gravel plains of Abu Bahr, we ran into a herd of gazelle and shot one. Johnny and I went off after the rest, but only shot some pictures of them and let them go. We told the soldiers that the herd had escaped into the hilly country to the north.

Taking off from a point we had mapped a month ago, we went south along the sand on the eastside of Abu Bahr. The terrain here consists of long straight *uruq* sitting on the flat plain. Some of the ridges run for more than 20 miles, straight as a string and three or four hundred yards wide. It was hot; there was a south wind, and it was miles between bushes – dead or alive.

The next day we wandered eastward following the *hautas* between the *uruq* and then, about noon, cut back south to the edge of the uninterrupted plain. About four o'clock, the older of our two pickups stopped. Salih, who was driving it, said it was beginning to make a noise. The rear wheels were locked tight when we tried to push it, so we made camp out in the middle of the flat gravel.

In the morning we left a driver and a soldier with the pickup and shoved on southwest. At noon we were opposite the south point that we had reached on the west side of Abu Bahr a month ago and in the sand that we believed cut the big plain in two. The lorry stopped to make camp, while we crossed the sand out onto the southern plains to a point south of Philby's desperate route. He marched west out of the middle of the Rub' al-Khali for 12 waterless days to the settlements in Wadi Dawasir and almost didn't make it. The day before had been hot, and a strong south wind whipped sand into our eyes every time we crossed an *irq*. This day was hot, but the wind was gentle.

A great uruq *along the eastern edge of Abu Bahr*

Next morning we intended to go west and tie in with our previous work to see if the sand extended clear across to the west side. But we awoke to a whistling north wind that filled the air with sand and made us give up after about 10 miles, as we weren't sure that we could find our way back to the lorry, map or no map.

With our old tracks and the automatic gyroscope Khamis has in his head, we made our way back the 60 miles to the pickup, pitched our other tent and sat inside all afternoon while the wind howled and the sand roared across the plain and beat on the tent, entering and descending in a fine spray. Even reading was disagreeable, as the pages were covered with sand between turnings, so I mostly lay on my bed with my *ghutra* over my face and dozed.

The morning was clear, cool and calm. We started work on the broken pickup. The wheel locks showed no intention of coming off easily, and we had no wheel-puller, so we removed the whole rear axle, differential and all, from the truck. Then we struggled to find some way to grip the hubs of the two wheels so we could pull the damned thing apart. At last, by anchoring one end to the second pickup and pulling on the other with the autocar, it popped open. A bearing had broken, and the differential was all chewed up, full of gear teeth, roller-bearing parts, and so on. We finished putting it back together about an hour before sundown.

Today we sent the Autocar, towing the pickup, to a rendezvous at a dune on the north edge of Abu Bahr. With the sedan and other pickup, we went southwest to find out about that sand cutting across Abu Bahr. In that sand "the earth is alive;" that is, it rained there last spring and the sand is covered with green grass and bushes, a fine place to find *wudhaihi*.

The sand does cut clear across, and about eleven o'clock we found our old tracks and tied in our map work. No sign of *wudhaihi*, but when we turned to go back north and east, we found tracks and tracks, all no more than a day old. As the wind was from the southeast, we traveled northwest in the direction the oryx should have gone in order to flee from the noise of our cars. Eventually we left the sand and found no more tracks.

About noon, Khamis spotted tracks of five *wudhaihi* heading northeast, the direction we had to go. We decided to eat lunch, follow these tracks, and if we found something well and good; if not we were going in the right direction. At lunch, I spliced a loop in the end of a piece of rope and gave a poor demonstration of how cowboys lasso cows. The soldiers were unimpressed.

In less than half an hour, we caught up with the herd, three big ones and two smaller ones. I snapped pictures and took movies while the soldiers knocked off the three adults. They must have weighed over 200 pounds apiece and had a total of about 15 feet of long, sharp horns. I shot more movie film while we followed a wounded one. Then we set off after the two smaller ones and tracked and tracked and tracked, part of the time with one or the other soldiers running ahead of the cars.

It was late, so we decided that if we didn't see them in five minutes, we'd press on. The tracks got fresher until Abdullah, a pint-size soldier, spotted them. We stopped as soon as we could catch up with the pickup truck. Johnny hopped in and drove after one of the smaller oryx as I stood on the running board with my lariat. It took me about four tries before I found out what to do about the wind and how to hang onto the running board with one hand. When I finally dropped the rope over his neck, he wasn't even breathing hard.

He was a savage little devil, kicking and butting at us until we trussed him up and put him in the back of the truck. The sedan was chasing the other *wudhaihi*, trying to wear him down, so we chased the sedan, pulled alongside the little oryx, and I roped him on the second try. The Arabs thought my lariat work was swell and marveled aloud about where did I ever get the idea to use a rope like that.

The two baby oryx Butch and Tillie

They were male and female; we call them Butch and Tillie – *tully* is Arabic for a small *wudhaihi*. We put them in the back seat of the sedan with Abdullah, as he was the smallest soldier and there wasn't much room in front beside our portable radio. For about an hour, they gave him plenty to do. As he said, "When one rests, the other one works."

If they pull through, and we are going to do all we can to see that they do, we are going to write to a zoo in the States to see if anyone wants them. We'll try San Francisco first, where we'll have a chance to see them again. In spite of "cute" being already heavily overburdened, that's exactly what they are. Their toughness, aggressiveness and all around cussedness only accentuates it.

Tomorrow we will be in Jabrin if all goes well. Tonight we asked Khamis if it would be a good idea to send one of the big *wudhaihi* to Bin Jiluwi. He thought it would be. As we are going to send the lorry in for supplies, we thought it would be easy enough for the driver to drop it off on his way through Hofuf. Khamis didn't think much of the idea.

We pressed him a bit before he explained, "Well, if we just send it up and the lorry is going in anyway, it wasn't so much. But if we send a car in especially to take a *wudhaihi* from Abu Bahr to Emir bin Jiluwi, that would be a big thing with the people." Face, it is. Always one must keep or make, whatever is the proper expression, as much face as possible. So we shall send the garrulous governor meat by special delivery and probably earn more good will than we could otherwise earn with 10 times the expenditure.

Bismarck – January 24, 1940

We are now embarking on 1940; everyone is upset over a book called *Grapes of Wrath* about the migrant workers from the Oklahoma "Dust Bowl. It's by John Steinbeck, and the language is perfectly vile. Also people are going slightly mad over a song which is as old as I am, "Oh, Johnny." At any rate, I promised that I would send my feeble poetic efforts.

Abroad Thoughts from Home (apologies to Robert Browning)

Why is it now that I must be
So consumed in reverie
Of sun and sand and always you
Wondering if these things are true?

Why can't I seem to concentrate
On work I know must not wait?
Thoughts that start out logically
Always end on a ship at sea.

Before me is a calendar
And I know the time's not far
Yet the months plod slowly on
As I become a very dull automaton.

March 3, 1940
Camp Jabrin

Kath, you astonish me with your verse. You must do more of it. The latest is excellent, especially since I can change the title from "Abroad Thoughts from Home" to "Abroad Thoughts of Home" and "sun and sand" to "the prairie." You know, Kath, if I could only learn enough Arabic to understand some more Arabic poetry, it would be of fun translating it, especially some of the Bedu songs.

Few are written, and most of the English translations are lousy. They have poems and poems, and some, nay most, have a fine stirring rhythm. In many of them, line after line will rhyme. There is a fine one about Ibn Saud's attack on Riyadh, how the guide lost his way to the only place where they could water the camels without fear of discovery before the last dash on the city. Abdul Aziz had only 30 men, and the regular garrison was more than 80 established in a sort of citadel within the walls. We might try it when we come back – I'll translate, and you make the poetry. Khamis told me the other day that I learned Arabic faster and better (now) than any of the other *sahibs*. Lucky I have big shirts, as I dislike sewing on buttons; Khamis has been with the company ever since 1933.

Our two young ones, Butch and Tillie, arrived at the Jabal in good shape and by now should be bursting with goat milk. I guess they caused a mild sensation, even competing with Abu Hadriya, which came in the night before – it's an oil well! It seems that there had been a big argument about Abu Hadriya, with one faction in favor of deepening the hole and another group saying that the well was already at 10,000 feet and there wasn't any oil in the thing. Finally a cable was sent from San Francisco with orders to suspend the operation, but the hole was going well so the cable was conveniently misplaced, the drilling continued and now there is oil.

The oil at Abu Hadriya means a great deal, as we have several similar structures from which we can now expect a 50-50 chance of getting oil. Before this, we had no idea of their significance as possible oil producers. Now the company will start drilling another structure at a place called Abqaiq, halfway between Dhahran and Hofuf, on the edge of a great belt of sand dunes. Max has been all his life looking for a place like this, and now he'll soon find out if he's right. This is going to be a great oil company and a good place to make a future.

March 11, 1940
Camp Jabrin

How are you? I am all right. My Mom has many of the letters I wrote from St. Benedicts when I was 9 years old. They all start out as above, then follows, "Please send me.....," and "Your loving son." Very informative.

Day after tomorrow we start out on our big trip to Laila, Sulaiyl, and all points southwest. Laila should have a brass band for us, as no European has been there since Philby visited 23 years ago and put it on the maps. He went to Sulaiyl on the same trip and returned there eight years ago when he passed through on his way out of the Rub' al-Khali.

He was on camelback, whereas we can scurry about in Fords and look at the country to the right and left. Khamis says there are mountain goats in the Tuwaiq Mountains. They are an animal the size of a goat and have big curled horns and a beard, which ought to make them a goat, but I don't imagine we'll see any. That whole part of the country has been several years without rain, so the hunting probably will not be good. We hope that the geology alone will provide plenty of excitement. Our map this year will certainly be a whopper.

The war news doesn't sound encouraging, with talk of the Allies giving active aid to Finland and possibly declaring war on Russia. We also heard the reports of conferences in Turkey between Allied generals and the Turks. It might be that come summer the Mediterranean will be closed, though I think it unlikely because the Italians seem to be drawing closer to the Allies. Anyway, should it be so, I will whistle across the Pacific to you.

I really haven't anything to tell you about, Kath, except that I love you as always and forever.

We've been trying to do some work around here, without much success. Three days in a row it was so hazy by 10 in the morning that we had to give up and come back to camp. There is a truck coming down here with gasoline for us tomorrow, and this will bridge the gap between my last and my next letter, when we return from the trip in a couple of weeks.

Our current joke is Bill Seale's return to his camp, 80 miles north of us. His wife arrived about two weeks ago, so Bill went into the Jabal about three days before she arrived. For the last five or six nights, we have heard him saying on the radio, "Well, I think I'll be down tomorrow, boys. Anything you want me to bring?" and thusly each night until tonight, when he finally arrived.

At Christmas time, I ordered a couple of Mosul goat hair rugs from Iraq. In the last mail I received a notice stating that the sellers wanted double the quoted price, so I cancelled my order. They are fine rugs, soft and wooly, but I guess we'll have to do without them for a while. Then, too, I was going to buy several Arab brass coffee pots to take home as presents. They are about the best souvenirs from this country. When Salih went into Hofuf a few days ago for groceries, he was to place the order. Now he reports that the price has nearly doubled because the Americans have been coming to Hofuf to buy them and ruined the market. He says that when he returns, he will see about them, and after his refusal to buy the first time the price probably will be down again.

One of the best stories concerns a stone pot Ken Parsons bought. Ken was quite proud of it. It was hollowed out of a soft sort of soapstone. Salih tells us that there were quite a few of these in Hofuf, most of them brought back from Mecca by pilgrims returning from the Hajj. They are said to have come from Teheran, Persia. In Hofuf, they were merely curiosities that sold for a rupee or less. Ken paid nine and thought he had turned a bargain!

Salih filled me in on the merchants of Hofuf. Nearly everyone who buys for someone else, or takes a buyer into a shop, gets a commission from the seller. There are quite a number of people who make their living by helping strangers, such as the Bedu, do their buying. Spotting a stranger, they offer to go along and see that he doesn't get overcharged. The merchant then doubles the price and the helper gets half of the increase over the normal price.

March 16, 1940
Camp Jabrin

This should be a surprise after my threat of no letters for at least a couple of weeks. Dick Bramkamp came down here three days ago, and we were all set to go on our trip, except for one small detail. We hadn't received notice of the government's permission for the trip. We've sat and stewed and fumed, and no permission has arrived. Dick is going back to the Jabal tomorrow, and the trip will be delayed at least a week.

It seems that the fat-headed Government Relations Department, instead of sending in a politely phrased request that we might be allowed to make this trip into territory outside of our concession, "notified" the government that we were going on such and such a date. The government, quite justifiably, came back and asked if the Relations people knew that the proposed route lay outside of the concession. Now the thing is all gummed up with inquiries, offended dignity, and so on. It is the first time such a thing has happened to us. Max was out in the desert, but he came back to the Jabal yesterday; I can well imagine that at least some of his remarks could not be repeated in the mails without fear of prosecution.

We always had a clean shirt every morning, but we seldom took a bath – it was too cold, and besides that, there wasn't enough water. Years afterwards we were discussing how it's perfectly possible to go without a bath for a long time; we didn't get sick or anything. Dick Bramkamp, who was usually in Dhahran, would come to visit us for three days at a time to look at our fossils and help us along; finally confessed that it took him at least half a day to get used to us.

The plans for my homecoming are somewhat nebulous. I am desperately trying to find out if I must go across the continent to say hello in San Francisco before I go home. The opinion seems to be that I must, but I am obtaining a solemn and authoritative pronouncement on the question. Everyone has decided that I must buy a car. As a start, I have written to my Dad to see what sort of deals he can make with the dealers at home to have one delivered in New York. The how, when, and where are still in abeyance. I might even end up coming across the Pacific.

Tonight we had dinner with Bill Seale, Walt Grumm and Rudi Gierhart, who have their camp pitched just across the sand ridge from ours. The chicken dumplings were excellent. How are you on chicken dumplings, Kath? Matilda sent us a small box of cookies with Dick and, hence, still holds our No. 1 rating amongst Arabian wives.

They are building a swimming pool at the Jabal, fixing the golf course, and preparing the bar to receive alcoholic beverages, which now have been permitted by the government. The company is putting in landscaping around the houses, and Bill Seale says he helped order a whopping lot of about 70 different kinds of plants from India, so it will be quite the place when we return.

Bismarck – February 12, 1940

Please let me know soon about your plans for me. Your letter sounded as though my leaving in June is now but another dream gone astray. All I ask that we be together alone for awhile before you come home. You must know how important that is to me. It will be wonderful to spend Christmas in Hawaii. Do you think we could? Good night, sweetheart. Will you be my 1940 Valentine?

Bismarck – February 16, 1940

How is my little valentine? I seriously considered sending the following cable:
> If you love me
> Like I love you
> RSVP
> PDQ

Darling, I have your little problem all worked out; in fact, I think that the company should give us a reward for such a brainstorm. Why don't you come home this summer, take your vacation, renew your contract in the fall and go to work as Max's assistant? Then I could go with you. It seems a waste for you to take local leave this summer and then just diddle around doing nothing in October and November.

In a gentle way, your last letter warned me to give up hopes of coming in June. I guess I must be made of cast iron or something now because I don't feel a thing anymore. I suppose subconsciously that I expected it. I have acquired a handy mechanism, which I shall term the alternative device. I always make two plans, one that is a beautiful dream and one that will work. The workable one is meeting you in Hawaii, and perhaps you should accustom yourself to it, since it is probably all that you will hear from now until Christmas.

The war news is dreadful with the Russians wiping out the poor Finns, and Japan in such a stew about our treaty. I think you had better come home this summer.

March 21, 1940
Camp Jabrin

The first day of spring, and what a day! Not a cloud in the sky, yet you can look straight at the ghostly white disc of the sun. The tent is flapping and whipping in the gusts that drive the sand in sprays and make a blizzard of dust that is much worse than anything I've ever seen in North Dakota.

Yesterday morning, a south wind rose with the sun until its dust obscured all our landmarks, and we had to retreat to camp. This morning the wind switched to the north, and I buttoned up the tent. An hour later we could barely see our gasoline dump, which is only a hundred yards away. And so we sit in camp another day.

Two letters from you in last mail, day before yesterday. You must have second sight, Kath; your "brainstorm" is exactly what I was writing to you when you wrote your letter. I hope to be home in August. And Kath, we have a house assigned to us; a notice came in this last mail: "To be ready Nov. 30, 1940." We won't be here by then, and as it won't be ready by then, everything should work out beautifully. I will ask Matilda Armstrong for a list of things you should bring. Before she came, she made quite a raid on Woolworth's for paring knives and such stuff as cannot be found for love nor money here.

Dick Kerr, in telling me about his wife's arrival, said, "I told her to pile all of the linen in a heap and stuff it in boxes, blacken the pots, get the dishes greasy and don't bring a phonograph. But did she? No. She went to the office in San Francisco, and they told her to take anything she liked, Of course, I, having been here only four years, would know nothing of the conditions. So the linen looked as if it had been taken off the shelf and the price tags pulled off; she paid four rupees duty on a two-dollar toaster that we had won in a contest eight years ago; the silver plate we've had for 15 years showed up in its velvet lining without a scratch or blemish, and we had $300 worth of phonograph records impounded in customs."

The company furnishes sheets, blankets and so on, but most people bring their own. I wouldn't recommend letting the laundry have a chance at any especially good sheets or pillowcases. We are betting on the laundry being considerably reformed now that there are more wives in camp. They'll not grumble and swear and do nothing about it, as we do. The seismograph camp sent in a bunch of wool blankets to be laundered and got them back reduced from seven feet in length to slightly over five. Not officially confirmed, I believe the married people's food allotment is $50 a month – nearly everything is purchased through the commissary.

The Armstrongs had their house painted after Matilda arrived, so they lived in various rooms by turns while the painters had at the others. Great business, these houses, I understand from some of the plumbers, painters and carpenters in the Jabal; also a study in wives. Some of them have a hard time getting anything done, but I notice others, with more tact and good humor, get nearly anything they want right now.

You undoubtedly will have a lot of spare time, so if there's anything you've always wanted to do, this is the place to do it, Kath. Bill Seale was saying last night that his wife was studying public speaking. "Now why in the hell anyone her age who has had five boys wants to study public speaking I don't know, but if it makes her happy it's all right with me."

Matilda brought over about half a trunk of yarn that Army jollied the Customs into passing through without duty. As a starter, Kath, it's practically decided, except for asking your opinion, that you are going to teach me French. The new swimming pool and the tennis courts will be right handy. The golf course is being improved, though I'm not optimistic over the prospect of any amount of "improvement" making it into a decent course.

We probably shall have many arguments, my darling, but if God wills, we will compromise, and you can have your way. Now, for instance, buying rugs. You are forbidden Oriental rugs until you've been here long enough to know something about them. This is only to save our guests the embarrassment of admiring a lot of trash.

One time Florence Steineke bought two carpets in Bahrain, and I met her at the boat when she came back. I took the rugs into the Customs for Max to clear later on, but Florence asked me to find out what the Customs valuation would be, though she wouldn't tell me what she had paid for them. A Saudi Customs man knows the value of rugs thoroughly, as they are a principal native import. All Arab houses are furnished mainly with rugs and cushions on which the higher-class Arabs spend most of their time sitting and talking. These experts thought 75 rupees apiece was a fair value, and one of them was inclined to make it less than that.

I found out from Max afterwards that Florence had paid twice that, about $50 each instead of $25! I fully realize such prohibitions are effective only from a safe distance and have no doubt they will undergo some slight modifications when you have me close in hand.

I would say the tea reader is moderately encouraging about living abroad and bringing a baby home. I shall do my best to keep you from being unhappy. If you want, I will teach you Arabic so you can talk with the Bedu women, which ought to help cure a normal amount of unhappiness.

Speaking of Arab women, one of our Bahraini drivers told us the other night about the Bahrain government's efforts to clean up and improve the sanitary conditions on the island. One new regulation requires all babies to be delivered in the hospital, if possible. The soldiers fairly rocked with laughter at the idea of anyone going to a hospital for such a simple thing as having a baby.

The driver's wife is pregnant in Bahrain, so he is worried over the prospect. It is hard to account for this attitude, as they all consider hospitals fine places. I suspect that their holy men oppose the treatment of women at the hands of infidels. They wanted to know if it were true that all English women had their babies by Caesarian operation, "cut out of them," in their words. Another reason may be, as they joked with the poor driver, that they are actually afraid the women in hospitals may be raped. Curiously the Arabs seem to have great affection and genuine respect for their mothers, but otherwise women as a class are drawers of water, hewers of wood, producers of children (girls not counting), and a God-given means of satisfying man's concupiscence.

(Excerpts from a letter from a favorite cousin, Jane Williams) "Well – we, the family, heard you were married sometime in November. You can imagine the conversation. It seems that Uncle George was in North Dakota on business, and someone there told him. He, of course, said it can't be true or he would have known it. They said the girl was getting ready to go over to Arabia and that your family had a fit about it.

"To be perfectly honest, I must confess it didn't sound much like you; on the other hand, I thoroughly enjoyed it. You have always been such a fair-haired child that no one ever dreamed you would do anything not strictly in the accepted fashion. Anyhow, if your wife (gosh, that sounds funny) is going abroad, she undoubtedly will sail from New York. Why don't you give her my address? She could stay with Jane Connolly and me while she is in New York. We are taking a new apartment the first of March.

"Lest I forget, let me congratulate you on your marriage. I think it is grand and hope you come home soon so you can be a proper family man. I still think you should tell me more about it, or your plans or something. If there is one thing I haven't the slightest intention of accepting from you, it's an attitude of indifference. I guess that isn't what I meant to say, but what I mean is that you have always been my favorite cousin, and I intend to keep it that way.

"P.S. (This in pencil) I'm glad you didn't marry that sissy girl from Grafton."

March 26, 1940
Camp Jabrin

Yesterday we had another sandstorm more violent than any we've had before. Tonight we received permission to make the Laila trip and shall be off in two or three days. I still love you, but do not expect any mail from me for two or three weeks.

Bismarck – April 19, 1940

You said you wanted my police description – how disillusioning for you, but here it goes! 5'6 1/2" tall, waist 25, hips 34, bust 33, dress size 14, hat size 22, gloves 6 ¾ and shoes 8AAA.

I love white turbans and white gloves and spicy perfume. My favorite dress colors are black and white. I adore huge chunky jewelry and tall dark men with curly black hair and twinkly brown eyes.

You are planning on my meeting you, aren't you? Because if you aren't I'm coming anyway. I'm afraid that your folks will be a bit upset, still not believing that we are married, but it might be sort of exciting, this living in sin. I know you think I'm wicked, but everything seems exciting and funny now – even trouble.

Oh, yes, about Jane, had you forgotten that we are old school mates? I remember her as a vivacious, ashen-blonde and a bit sophisticated. I'm anxious to see her again and can tell she will be eager to help me reform you from a fair-haired childhood.

Kathleen dressed for a formal night out in San Francisco, 1940

A samra *tree in Wadi al-Shadiya, northeast of Sulaiyl*

Chapter 16
"To Laila, Sulaiyl and the Wadi Dawasir"

April 17, 1940
Camp Jabrin

Fixing cars, shooting stars, and long days completely wrecked my good intentions of writing a little to you each day of our trip.

First off, besides our own crew, we had to take 10 soldiers from Hofuf with us, which meant we needed an extra Autocar truck to haul them. Salih's eyes grew wide when he saw the contingent arrive. He said, "The field parties have never seen soldiers like these before. These are soldiers of war."

Their Emir was one Muhammad bin Mansur, chief tax collector for Bin Jiluwi, sent by special designation of the King himself. Of his nine soldiers, all tough-looking customers, four were also Emirs occasionally sent out from Hofuf in charge of their own detachments. They had on their Sunday clothes, and in addition to knives and cartridge belts, (practically standard dress for a desert Arab) most of them wore bandoleers and carried Mauser pistols.

On April Fool's Day, Johnny, Dick Bramkamp and I, 15 soldiers, our soldier's cook, our cook, our houseboy and three drivers left here in two Autocars, two pickups, and a sedan. The Emir rode in the sedan with us, as befitted his rank.

The first day out, while our convoy stopped for lunch on the east side of the Dahna, Johnny, Dick and I went ahead with the sedan to scout a road for the trucks. On our return, we had our first of the rosewater-flavored tea.

One of the soldiers named Faraj is Bin Jiluwi's special tea maker, but since Bin Jiluwi was in Riyadh visiting the King, Bin Mansur brought him on the trip. A burly, grinning fellow, he had a favored place and rode with Johnny in the pickup whenever we had to take one of the guides in the sedan. He had the rosewater in an old John Haig bottle that was carefully handled. The tea was fine, neither too sweet nor too bitter, and the rosewater was just enough to give it a rose smell without affecting the taste.

That night we camped west of the Dahna sand in a rocky, desolate region called the Haraisan. Muhammad bin Mansur was somewhat puzzled by our work, especially the business of driving the sedan in the straightest possible line, up and down hills, over rocks, bushes, and gullies. It wasn't until we started home from Sulaiyl that he began to realize that hunting was only incidental to the work and not our chief interest in life.

As we came from the east across a flat plain, the palms of Saih and Laila showed up first as dark blobs dancing in the mirage and gradually settled down to dark masses of trees as we approached closer. There were a lot of outlying ruins of mud *qasrs*, reminders of the turbulent times before the peace of Ibn Saud. The two main towns, Laila and Saih, are about three or four miles apart, separated by a belt of dunes. We crossed them and made camp on a sandy plain about a quarter of a mile away from Laila. Actually both Laila and Saih are made up of several small villages, but the palm trees all merge together. Laila is the seat of the governor and the only town with a market place.

The soldiers of Muhammad bin Mansur

Bin Mansur put on his fanciest clothes and sent three of his soldiers into town to announce our arrival to the local Emir. Quite a few people, accompanied by a horde of ragged small boys, came running out to see our caravan, but no one came very near. In a little while, the Emir and all the soldiers set out for town in the small cars to pay their official respects.

Our own Emir, Abdul Aziz, was quite overshadowed by the entourage from Hofuf. Laila is his hometown, so he went off to his family. Muhammad bin Mansur came back about an hour before sunset to say we had been invited to dinner with the governor. We unpacked our *bishts* and our fancy white *ghutras* and put on clean shirts. As dinner was arranged for our convenience, we went in at eight o'clock, after we had radioed Dhahran. Winding our way over irrigation ditches and through narrow streets, the effect of our entrance was marred somewhat because the sedan developed a short circuit in its lighting system, so our parade was lead by a pickup truck.

The Emir of Laila was in Riyadh, so his son greeted us. We arranged ourselves along the wall of a large courtyard covered with carpets and lighted by a few feeble kerosene lanterns. As headman of our party, I sat beside the Emir's son. I believe his name was Muhammad, but it didn't matter, as we addressed him in the third person as "Oh, Emir."

After a round of coffee and tea, the servants brought in two huge round platters and placed them on foot-high pedestals in front of us. The host does not eat with his guests, but the rest of us crowded round, kneeling on one knee with the right hand in action. The platters were heaped with boiled wheat gruel, overlaid with rice, and covered with the broken-up carcasses of a whole sheep and numerous chickens, all more or less soaked in animal fat and ghee.

The Emir, Bin Mansur, and his soldiers saw to it we had plenty of detached pieces of meat – it's sort of awkward trying to rip chunks off a shank of mutton with your right hand only. In the Aflaj, the name of this entire province, rice is a luxury because of the distance to the coast; homegrown wheat is the staple of their diet. I like it better than rice, and it's easier to knead into a ball to pop into your mouth. The food was well cooked, so we all feasted. When we finished, we wished the blessings of God on our host, who replied in kind; then we washed up and left.

We had ceased our map work east of Laila in order to make camp before dark, so the next day we resumed there and mapped our way around the south side of Saih. Here we found several massive clay *qasrs*, one in good preservation, and the marks of walls and buildings of a fairly large town. The structures seemed to be very old, but no one around here knew much about them. The *qasrs* are called "Qasrs of Ad." Ad was the great semi-mythical king of the lost city, Wabar, in the Rub' al-Khali. He is mentioned in the Koran as an example of a proud monarch overtaken by the wrath of God.

A little farther on, we visited the northernmost of the great springs that at sometime in the past supplied water for an extensive irrigation system, as seen by the ruined network of old canals. Some of the canals still divert water to the gardens of Saih, though the flow is sluggish. They must be nearly choked with the debris of centuries.

The canals are of a type called *khariz*, which still can be seen in many places, including the Qatif oasis just north of Dhahran. At first the canals were open ditches, as at Qatif; later they were covered to keep out the wind-blown sand, and manholes were put in at intervals. Eventually sand dunes began to encroach on the manholes so the farmers built up the masonry around them to stay above the sand level. Now in Qatif there are many places where the sand dunes have passed on to leave the manholes standing along the course of the canal like a row of tall chimneys. The manholes in the canals from the Aflaj wells may have been built when the canals were originally dug, as some of the ditches are very deep.

The next day we came back and spent the whole morning mapping the six wells. The deepest was 85 feet of clear blue water. We went swimming in the largest one. Three-quarters of a mile long by a quarter mile wide, it is undoubtedly the largest permanent lake in Arabia. All of these wells had abandoned canals that stretched into the now-barren desert.

The second night in Laila, we had dinner with our own Emir, Abdul Aziz. It was chiefly noteworthy for the display of the sheep on our platter. The sheep's head was placed upside down, so the jaws were flopped wide open. Johnny was particularly taken with the one-handed wrestling with the intestines; they showed remarkable toughness and elasticity.

Then Faraj had quite a struggle popping out one of the sheep's eyes, but he finally worked his thumb under it and made it all right in the end. It's just as well that the light was dim; we had dinner later at Sulaiyl with Muhammad bin Mansur in the light of our own Coleman lanterns, and though the rice was excellent, the sheep didn't appear too appetizing in the glare.

The Aflaj has changed considerably since Philby's visit 23 years ago. In that year, the *wadis* coming down from the Tuwaiq Mountains flowed seven times. Now it has been nine years since the last general rain. In the shallow *wadi* beds east of the settlements and on the 10-mile broad plain to the west, numerous thickets of large thorn trees attest to the former rainfall. Now the ground is almost bare of bushes and grasses.

Nearly all of their sheep, goats and cows have been killed because there is only enough fodder to feed the donkeys that draw the water for the gardens. Prices for dates and nearly all foodstuffs are four to five times as great as in Hofuf.

The third day we made a trip up one of the main *wadis* into the Tuwaiqs. It was great for geology, because all the rocks are exposed in the canyon walls. We reached Wasit, a small town whose palms stretched for nearly a mile along the *wadi* bottom.

Except for our arrival, so few people appeared to visit our camp at Laila one might have thought that the town was deserted. We later found out that the people had been ordered to stay away from us, but at Wasit we were the first foreigners in the first cars ever to be seen, and the people came running. The black-masked women sat at a respectful distance, but the men came close. We climbed a low cliff to photograph the town, which was alive with a great hum of voices, and I could hear the Arabic word for cars, *Sayaraat,* shouted from half a mile away.

From Laila we went south, keeping well east of the torrent gullies coming down from Tuwaiq, and past the towns and ruins of the Aflaj scattered along for some 20 miles. The day was hot with a south wind, but at sunset black clouds came up from the west along with a north breeze. About midnight we awoke to a terrific blast of dust and south wind accompanied by lightning and thunder. We covered everything and rolled up our beds and put them in the kitchen tent. With all the fuss, there was less than 15 minutes of rain, so we unrolled our beds in the kitchen and slept on the ground the rest of the night.

In the morning the *shamaal* came out of the north, and by eleven o'clock the sand and dust so filled the air, it was impossible to continue our map work. That afternoon we went up a small *wadi* into the Tuwaiq Mountains. Our road was finally blocked by pools of rainwater from the storm of the previous night. We spent several hours examining the rocks in the cliffs, while the soldiers had a good time bathing and sleeping in the shade of some big thorn trees.

On the day before yesterday, we had made camp near one of the few wells on the road to Sulaiyl, but on our return from this *wadi,* we learned that, after straining out most of the worms, the men had managed to fill only one barrel with very bad water. So the soldiers went back to the rain pools and filled up with water. Though this water was cloudy with dirt and sand, it wasn't muddy and it was worm free.

The following day there was more wind and dust as we continued to drive south. By noon of the next day, we were at Sulaiyl, the oasis at the east end of the great gap cut through the Tuwaiq range by Wadi Dawasir. We pitched camp before a large, friendly audience of local people.

The qasr of Hamam, northeast of Sulaiyl. Of the 17 palm trees and two ithil *trees of Philby's visit in 1918, only one lonely* ithil *tree had survived.*

Our warm reception in Sulaiyl was quite a contrast to Laila. We had entered Laila only twice in the evening for dinner, so we encountered no hostility, but our party did. It seems the Lailaites would not return the "*Salaams*" of our soldiers and had even refused to sell meat to "the servants of infidels." Though it is said they refuse to "*Salaam*" all strangers, Bin Mansur's men considered this to be an affront not only to themselves, but to Ibn Saud, as they were his representatives.

After our return here, we heard the soldiers had decided that if we camped at Laila on the return trip, they would go into town and beat anyone who did not return their "*Salaams.*" They would have been quite capable of it, too, and if need arose, they carried enough ammunition on their persons to stage a small war. At Sulaiyl, the Emir was kept busy receiving and returning invitations to coffee, and the people even returned the "*Salaams*" of us infidels.

Sulaiyl is a medium-sized town of 2,000 people with two or three mud villages clustered around the outskirts of the palm groves. The trees are irrigated from wells 75 feet deep; the water is drawn by camels. More recent rains in the last two or three years make the desert a little greener than around Laila. The Wadi Dawasir here cuts a great gap in the Tuwaiq Mountains. There are many small settlements in the valley, but the main group of towns lies about 40 miles west of Sulaiyl. We did not visit them, as our work took us only to the west side of the mountains. It was just as well, as the towns of "the Wadi" have a worse reputation for fanatical bigotry than even Laila.

On the second day in camp, we came in from work to find a young lad between 8 to 10 years old with a badly swollen leg that was festered and scabbed from ankle to knee. He had fallen off a camel and hurt it. It had swollen up, and after 25 days the pus had broken out in running sores. This had been six months ago.

He was a manly little fellow who moaned a little, but did not whine or cry, and almost invariably addressed me with, "God lengthen your life, 0, my uncle." I told him to soak his leg twice a day in hot water containing a little salt and keep a clean cloth over the sores to keep out the flies. When he came back the next evening, I was surprised to find that the swelling had gone down, and it did look better. I gave him a handful of clean cloths and a couple of Maria Theresa dollars amid general benedictions by him and his friends.

If he continues the soaking as directed, he might recover; that is not die, though the leg probably will be nearly useless. These people have a remarkable resistance to infection; six months of such would, I suppose, kill an average American.

The morning we left Sulaiyl, we came out from breakfast to find another young boy of about 12 laid on a crude stretcher near our tent. His tearful father implored me for medicine; the boy was paralyzed from the hips downwards. In these cases, all you can do is take refuge in their fatalism, which they dare not deny, small though their comfort may be. "God has sent this on him, and if He wills, He will take it away. God is kind. I can do nothing for him, as I have no medicine for this sickness." God is kind, *Allah Kareem,* is the retort unanswerable.

We started out the first afternoon by crossing over to the south side of the w*adi* – Sulaiyl is on the north bank – and working westward. We confounded the local wisdom about roads because on our return Bin Mansur, before he heard where we had been, told us he had been collecting information and everyone said we could not cross anywhere nearby and would have to stay on the north side.

*The qasr and well of Hisy, the first watering place
south of Sulaiyl on the road to Najran*

I suspect that this was quite to his liking, as there was a great, flat thorn-tree-covered plain to the northwest that looked like a fine place for gazelle. However, we had crossed the *wadi* and persisted in our madness by crossing again the next morning to pick up our survey from where we had left off. This time we picked another route because our first crossing through the bushes and great sand mounds of the *wadi* bottom was the worst strip of terrain I have ever driven. The task was complicated further by the need to drive in a straight line as we traversed from one hill to another.

The third day we went south to within our new concession territory, which begins 30 miles south of Wadi Dawasir. We are the first Americans to ever visit this area.

We had lunch at a place called Hisy. A drawworks over the well, operated by a donkey, watered a small garden; next to it, there was a mud fort occupied by a Dawasir family. There was a large pile of dry seeds from the bright yellow desert gourd called *sheriy*. It is about the size of a canteloupe and looks as if it ought to be good to eat. I suppose that nearly every geologist over here has a hunch that they are not as bitter as they are reputed to be, until he has tried one. These seeds must be a poor sort of food.

The soldiers made coffee in the shade of an overhanging cliff and had guests from the fort, including a very old man who was so dried up and wrinkled that he looked like a human prune. He was a good-natured old chap and laughed at the soldiers' jokes. His voice was low and husky; it was evident that it took some effort for him to speak, but he was easy to understand, probably because the effort made him more simple and concise than most Arabs. The soldiers said he looked old enough to be the brother of Ad, the King of Wabar. They asked him, "0, Brother of Ad, how old are you?"

He replied, "*Mubty,*" which cracked up the soldiers. It roughly means older than ancient, but is a difficult word to translate exactly. Ours were the first cars he had ever seen. When the men asked if he would like to ride in our sedan back to his *qasr*, he answered, "I will go by foot. I have gone a long way on these feet."

On our way home we shot several gazelle; on the whole trip there was hardly a day when we didn't have gazelle meat. We took three days to make the trip back to Laila, as we stopped for a day and a half to do some work near the midpoint, Khafs Maqran. At Laila we stopped only long enough to take on water. We made camp west of the Dahna, worked around the neighborhood and discovered some of the most important geological information of the whole trip. The same afternoon Muhammad bin Mansur went out with the second pickup truck and shot 16 gazelles. Apparently the Emir is never satiated.

Three generations. The old man, Lord of the Qasr of Hisy, was undoubtedly the oldest human being I had seen in Arabia

Bismarck – March 26, 1940

Don't you know that I will be a nervous wreck if you don't get home soon and if you don't come some other way than the Atlantic? Honestly I shall worry every minute. I'd almost rather have you stay, and that's saying something. The Atlantic is simply laden with magnetic mines, and they have no respect for any ship, regardless of national affiliation. I love you so much, and now that you are so near I simply can't lose you.

Why don't I like New York? I don't like the dismal hours I wept alone in a hotel room and the last night holding you in my arms and knowing that you would go and that I might never have you just like that again. Eating crumpets and tea alone when my head ached from emptiness. New York to me is gray and cold, and hope is gone. San Francisco is warm and sunny, even in the fog, because it's new hope and full of so many foolish, wonderful dreams.

No fooling, my knees won't be able to hold me up when I see your little old countenance beaming over the deck. This Johnny person sounds like an obstreperous upstart, the very idea of putting ideas into your head about me not staying up after 9 p.m.

During our trip to Wadi Dawasir, Khamis came to me and asked if I thought that the North Star had moved. At first I didn't know what he meant, but he explained some more and said that as far as he could tell, the North Star wasn't in the proper place. Since he had never been this far south, I assumed at the time that because we were in an unknown country, maybe his built-in compass was a bit off. It wasn't until many years later that I realized that he was indeed right. Having traveled about three degrees of latitude or more than two hundred miles farther south than he had ever been, Khamis was now seeing the North Star from a completely different angle, and it would be right to say that that it had moved. I doubt if there are more than a half a dozen men on earth that would have noticed the difference.

Khamis with two of Bin Mansur's soldiers in the Wadi Dawasir. The Tuwaiq Escarpement is in the background.

April 20, 1940
Camp Jabrin

Max brought me five letters from you, and I was very *mabsut*, happy. As is usual when he is here, there is a whirlwind of activity. Up at five this morning, we have been working almost continuously until now, after nine at night.

We are to go in from the field May 15, and I hope to leave here for you and home between the 15th and 20th of July. If the war doesn't spread, the usual method of going home is by boat to Basra, Italian airline to Genoa, and Italian or U.S. Line boat to New York. Thus, I should be in New York about the second week in August. Apparently I must go to San Francisco to check in, make arrangements for the return trip and so on, and then we start our vacation.

April 26, 1940
Camp Jabrin

The weather has at last caught up with us, and it is blistering hot. We start work at 5:30 a.m. At lunchtime we hunt around for a shadowy cliff or the rare tree and doze and sweat for two or three hours at midday. The tent cools off about two hours after sundown, while we sit outside and read. Even though I spent a couple of hours sewing cheesecloth curtains over the doors to the tent, we are honored tonight with a horde of various sorts of small bugs. After six months at this campsite, we are finally moving about 30 miles away to the top of a hill. This sand cup we are in was a fine location in the winter, but now it acts like a sort of superheated reflector.

Our generator ran out of gasoline, so we're now using a Coleman that has an advantage over the electric light in that it incinerates a certain number of the more active bugs.

In reply to your sketch of your office, I send one of ours. In hot weather we have two doors; in cool weather, only one, its location depending on the wind's direction. This sketch is the daytime arrangement; at night, Johnny pops another tin trunk out from under his bed, and I drag the medicine chest from beneath mine. I have not shown my four pairs of shoes, all in the last stages of decay. Johnny has only one whole shirt. It's good that we only have a couple of weeks left in the field.

Keep me away from your Arabic-speaking Syrian friend or else prime him beforehand, so we can make words at one another and I can keep my reputation as an Arabist intact. Did I not tell you about the storekeeper in Beirut to whom I spoke in Arabic for about five minutes before he asked me if I were a Bedouin? We got along fine, but I was definitely not speaking the Arabic of the Syrian towns.

I am not quite certain on the question of breakfast in bed for slaves. It is said that the Koran enjoins the kind treatment of slaves, and in this Moslem country you should have some hope on that score. On the other hand I am not sure, after observing the treatment of wives, as to whether the precept applies to female slaves. I shall probably weaken and come running when you crack your whip.

The war seems to be steadily increasing in volume. From all I can gather, the Germans bit off a large chunk in Norway, and, as far as their navy is concerned, the campaign has been little short of disastrous. The big danger in the north for the neutrals is that the Allies will press the Germans so hard in Norway that Hitler may try to relieve his forces through Sweden and/or by creating a diversion in Belgium and Holland.

The soldiers' saluki is barking, so either our truck is coming or our nightly visitor, the hyena, is at hand. Said hyena has never been seen, but he leaves fresh tracks around the camp. No sound of the truck, so it must have been the hyena.

Bismarck – March 30, 1940

It is just not possible for me to keep my mind on anything but summer and you. I intend to go home to Medora and rest for two months, and then you shall have no rest for the remainder of your life – isn't that simply awful to look forward to?

I have visions of myself a nervous wreck by August. My supervisor says that I look like a different person already. Guess she was afraid I was getting to be a bit of a hag or a crank. I'm sure the girls did. Mother marvels that I managed to retain my youth as well as I have amongst these old maids, but then I guess I have held my own quite well – though I'm sure they all think me to be an utter flutterbug.

Goodbye, my love, and Phooey! to Johnny.

April 29,1940
Camp Jabrin

Our truck goes in tomorrow, so I must finish this tonight. It is still hotter than hell. We found out today that the new area we are working is so darn complicated it will take more than a couple of weeks to finish it properly, and even then it is doubtful if we'd know any more about its oil possibilities than we do now. All of this means that we may go in before the 15th of next month.

It occurs to me that maybe you are not particularly enthusiastic about coming to New York to meet me. If so, speak up, my lass; if you do not relish the trip, I will meet you in North Dakota, and we will go on to San Francisco together, spending some of the time and money saved on the New York trip in Yellowstone, Yosemite, and Sequoia. After three winters of flat Arabian desert, my eyes, despite the Kashmir and Lebanon treatments, ache for some forest-covered mountains. Anyway, my long-neglected wife, you name your heart's desires, and I shall do my best. I might, at that, enjoy riding in the mountains more than a New York nightclub, and it is possible that I might be prevailed upon to sleep in a tent.

They have a bar and beer in the Jebel now. It is sold only in glasses to make sure none is carried away to fall into the hands of good Muslims. Our last batch of groceries from the Jebel came down crated in empty Anheuser-Busch boxes. Johnny, almost foaming at the mouth, came in to tell me about it.

May 15, 1940
Dhahran

In from the desert at last, I have put off writing to you for a couple of days so I could sort of get straightened around and make a few inquiries about this and that. Yesterday I was told to put my trunks on a boat about to sail from Bahrain, so as to have them home before I arrive, but last night's news was so disquieting, I have decided I am in no hurry to send my trunks. I may be coming home via the Pacific right along with them. It certainly looks as if the Italians are fixing to enter into the mess. If so, I shall certainly not be crossing the Mediterranean. Army is considerably worried, as Matilda is now in Genoa on her way home. She should catch a boat out of there the day after tomorrow.

Yes, we undoubtedly need a car. Unless you will be absolutely desolate, I vote against a convertible coupe as not having as great a resale value as a sedan or standard coupe. My old car I sold in Linton before I came over here and applied it on my debts. Didn't you know, Kath, you married me in a most deplorable financial condition?

The time of our departure for Arabia will depend upon my arrival. I will have about two and a half months of vacation due me. I will probably spend anywhere from a week to two weeks in the San Francisco office – say three months total.

The Mass yesterday was probably the first in Arabia for hundreds of years. Two days ago, Ted Clausing, a chap in the marine department, drove his car off the pier at Ras Tanura and was drowned. They wired for Fr. Lewis, that night and he came over from Bahrain today.

Investigation determined that Mrs. Clausing was a Catholic, but Ted was not. I was drafted to set up the altar in the auditorium until this information left my arrangements in the air. After talking with Mrs. Clausing, Father appeared and said, "Yes, I will say Mass. He might have wanted to become a Catholic, and, anyway, he is a Christian in a far away land." So we had a regular requiem Mass, and probably two-thirds of the audience didn't know what it was all about, especially as there was no sermon.

Father Lewis has been in Bahrain for just a year and has already built a new church, is starting a school in loaned rooms this fall, and will build a school later if attendance warrants. "And the big joke is with no money. Ve'll show dem what we Catholics can do." Says he has an assistant coming, "Only 25, but with a voice like Caruso."

I am going to try sending this by Transatlantic Clipper, Kath, in hopes that it will reach you somewhat sooner than regular airmail. I'm told that letters so sent have made the trip in nine days.

Bismarck – June 4, 1939

Just received your letter of May 15th, which came by Transatlantic Clipper. I shall try sending mine that way since this undoubtedly will be the last to you. The thought of waiting until September for you makes me fitful but I'd rather you were safer. I am sure you'll start as soon as you can. I have decided that I shall meet you in San Francisco; we have waited so long, and we simply must be together alone. Coming to North Dakota directly would mean a good many family complications, which will probably be more humorous than tragic at a later date.

I have lost all capabilities for formulating an expression of my love for you; if only you could know, but I am sure you do. Be safe and come home soon.

May 31, 1940
Dhahran

I haven't written sooner because I was unable to tell when and how you might expect me. Today it is settled. I have a reservation on the *S.S.President Garfield*, an American ship due to leave Bombay on July 10th, or later. It seems the best all around arrangement.

The big factor of uncertainty is, of course, Italy. The *President Garfield* is one of the boats on the around-the-world run, going west from New York and returning there across the Atlantic. By catching it at Bombay, I have three ways of getting home: through the

Mediterranean on its regular route, around the Horn and across the Atlantic, or back across the Pacific, in case the Mediterranean is closed and the Atlantic too risky.

It is still difficult to make any plans, but at least I shall get there. It would be faster to fly to Hong Kong and catch an American boat across the Pacific. However, should Italy go to war, it is likely that the airlines here would either cease or be reserved for military personnel, and I would be left stranded with no reservations on a boat.

The French news tonight sounded ominous; they all but said that the entry of Italy into the war was inevitable. It is hard to see what Italy will gain by war. If she and Germany win, Mussolini, as Dick Kerr says, will have the seat of honor at the foot of the table. Win or lose, the Italians will take a terrific walloping from the Allies in the process.

June 29, 1940
Dhahran

Don't ask me how I am coming home. No one knows, least of all me, but I shall come home to you as soon as I can. Boat service in the Persian Gulf has been cut down, at least temporarily, to one slow boat a week. The immediate game is to try to get Army Armstrong and me out by plane to catch the *President Garfield* from Bombay, in which case we will sail around the Cape of Good Hope and on to New York. Another possibility is a plane to Singapore, plane or boat to Manila, and thence across the Pacific. Still another is to wait a month and catch the next President boat in Bombay.

It is kind of hard to make plans, my darling, when we don't know just when or where we should make them. There is also some doubt as to whether we will be coming back here at all. It depends on the war. The company may cut exploration to a minimum, so that they wouldn't need many geologists. No one here knows just what will happen, nor, I suppose, does any one in San Francisco know more. Anyway, by the time I get home and have some vacation, the situation may have clarified somewhat. We shall see.

Going Home

July 15th, 1940, Army Armstrong and I left Bahrain on a BOAC flying boat to Calcutta. From there, we flew a small four-engine monoplane over the mountains into China and landed in Hanoi, where the Japanese were already in evidence at the airport. We flew on to Hong Kong, waited a week, and then took a Martin Flying Boat to Guam, Wake Island, Midway, Honolulu and, finally, San Francisco and Kathleen.

Kathleen with Tom in San Francisco – 1940

We went on a short holiday and returned to San Francisco, where I did some work for Doc Nomland. Then we went on vacation, making our way back to North Dakota. While we were at her parents' house in Medora, the Italians bombed Bahrain and Dhahran, which ruined our plan to return to Arabia together. Though this attack turned out to be a harmless accident, at the time it was serious enough that Casoc refused to let any dependents travel to Arabia. I had no intention of leaving Kathleen again, so at the end of vacation, we returned to San Francisco via several places where I thought I might be able to find a job, but the job market was still poor and I found no decent prospects.

In San Francisco, we lived in an apartment while I did a series of jobs for Doc Nomland and tried to either obtain permission to take my wife to Arabia or be reassigned to another country where she could accompany me. Both efforts were in vain. Finally Doc Nomland ran out of jobs for me to do; it was after Christmas, and I had to make a decision.

Years later, Kath told me that Max had taken her out to lunch and said, "Kathleen, you just have to let Tom go back to Arabia; you've just got to. It's going to be a big operation, and some day he's going to run the whole thing. You've just got to let him go back."

So, I went back to Arabia.

l-r. Phil McConnell, author of **The Hundred Men,**
Max and Dick Bramkamp in the late 1940's

Epilogue

It took Tom 15 days to travel to Arabia in 1937; the second trip back took more than two months. Tom and Kathleen sailed together from San Francisco to Honolulu, and the day after they arrived, March 7, 1941, they once again had to say goodbye.

Traveling aboard the *S.S. President Jackson* to Kobe, Japan, followed by Shanghai, Hong Kong, Manila, Singapore, Da Nang and Colombo in Ceylon, he finally arrived in Bombay, India, nearly six weeks later. After languishing in Bombay for two weeks, he managed to hitch a ride on an empty tanker returning to Bahrain and finally landed at Jabal Dhahran on May 17, 1941, to discover that he was the first American to arrive at Casoc in 1941.

Virtually all of the other Americans who were traveling were leaving the country, and Dhahran was becoming deserted rapidly. In January of 1940, there were 360 Americans and 3,500 Saudis working for the company; by the time he arrived, there were fewer than 300 Americans and 2,300 Saudis remaining in the workforce. By the end of 1941, at the time of the Japanese attack on Pearl Harbor, there were barely 100 Americans and 1,600 Saudis working at Casoc.

This was the time of the Hundred Men, so well documented in Phil McConnell's book of the same name. This skeleton crew responded to serious shortages of manpower, supplies and transportation with creative thinking. In one example, most of the materials necessary for drilling the first well at at Abqaiq, Abqaiq No. 1, now the single most-important oil producing center in the world, were hauled to the new field by a massive camel train organized by Khamis and Cal Ross.

Casoc's primary mission was to keep the Bapco refinery in Bahrain topped off, as its rated capacity exceeded the actual production of the Bapco field. This refinery was of critical importance in the war effort because Bahrain was three tanker-days closer to Suez than the refinery in Abadan. Given the general scarcity of tankers at that time in the war, three tanker-days were precious indeed.

All the field parties had been disbanded, and the geology department was reduced to Max, Dick Bramkamp and Tom as Max's assistant. After a great deal of discussion with Max, Tom made one of the most important decisions of his life and left geology to work for Roy Lebkicher in government relations.

(The following is excerpted from Tom Barger's papers, circa 1982)

Before I made up my mind to take the government relations job, I also talked to Roy Lebkicher who was in charge of organizing Casoc's Government Relations Department. Originally a geologist, Roy had been drafted into negotiating concessions for the company and, by now, had been working in Standard Oil of California's London office for some time. He was not only a competent man, but also a congenial, well-liked person who was respected by everyone who knew him. Roy's plan was to set up a service within Standard of California, in which the personnel would be people who knew the language and culture of the country in which they were operating, so they easily could carry out the routine details of the job. This department was to be methodically organized in such a way that once it was in operation, it could be used as an organizational model for similar units in Standard Oil's other foreign operations.

While trying to decide about working with Roy, I was still worrying about the prospect of becoming a father. Kathleen was pregnant when I left her in Hawaii, and the baby was expected around the first of September. This most wonderful addition to the human race, Ann Elizabeth, was born on the third of September, but I didn't learn about it until the cable arrived on the ninth. By this time, I was a nervous wreck, so I was overwhelmed with great joy and much relief when Floyd Ohliger came to me with the telegram announcing her birth.

On the twelfth of September 1941, I began my career in government relations with a staff of six men. First of all there was Floyd Wellman, a carpenter and all-around handyman, who had learned sufficient Arabic to handle drivers and the myriad problems we had with mechanical matters. Floyd was a mature, level-headed man who took much of the burden of routine requests on himself.

I had four translator/secretaries, none of whom would have qualified for such a position in the United States. I also had a typist as well as a tall, slow-spoken, somewhat taciturn Somali driver by the name of Juma'a. It took awhile to get to know him, but Juma'a was an absolute jewel, a born diplomat in his quiet way – absolutely trustworthy and a joy to have around.

My opposite number, the government's local representative was Shaikh Abdullah Al Fadl, who reported directly to Shaikh Abdullah Sulaiman, the King's right-hand man. Abdullah Al Fadl was a real gentleman, utterly honest, open and frank, with a good sense of humor. He disliked some of the wrangles that we became embroiled in – not necessarily he and I, but wrangles with third parties that sometimes put us both in uncomfortable positions. His English was quite good. He had been in the diplomatic service, and when he finally left his post in the Eastern Province, he became the Saudi ambassador to Syria.

Shaikh Abdullah Al Fadl was a Najdi from central Arabia; his assistant, Salih Islam, was from the Hejaz on the western coast of Arabia. When Salih first took the position of assistant to Shaikh Abdullah, he decided that he ought to learn English. To do so, he started out with a dictionary, and by time he got to C, he decided that there had to be an easier way to learn English than using an Arabic-to-English dictionary. Several of us helped him to study, and he became a great reader of English books, devouring about one a week, which I brought him from our library. He was not so adept with spoken English because he had no formal training in grammar, and his mastery of the nuances in spoken English left much to be desired. On the other hand, he understood written English superbly.

l-r. Salih Islam, Shaikh Abdulla Al Fadl and his brother, Abdul Wahhab Al Fadl, in the late 1940's

Salih Islam was a man of considerable vision. He did not shrink from making unpleasant decisions, as some others in the government were prone to do. In my judgment, he was absolutely fair in the various matters of controversy in which the company from time to time became involved, and he was, as I was fond of saying, the first "Saudi" that I had ever met.

This meant that without any qualifications, he regarded himself as a citizen of Saudi Arabia. Almost without exception, everyone else – government officials and all – would define themselves according to their traditional family or territorial background. If you asked a man who came from central Arabia what he was, he would say a Nejdi; if he came from Jiddah, he was a Hejazi. If he came from the desert, he might be a Murra, or as in Khamis's case an Ajmi from the Ajman. But no one else in those days would have said he was a Saudi. It was only after the development of a stronger central government bureaucracy that people began to think of themselves as Saudi Arabs.

It was fitting to me that Salih was responsible for perhaps the single most important element in the early development of a Saudi consciousness. After Pearl Harbor, the government decreed that all personal radio receivers were to be confiscated as a national security precaution. Naturally this caused a great howling in camp where our only connection with the outside world was the radio. We went to see Salih, and he was more outraged than we were. He said that if the government took the radios from the people, they wouldn't be able to hear what the government said. Facts would be replaced with rumors and lies. He took that argument to Riyadh and eventually prevailed; the ban was lifted. The increasing proliferation of personal radios, and the reporting of news from other countries that designated the Kingdom as Saudi Arabia, instilled in the people a sense of nationhood. They came to consider themselves as Saudi citizens.

And so began Tom's career in government relations. In 1944 the name of the company was changed to the Arabian American Oil Company, Aramco. Along with the name change came the understanding that the company would accelerate Saudi participation in the company's operations. Tom realized that this would not be accomplished without decisive action on his part. In 1948, he wrote an internal report that defined in broad outline the problems faced by Aramco and called for company programs designed to increase Aramco's social, educational and economic involvement in Saudi Arabian life. In particular, he advocated establishing training programs for young Saudis so that they could advance within the company along with their American counterparts. The farsightedness of this report assured that the company and Tom Barger would have a long and fruitful association.

Max Steineke continued as Aramco's chief geologist until 1950 when his health began to deteriorate. In Dhahran at the inauguration of Steineke Hall, Aramco's guest house for visiting managers and consultants, F. A. "Fred" Davies, Aramco's chairman of the board and a geologist himself, honored Max for his vision in these words: "It was Max's unflagging optimism that had a lot to do with the decision that was made at the time to carry the drilling deeper to a horizon that had never been tried and in which oil had never before been found. The result of that deep test was Well Number Seven and the first discovery of Saudi Arabian oil in commercial quantities."

In 1951 Max was awarded the Sidney Powers Gold Medal Memorial Award of the American Association of Petroleum Geologists, the greatest honor within his profession. At the ceremony, Max was cited as the man responsible for "the structural drilling method, which was so widely applied later in Saudi Arabia and has resulted in the discovery of so much oil. The methods he developed in the area probably resulted in the discovery of greater reserves than the work of any other single geologist."

His eventual passing in 1952 at the relatively young age of 54 brought great sorrow to all who knew him. In the closing words of the citation delivered at his award ceremony, "He never shirked hardship and never asked those who worked with him to do as much as he did himself. He always gave full credit to others, and for these just and friendly qualities he became a natural leader."

A desert companion and a true friend of Steineke, Khamis bin Rimthan continued working for the government as a soldier-guide until 1942, when he joined the company. He earlier had bestowed on Max an honor, that was in Max's eyes, the Bedouin equivalent of the Sidney Powers Award. It occurred during one of their last trips together to the Wadi Dawasir.

In that area there is a stubby *jabal* with vertical sides and a flat top. Its name was *Um Ruqaibah,* Mother of the Neck, but Khamis said that the Bedu had changed the name to *Usba' Steineke,* Finger of Steineke, and no one uses the old name anymore. Steinke overheard this reference to his finger and was told that the *jabal* had been named after his short finger, the one that had been amputated following an infection. It seems that this was one of the few times in his life that Max was at a loss for words.

Khamis worked for the company as a guide and advisor until his early death at age 50 in 1959. Though he knew more English than he ever let on, he never learned formal English and turned down many opportunities for advancement as an employee. A proud Bedouin, he preferred to live his life in his own way, and that integrity, as well as his gentle manner, resulted in a contented man, wealthy in friends and their respect. In 1974, Aramco named a newly discovered oil field the Rimthan field in honor of Khamis.

In February 1945, more than seven years after they were married, Kathleen joined Tom in Saudi Arabia, and they finally began an actual married life together. They had five more children, four of them born in Saudi Arabia, and, eventually 13 grandchildren. Ever since she was a young girl, Kathleen had dreamed of living in Arabia, and she made the most of what in the early days was a difficult situation for a young mother and housewife. She helped to organize the Hobby Farm, a riding stable for employees, so that she could ride in the desert and perform in Arabian rodeos, the main difference being that they were more genteel affairs called gymkhanas.

She was Tom's best friend, his confidante, and last, but not least, a professional hostess. Throughout most of their time in Arabia, there were no hotels or restaurants, so the hundreds of visitors who came to Aramco annually were feted at the homes of Aramco executives. Kathleen, who had grown up on a dude ranch in North Dakota, knew how to feed and entertain dozens of guests at a time, and in Arabia she applied that expertise with grace.

Her energy was boundless, and when she and a group of dedicated Aramco women began raising funds for the Pontifical Mission for Palestine, a charity mission to help the millions of Palestinian refugees and their descendants displaced by the Arab- Israeli war, Kathleen became relentless. Stories are told about her tracking down hapless Aramco old-timers at dinner parties and hounding them into donating their blood and pledging the blood stipend to the Pontifical Mission.

Tom worked as director of local government relations, company representative to the Saudi Arab government and manager of concession affairs. Additionally, he was a member of several Aramco committees appointed to establish long-range plans and policies. One of his proudest achievements was his contribution to the development of Aramco's home ownership program, which had helped more than 7,000 Saudi Arab employees finance their own homes by 1969.

In 1957 he was named vice president and assistant to Aramco President Norman Hardy. A year later he was appointed to the Aramco board of directors. In 1959 he succeeded Hardy as president and became chief executive officer after Mr. Hardy retired two years later. With the help of hundreds of superb professionals, Tom Barger presided over an unprecedented expansion of the company's oil-producing capacity. During his ten years in office, Aramco's output tripled from one million barrels a day to three millions barrels a day. Aramco was now far and away the largest independent oil-producing company in the world.

In 1968, he was elected chairman of the board of Aramco. A year later he retired to La Jolla, California, after spending more than half his life in Saudi Arabia. Two years later, after a long bout with cancer, Kathleen died on Christmas day, 1971, at the age of 54. It seemed unfair that someone so in love with life should die so young, and she was dearly missed, but never forgotten, by all who knew her.

Tom was then blessed with the second Kathleen in his life. Kathleen V. Loeb, who had lost her husband, Arthur, three years before, was the sister of Tom's best friend in college and had been a close friend and pen pal in his early life. After hearing quite belatedly, and coincidentally, of Kathleen's passing through her daughter, whose college roommate was the daughter of an Aramco employee; Kitty sent Tom a letter of condolence. Neither of them was quite prepared for the ensuing whirlwind courtship, which resulted in their marriage in Brevard, North Carolina. With three daughters of her own, Kitty became the mother of nine, and she and Tom presided over a growing tribe of grandchildren and great-grandchildren

In retirement, Tom served on the boards of a several major corporations, including Northrop, California First Bank and WD-40. He also consulted on Mid Eastern Oil Affairs for a variety of companies, lectured often on oil and politics and wrote, among other things, a book for the Center for the Study of Marine Policy entitled, *Energy Policies of the World: Arab States of the Persian Gulf.*

As fate would have it, one of the finest moments in Tom's career occurred fifteen years after he had retired. When King Abdul Aziz granted the original oil concession to Casoc, it was with the understanding that Saudis were to be trained in the oil business. At the time, this proviso was regarded by many as so much lip service, but Tom and a few others were convinced that this was not only desirable, but absolutely necessary. Throughout their careers, they worked to assure that Aramco's Saudi employees had world-class on-the-job training and virtually unlimited access to higher education.

In 1984, Shaikh Ali bin Ibrahim Al Naimi, the son of Bedouin parents who had started working for the company at the age of 12, became the first Saudi president of Saudi Aramco. Despite Tom's struggle with the illness that would eventually take his life, he cabled his congratulations to Ali. This was Shaikh Al Naimi's reply:

"Thank you for the kind congratulatory cable. I am proud and honored that you were one of the pioneers in shaping many a young Saudi Arab career. You, of all of Aramco's leaders, had the greatest vision when you supported the training effort of Saudi Arab employees during its early days of infancy. That visionary support and effort is bearing fruit now, and many executive positions are filled by Saudis because of that effort.

Thank you, again, and may God bless you and ease your current affliction, Ali I. Al Naimi"

Tom was extremely pleased to know that his efforts had made a difference and proud that he had been able to help honor the promise made to King Abdul Aziz so many years before. Had he lived longer, he would have been delighted to know that in 1995 Shaikh Al Naimi was made the Kingdom's Minister of Petroleum and Mineral Resources.

After nearly two years of a debilitating struggle with Parkinson's Disease, Tom Barger passed away June 30, 1986, at the age of seventy-seven. His son, Timothy, ended the eulogy at his father's funeral with the following words:

"The phrase 'Goodbye' isn't used in the Arabic language. Instead, they say, *'Fi aman Allah,'* which means 'Go in the care of God.' Dad, on behalf of all of us who loved you so very much, God bless you, and *Fi aman Allah.*"

Appendix One – The Water Wheel

Text of a Farewell speech given by Shaikh Muhammad 'Aqil, Director-General of the Dhahran Electric Power Company, at a retirement dinner for Thomas C. Barger, August 1969

Dear Mr. Barger,

I am pleased to present you this wooden wheel as a reminder and a symbol of our past poverty.

Mr. Barger, farmers in the Kingdom once used this wheel, along with donkeys, oxen and camels, to draw water from a depth of 100 to 500 feet. Such meager water as was drawn was not intended to provide drinking water, it was intended for farming. Just imagine the trifling amount of water produced by this wheel, and compare it with the tremendous prosperity ushered in by you and your colleagues as a result of your efforts to discover the black gold in our country.

Thanks to this discovery, the wheel, the donkey, the ox and the camel have been replaced. Now we have "wheel-less," highly productive water wheels operated by Blackstone, Ruston and whatnot engines; I really don't know all their names, as I am not a farmer.

Mr. Barger, thanks to these mechanical devices, the farmers in our beloved country have been able to do away with strenuous work and concentrate on developing their experience to the benefit of the people, who now enjoy unprecedented prosperity.

Mr. Barger, on the occasion of your departure (I use the word advisedly rather than "retirement") for your beloved America, please accept this wheel as a memento. You may keep it or you may throw it overboard into the ocean deep on your way home – the time for such wheels in our country has gone, never to return. And for who are we to thank for this? No doubt you, Mr. Barger, and your respected colleagues. to whom the people of this country are, and will be, eternally grateful for the happiness you have been instrumental in bringing about.

After 32 years of continuous service, crowned in brilliant success as the black gold gushes out of our land to bring prosperity to this country, I wish you a speedy and safe return home.

Appendix Two

Minutes from the Executive Committee Meeting of the Arabian American Oil Company held in New Your, New York, August 5, 1969

"The Secretary advised that Mr. Thomas C. Barger, Chairman of the Board of Directors of the Corporation, had submitted his resignation as Chairman and as a Director of the Corporation, effective August 31, 1969, so as to enter retirement. Then, upon motion duly made and seconded the following preambles and resolution were unanimously adopted:

"WHEREAS: For 32 years the Company has drawn in full measure on the talents, vision and dedicated service of Thomas C. Barger and,

"WHEREAS: The Board of Directors wishes to pay tribute to the man whose name is justly identified with the highest aspirations of the Company and the country in which he has lived and worked.

"RESOLVED: That the following statement be recorded in the minutes of the meeting:

"Born in Minneapolis, Minnesota, Thomas C. Barger became a North Dakotan soon afterwards, receiving his early schooling in Linton and graduating from the University of North Dakota in 1931 with a B.S. degree in Mining and Metallurgy. Six years later, following various jobs in the mining industry and a period of teaching at his Alma Mater, he was approached with a job offer from Aramco's predecessor, the California Arabian Standard Oil Company (Casoc)

"In December 1937, at the age of 28, Thomas Barger arrived in Saudi Arabia to work as a geologist. He quickly demonstrated a keen interest in all aspects of his new surroundings – language, customs, history, traditions, flora and fauna. As one of the pioneer explorers, he spent the first four years with mapping parties and was working in the Rub' al-Khaili when word came in that Dammam No. 7 had located Saudi Arabia's first commercial oil.

"Thomas Barger's eagerness to confront new challenges made it a foregone conclusion that he would be among the 'One Hundred Men,' who stayed behind during wartime to mind the store until the massive postwar expansion could get under way. It was predictable too, that his interest in and knowledge of the country and his developing proficiency in Arabic would channel him into government relations work, where he made important contributions from 1941 through 1957.

"During those 16 years he held such key posts as Assistant Manager, then Manager of Government Relations; General Manager, Concession Affairs; Director, Local Government Relations; and Company Representative to the Saudi Arab Government. Commanding early respect for his judgement and foresight, he was given a variety of special assignments. The upshot of one study was the Home Ownership Program, under which more than 7,000 homes have been financed by Saudi Arab employees.

" On December 31, 1957, he was elected a Vice President and named Assistant to the President. He succeeded Norman C. Hardy as President on May 20, 1959. He was named Chief Executive Officer on December 1, 1961, and Chairman of the Board on May 7, 1968, the post from which he reitires. He has served on the Trans-Arabian Pipeline Company's Board of Directors and was Vice Chairman of the Aramco Overseas Company.

" Thomas Barger looks back upon a career that must seem in many ways like an impossible dream. When he arrived , not a barrel of oil had been shipped. Today Aramco has produced more than ten billion barrels of crude oil and Saudi Arabia ranks among the top six oil-exporting countries. At one time, twice as many employees as the Company now has were producing about one-third the oil and less than half of the work force was Saudi Arab. Today, with production of nearly 3 million barrels daily, more than 80 per cent of the employees are Saudis.

"The communities of al-Khobar and Dammam were tiny fishing villages when he stepped ashore in 1937. Today they are bustling commercial centers with factories on their outskirts. Farmers of the area have made such rapid strides that they can serve the local demand as well as export produce to nearby countries.

"Thomas Barger would attribute little of this progress to his own hand, turning the credit to the ability of Saudi Arabs to absorb so much training in so brief a time; and to the vision of Saudis in pioneering business ventures when they were, at the outset, short of capital and experience. But he believed those miracles could happen and lent his strength to these efforts at every opportunity.

"If only because of extraordinary talent, Thomas Barger would have left a profound mark on the Company's course over the past three decades. However, his contribution has been of far greater magnitude than one based on ability alone, for he has combined integrity with intellect, dignity with dilligence, compassion with competence. The Company has become imprinted with the Barger philosophy of concern, which entwines the interests and the needs of the Company, its employees, and the Kingdom of Saudi Arabia.

"The Board of Directors, officers and employees have been enriched by their associations with him. They will be immeasurably dimished by his absence from their councils. No higher tribute can be offered than to pledge that the Company will determinedly pursue the high ideals and worthy goals to which he dedicated his career."

Sincerely,
J. J. Johnston
Vice President and Secretary,
Executive Committee,
Arabian American Oil Company

Appendix Three

The following was written by Kathleen Ray Barger, circa 1970

It was a very special rocking chair – large, soft and deep. Covered with scuffed brown leather, it had soft arms that a 9-year-old, tomboyish girl could swing her legs onto and fold up into a comfortable reading position. With cedar logs crackling in the big fireplace, that end of the old log lodge was cozy and warm on cold days , yet cool on hot days when it was a refuge from the hot North Dakota summer sun.

Here in this old chair I devoured John L. Stoddard's lectures. The entire set somehow had drifted down to us from the first dude ranch in the world, the old Eaton Brothers Custer Trail Ranch located near Medora, North Dakota. I know it was founded in the early 1870's because my maternal grandfather worked there as a dude wrangler when he was seventeen years old.

John Stoddard was a 19th-century traveler whose writings opened the world to me. After reading the entire set of travel books in that old leather chair, I decided that I must see the Taj Mahal, visit Venice and that I would live in Arabia. I called these my prophetic dreams, for dreams they were, but I knew that they would happen. Unlike Schlieman, who had a dream that he would find Troy, and then worked like a Trojan for years to accomplish this, I simply went about the business of being a small girl who enjoyed herself too much to worry about fulfilling her dreams.

My second prophetic dream took place at the University of North Dakota. I went, rather reluctantly, to my first meeting of the Newman Club, the Catholic students group at the university – reluctant because I had an infection on the heel of one foot and was forced to wear a black satin mule on that foot. I was a new student and aware that eyes were on me; all that racket from the black satin mule made me more than a little conspicuous. Watching my noisy entrance with amused, dancing, brown eyes was a young man in the front row. To my utter amazement, I found myself going to that front row, where I sat down next to the dancing eyes.

When I looked at him, I wanted to laugh out loud. I suddenly knew that this was the man I was going to marry, the man who would be the father of my six children. It was as easy as that! I've always wondered what would have happened if he had been a mind reader instead of a mining engineer. I soon learned that he was an old 26 to my 18 years. A professor in the Mining School, he was present that night in his role as faculty advisor. These things may all seem unrelated, but this ancient professor was the one who was sent to make all my dreams come true.

Bibliography

Antonius, George. *The Arab Awakening*. New York: Lippincott, 1939.

Atiyah, Edward. *The Arabs*. New York, 1968.

Armstrong, H.C. *Lord of Arabia*. Beirut: Khayyat, 1954.

Brockelmann, Carl. *History of the Islamic Peoples*. New York: Putnam's, 1947.

Belgrave, Sir Charles D. *Personal Column*. London: Hutchinson, 1960.

Burton, Sir Richard F. *Personal Narrative of a Pilgrimage to Al-Madinah and Meccah*. London: Bell, 1898, and other editions

Cheesman, R.E. *In Unknown Arabia*. London: Macmillan, 1926. *

De Gaury, Gerald. *Arabia Phoenix*. London: Harrap, 1946.

Dickson, H.R.P. *Kuwait and Her Neighbors*. London: Allen & Unwin, 1956.

. . . . . . *The Arab of the Desert*. London: Hodder and Stoughton, 1957.

Dickson, Violet. *Wild Flowers of Kuwait and Bahrain*. London: Allen & Unwin, 1955.

Doughty, C.M. *Travels in Arabia Deserta*. 2 vols. London: 1921. New York: Random House, 1946. *

Eddy, William A. *F.D.R. Meets Ibn Saud*. New York: American Friends of the Middle East, 1954.

Facey, William. *The Story of the Eastern province of Saudi Arabia*. London: Stacey International, 1994.

Glubb, Sir John Bagot. *A Soldier with the Arabs*. London: Hodder and Stoughton, 1957. *

Hart, Parker T. *Saudi Arabia and the United States*. Bloomington, Indiana: Indiana University Press, 1998.

Hay, Sir Rupert. *The Persian Gulf States*. Washington: Middle East Institute, 1959.

* indicates that the Title or Author is mentioned in the text.

Helfritz, Hans. *Land Without Shade*. New York: McBride, 1936

Hitti, P.K. *The Arabs, a Short History*. Princeton, N.J.: Princeton University press, 1949.

..... *History of the Arabs*. 10th edition. Boston, 1970.

Hogarth, D. G. *The Penetration of Arabia*. New York: F. A. Stokes, 1904.

Howarth, David. *The Desert King*. London: Collins, 1964.

Ibn Khaldun. *The Maqaddimah: An Introduction to History*. New York, 1958.

Kaplan, Robert D. *The Arabists*. New York: Simon & Schuster, 1993.

Kelly, J. B. *Arabia, the Gulf and the West*. London: Weidenfeld & Nicolson, 1980.

Lacey, Robert. *The Kingdom*. New York: Harcourt Brace, 1982.

Lawrence, T.E. *Seven Pillars of Wisdom*. Garden City: Doubleday, 1935.

McConnell, Philip C. *The Hundred Men*. Petersborough, N.H.: Currier Press, 1985. *

Meinertzhagen, Richard. *The Birds of Arabia*. Edinburgh: Oliver & Boyd, 1954.

Meulen, D. van der. *Aden to the Hadramaut, a Journey in South Arabia*. London: Murray, 1947.

...... *The Wells of Ibn Saud*. London: J. Murray, 1957.

Mountfort, Guy. *Portrait of a Desert*. London: Collins, 1965.

Musil, Alois. *The Northern Hejaz*. New York: American Geographical Society, 1926.

...... *Arabia Deserta*. New York: American Geographical Society, 1927.

...... *In the Arabian Desert*. ed. K. M. Wright. New York: Liveright, 1930.

Nance, Paul. *The Nance Museum*. Lone Jack, Missouri: Nance Museum, 1999. *

Nawab, Ismail I., Speers, Peter C., Hoye, Paul F. (eds.) *Saudi Aramco and Its World*. Houston: Aramco Services Company, 1995. *

Philby, H. St. John B. *The Heart of Arabia*. London: Constable, 1922 *

...... *Arabia of the Wahhabis*. London: Constable, 1928.

...... *The Empty Quarter*. New York: Henry Holt, 1933.

...... *Arabian Days*. London: Hale, 1948.

...... *Forty Years in the Wilderness*. London: Benn, 1957.

Stegner, Wallace. *Discovery!* Beirut: Middle East Export Press, 1971

Thesiger, Wilfred. *Arabian Sands*. New York: Dutton, 1959.

...... *The Last Nomad*. New York: Dutton, 1980.

Thomas, Bertram. *Alarms and Excursions in Arabia*. New York: Bobbs-Merrill, 1931 *

...... *Arabia Felix*. New York: Scribner's, 1932.

...... *The Arabs*. London: Butterworth, 1937.

Twitchell, K. S. *Saudi Arabia*. 3rd ed. Princeton, N.J.: Princeton University Press, 1958

Vidal, F. S. *The Oasis of al-Hasa*. Dhahran: Arabian American Oil Company, 1955. *

Wahba, Hafiz. *Arabian Days*. London: Arthur Barker, 1964.

Williams, Kenneth. *Ibn Sa'ud*. London: Cape, 1933.

Winder, R. Bayly. *Saudi Arabia in the Nineteenth Century*. New York: St. Martin's Press, 1965.

Winnet, F. V., Reed, W. L. *Ancient Records from North Arabia*. Toronto: University of Toronto, 1970.

Yergin, Daniel. *The Prize: the Epic Quest for Oil, Money and Power*. New York: Simon & Schuster, 1991.

Magazines

Aramco World is a bimonthly, full-color cultural magazine on the Arab and Muslim worlds, with emphasis on the Middle East and Saudi Arabia.

It is distributed free to readers who are interested in its areas of coverage. To request a subscription, write to Aramco World, Box 2106, Houston, Texas 77252-2106, USA.

Glossary

Agaal - The woven head rope Bedouin use to hold the ghutra in place. Also can be used to draw water or hobble a camel.

Aglaat - A well that is roughly the length of an agaal to its surface

Ain - A spring or well.

Ajeeb - Wonderful

Ajman - A large, powerful tribe in northeastern Saudi Arabia, their capital city was at Sarrar.

Al-Hamdulillah - Thanks be to God

Allah Kareem - God is generous

Awamir - A tribe renowned for being the most venturesome travelers of the desert, ranging from the Dhafra to the Rub' al-Khali.

Barasti - A hut made of palm fronds.

Bisht - A long robe

Chit - An Indian word derived from *chittie,* refers to a receipt or a disbursement note

Dahl - A limestone sinkhole varying in size from a small hole to a cavern

Dahna - A great sand belt that extends for about 800 miles in an arc from the Great Nafud in the north to the Rub' al-Khali in the south. It is a favored grazing ground of the Bedu in winter and spring.

Damusa - A small desert lizard

Dawsari - A man from the Dawasir tribe

Dawasir - A tribe based in the Wadi Dawasir

Dawsariyah - A woman from the Dawasir tribe

Delloo - A skin bucket for drawing water

Dhab - The spiny-tailed lizard, a heavy, plant-eating species that grows up to 20 inches in length.

Dhafra - A large sand mass that extends east of Sabkha Mutti into the region of Liwa. Now lies within the United Arab Emirates.

Dhow - A graceful Arabian sailing vessel

Dibdibah - A flat, gravel plain, also called *hadabah*

Dikakah - Terrain distinguished by knee high drifts of sand behind bushes, also known as *'affah*.

Eid Mubarak - Blessed holiday

Emir - The name for prince, chief or the headman in charge of a group of men.

Empty Quarter - In Arabic, Rub' al-Khali, the term used to describe the enormous sand region of southeastern Saudi Arabia.

Enshallah - If God wills

Faidha - A desert depression, often silty, with dense annual vegetation after good rains.

Fi aman Allah - [Go] In the care of God

Forayd - Little prominences

Gazelle - Graceful members of the antelope family that once populated the Arabian plains in herds of hundreds.

Ghutra - The headscarf that is secured with the *agaal*.

Gurbas - Waterskins made of sheep hide

Hajjel - A kind of rock grouse slightly smaller than a prairie chicken

Hauta - The flat rolling valley or strip between two *uruq*

Hubarrah - A game bird something like a sage hen and about the size of a young turkey (Macqueen's bustard)

Hutt - Put

Id al-Fitr - The Festival of the Breaking of the Fast, marks the end of Ramadhan

Ikhwan - The Brethren, an agrarian, religious movement founded by King Abdul Aziz

Irq - A long narrow Sand dune strip. A typical *irq* may stretch for miles in a north-south direction with a hard-packed, gentle, west slope and a steep, soft, east slope.

Ithil tree - Called a "salt cedar" in America, the ithil tree is a species of tamarisk native to central Asia (Tamarix *aphylla*)

Jafurah - A large sandy region that starts south of Hofuf and extends to the Rub' al-Khali

Jabal - An Arabic term loosely applied to hills, buttes, ridges and mountains.

Jamal - A mature male camel

Jerboa - A desert rodent, similar to the Kangaroo Mouse of the American deserts

Jumbia - Dagger

Khariz - Originally open irrigation channels that were covered over to keep the sand out. In time these became subterranean water canals accessed by intermittent manholes.

Khashem - Literally means nose, is used to describe a promontory or headland of an escarpement.

Khor - A salt water well, too bitter for people, but suitable for camels.

Kirwan - A type of bird similar to the stone curlew.

Leban - A kind of yoghurt

Manahil - A tribe based in far eastern Saudi Arabia and western Oman.

Manasir - A tribe ranging from the eastern base of the Qatar peninsula to the whole of the Dhafra.

Majlis - A parlor or meeting place

Mashallah - It is the will of God

Mesak Allah bil khair - Good evening

Mishash - A shallow, hand-dug water well, that is sometimes seasonally dry.

Mubty - Ancient

Mukhtal - In the speech of the Al Murra it means "hungry," but everywhere else in Saudi Arabia it means "crazy."

Murra (Al Murra) - One of the largest and most powerful tribes of southern Arabia, they were primarily sand dwellers, renowned for their large herds of camels and their tracking skills.

Naga - A milk camel

Nakhla - A palm tree

Nejd - The area of Central Arabia, capital at Riyadh

Punkah - A rope-operated, wing-like fan used to cool a room

Qa'adah - A huge sand mountain made of dunes heaped upon dunes.

Qadhi - A judge

Qasr - A large or prominent building

Qasrs of Ad - Large ruins of forts or palaces of Ad, the king of Wubar

Quadrille - A square dance on horseback

Qata bird - A type of sandgrouse

Qarn - Literally means "horn," often applied to a prominent conical hill or rock formation

Ramadhan - The ninth month of the Islamic year, Ramadhan is the month of fasting.

Ramlah - The Sand, a term used by the Bedu to describe the whole area of the Rub' al-Khali .

Raudhah - A desert depression, often silty, with dense annual vegetation, predominantly bushes, after good rains.

Rijm - A rock cairn often built on a *jabal* or high point by Bedouin to denote an important landmark.

Riyal - Saudi Arabian currency originally referring to a silver coin about the size of a U.S. fifty-cent piece.

Rub' al Khali - Literally means "the empty quarter" and refers to the great sand desert that covers about 250,000 square miles of southeastern Saudi Arabia.

Rupee - The currency of British India, formerly used throughout the Gulf countries.

Sa'ar - A tribe based in north central Yemen, south of the Rub' al-Khali

Sabkha - A salt flat caused by water seeping from below the surface. Evaporation deposits a layer of salt and forms a crust that is often cracked into countless irregular pieces.

Salaam aleikum - A traditional greeting that means "Peace be upon you." The reply is *Wa aleikum as-salaam*, " And upon you be peace."

Samra tree - A species of acacia tree recognizable by its flat-topped form, (Acacia *tortilis*)

Sayaraat - The plural of *sayarah*, the Arabic word for car

Shamaal - The Arabic word for north, it refers to a sandstorm caused by high winds from the north. *Shamaals* are a common occurence in the late spring and can last for weeks at a time.

Sheyl - Lift

Sidr - A very spiny large shrub of the desert, Ziziphus *nummularia*. The name is also applied to the cultivated tree, Ziziphus *spina-christi*.

Tayib al-ism - A good name

Thelul - A fast, riding camel

Tumulus - A burial mound made of piled stones

Tuwaiq Mountains - A long west-facing escarpment with gentle eastern slopes that extends for about 500 miles in a north to south direction, west of the Dahna in central Arabia.

Um Ruqaibah - The Mother of the Neck

Uruq - The plural of irq, the long linear dune forms that are common in the Rub' al-Khali

Usba' Steinke - The Finger of Steineke

Wabar - The semi-mythical city of fabulous wealth in southeastern Arabia, referred to by Bertram Thomas as "the Atlantis of the Sands." Also known as Ubar.

Wadi - A dry watercourse which can vary in size from a gully to a wide valley

Wahhabis - Western term for the religious conservatives and followers of the reformer Shaikh Muhammad ibn Abdul Wahhab.

Wudhaihi - The oryx, a large member of the antelope family. Mature oryx can weigh up to 200 pounds and have straight, tapering horns more than two feet long. Nearly extinct in modern Saudi Arabia.

Zaboon - A long, formal robe that is buttoned at the neck

Index